THE COMPETITION FOR DOLLARS, SCHOLARS AND INFLUENCE IN THE PUBLIC POLICY RESEARCH INDUSTRY

James G. McGann, Ph.D.

Lanham • New York • London

Copyright © 1995 by
James G. McGann, Ph.D.

University Press of America,® Inc.
4720 Boston Way
Lanham, Maryland 20706

3 Henrietta Street
London WC2E 8LU England

All rights reserved
Printed in the United States of America
British Cataloging in Publication Information Available

Library of Congress Cataloging-in-Publication Data
McGann, James G.
The competition for dollars, scholars and influence in the public
policy research industry / James G. McGann.
p   cm.
Includes bibliographical references and index.
1. Political planning—United States. 2. Policy sciences.
3. Research institutes—United States. I. Title.
JK468.P64M34   1994   320'.6'0973—dc20   94–37689 CIP

ISBN 0–8191–9750–5 (cloth : alk. paper)
ISBN 0–8191–9751–3 (pbk. : alk. paper)

 The paper used in this publication meets the minimum requirements of
American National Standard for Information Sciences—Permanence
of Paper for Printed Library Materials, ANSI Z39.48–1984.

To Emily, for her encouragement, patience and support.

My deepest thanks go out to my dissertation committee, Jean-Marc Choukroun, Tom Burns and Seymour Mandelbaum, whose patience, support and insights were invaluable. I am also indebted to Martin Myerson, John W. Gould and Bernard Cohen for taking time out of their busy schedules to read and comment on the book.

Many thanks are due to the individuals who took the time to fill out the survey and who never failed to answer my numerous and detailed questions.

Finally, a special thanks to my wife and family who encouraged me throughout.

TABLE OF CONTENTS

Section I: Public Policy Research Institutes in Context 1
    Chapter 1: Introduction – Methods and Motives 3
        Introduction 3
        Methodology 5
    Chapter 2: Think Tanks: I Know One When I See One 9
    Chapter 3: Developing a Working Definition of Public Policy Research Institutions 25
        1. Affiliated/ Non-Affiliated 26
        2. Diversified/ Specialized 27
        3. Academic/ Policy Oriented 27
        4. Partisan/ Non-Partisan 27
        5. Governmental/Non-Governmental 28
        6. For Profit/Not For Profit 28
        7. Degree Granting/ Non-Degree Granting 29
        8. Multi-Disciplinary/ Single Disciplinary 29
        9. Academic/ Policy Maker Constituency 29
        10. Contract/ Independent Research 30
    Alphabetical Listing of Think Tanks by Research Focus 33
        I. Diversified Public Policy Research Organizations 33
        II. Specialized Public Policy Research Organizations 33
            A. International Focus 33
            B. Domestic Focus 34
            C. State/ Local/ Regional Focus 35
            D. Economic Policy Focus 36
            E. Economic and Social Focus 36
            F. Defense and National Security Focus 37
            G. Environmental Focus 37
            H. Health Focus 37
            I. Other 37
    Chapter 4: Academics to Ideologues: Public Policy Research Institutions and the American Democratic Experience 39
        Brookings and the Rise of the Public Policy Research Institute 46
        Rand and the Rise of the Military Intellectual Complex 48
        The Urban Institute and the Rise of the Domestic PPRI 49
        The Heritage Foundation and the Rise of the Specialty PPRI 51
        Growth and Survival in the Public Policy Research Industry 53
        Chronological Listing of Existing Policy Research Institutions 55
Section II: Competition and Organizational Innovation 59
    Chapter 5: An Analytical Framework for Studying the Public Policy Research Industry 61
        Inputs and Outputs of PPRIs 63
    Chapter 6: Strategic Groups and the Strategy and Structure of the Public Policy Research Industry 71

    1. Academic Diversified 72
    2. Academic Specialized 73
    3. Public Policy Contract/ Consulting Institute 74
    4. Advocacy Tank 74
    5. Policy Enterprise 75
    6. Literary Agent/ Publishing House 76
    7. State-Based Think Tank 76
   Sample List of Firms by Strategic Group 77
        1. Academic Diversified 77
        2. Academic Specialized 77
        3. Contract/Consulting Institute 78
        4. Advocacy Tank 78
        5. Policy Enterprise 79
        6. Literary Agent/Publishing House 79
        7. State Based Think Tank 79

Chapter 7: Analyzing the Competition for Dollars, Scholars and Influence 81
    1. Academic Diversified – The Brookings Institution 82
       Institutional Profile 82
       Analysis of Strategic Dimensions 84
       Summary 86
    2. Academic Specialized – National Bureau of Economic Research 86
       Institutional Profile 86
       Analysis of Strategic Dimensions 88
       Summary 89
    3. Contract/ Consulting Institute – The Rand Corporation 90
       Institutional Profile 90
       Analysis of Strategic Dimensions 91
       Summary 93
    4. Advocacy Institute – Institute For Policy Studies 94
       Institutional Profile 94
       Analysis of Strategic Dimensions 95
       Summary 97
    5. Policy Enterprise – The Heritage Foundation 98
       Institutional Profile 98
       Analysis of Strategic Dimensions 99
       Summary 101
    6. Literary Agent/Publishing House – Manhattan Institute 102
       Institutional Profile 102
       Analysis of Strategic Dimensions 103
       Summary 105
    7. State Based Tanks – The Commonwealth Foundation for Public Policy Alternatives 105
       Institutional Profile 105
       Analysis of Strategic Dimensions 107
       Summary 109
   Overall Findings 109

Chapter 8: Conclusions and Implications For The Industry 121
    Market Interdependence 122
        A Funny Thing Happened on the Way to the War of Ideas .. 122
    Product Differentiation 127
        Politics, the Prince and the Policy Entrepreneur 129
    The Number of Strategic Groups and Their Relative Sizes 132
        Metamorphosis, Meaning and the Middle: The Brookings Institution 134
    Divergent Strategies and Strategic Distance 139
        Rand: Where Strategic Defense and Strategic Distance Meet 140
Chapter 9: Study Highlights and Suggestions for Future Research 145
Appendices 147
Bibliography 161
Index 197

TABLES

Table 1.1:	Strategic Groups and Exemplar Institutions	7
Table 3.1:	Characteristics & Representative Institutions	31
Table 3.2:	Summary Table of PPRIs by Research Focus	32
Table 4.1:	Existing Public Policy Research Institutes (By Period Founded)	45
Table 4.2:	Founding Dates of Selected Organizations	46
Table 6.1:	Strategic Groups and Exemplar Institutions	71
Table 6.2:	Historical Framework for the Emergence of Strategic Groups	77
Table 7.1:	Strategic Dimension Ratings for Each Exemplar Firm	112
Table 7.2:	Product Lines for 1989	113
Table 7.3:	Staff Compositions for 1989	114
Table 7.4:	Expenditures for 1989	115
Table 7.5:	Sources of Revenue for 1988 & 1989	116
Table 7.6:	Areas of Specialization	117
Table 7.7:	Total Income	118
Table 7.8:	Media-Related Outreach Activities for 1988 & 1989	119
Table 7.9:	Constituency Ranking	120

FIGURES

Figure 5.1: The Public Policy Research Environment 62
Figure 5.2: The Policy Formulation Process 63
Figure 5.3: Competition Among Strategic Groups 69
Figure 8.1: Competition Among PPRI Strategic Groups 142

Section I
Public Policy Research Institutes in Context

Section I will attempt to answer the following questions:

- What are the nature and origin of public policy research institutes?
- How do they differ from university research institutions, consulting firms, governmental research institutes and research and development centers?
- Why have they flourished in the United States?
- How have they changed over time?

CHAPTER 1
INTRODUCTION – METHODS AND MOTIVES

Introduction

This investigation of the public policy research industry grew out of a study I was charged to conduct for the Pew Charitable Trusts ten years ago. As the program officer responsible for the Trusts' public policy grants program, I was asked to try to make sense of the myriad of institutions supported by its grant-making activities in this area. The Trusts' grant-making program at that time supported public policy research at free-standing and university-affiliated research centers in the areas of domestic and international economics and social policy and security studies. To develop new funding guidelines, greater knowledge about public policy research institutes was required. What at first seemed to be a relatively simple and well defined project turned into a much broader study of the nature and origin of public policy research organizations in the United States. I discovered that very little scholarly research had been conducted on the role of non-profit public policy research institutes (PPRIs). This was surprising, given the growing number and importance of these institutions. The prospect of conducting a critical assessment of these institutions intrigued me because of PPRIs' reputed influence and the millions of dollars that are spent each year to support their operations.

Public policy research institutes, or think tanks[1] as they are more commonly called, first appeared early in this century as a part of a larger effort to bring the expertise of scholars and managers to bear on contemporary economic and social problems and to help manage the emerging federal bureaucracy.[2] Scholars and social reformers came to Washington after World War I to help elected officials develop policies and programs to alleviate human suffering and improve governmental efficiency. The Brookings Institution and the National Bureau of Economic Research, both established as a result of these social and political currents, continue to operate today to provide independent analysis of government policies and programs for decision makers in Washington. Rooted in the social sciences and funded by individuals and private foundations, these institutions operate outside of government and, for the most part, conduct their research and analysis independent of political parties and free from partisan interests. Over the last seventy-five years, scores of other public policy research institutions have come into being, each with its own base of financial support and distinctive approach to policy analysis.

---

[1] Writers on this subject often use these two terms interchangeably to describe institutions that engage in the research, evaluation and analysis of public policies and programs.

[2] For an excellent history of the intellectual and social forces that gave rise to the social scientist's role as policy expert, see James A. Smith, *The Idea Brokers: Think Tanks and the Rise of the New Policy Elite* (New York: Free Press, 1991). Also see J. S. Coleman, *Policy Research in the Social Science* (Morristown, NJ: General Learning Systems, 1972).

The last three decades have seen a dramatic proliferation in the number of public policy research institutes in the United States. While estimates of the total number of institutes vary according to how they are defined and who does the counting, current estimates reach between 1,200 and 1,400. However, if the universe is limited to institutes that are independent of government, colleges and universities, they total 112. A review of the various directories of public policy research institutes dramatically illustrates how this segment of the research industry has changed.[3] This information clearly suggests a pattern of sustained growth over time in the number and types of research institutes that compete for many of the same dollars, scholars and spheres of influence.

During this period, new entrants and existing firms in the industry have attempted to vary their strategy and structure[4] in response to the increased competition and other changes in the environment, such as the realignment of the Democratic and Republican parties. Public policy research is a growth industry, and new entrants to the field have shaken the monopoly once held by organizations such as the Brookings Institution and the American Enterprise Institutes for Public Policy Research. Over two-thirds of the existing institutions came into being between 1961 and 1986, and over one-half were established between 1970 and 1986.

The growth in the industry and the apparent trend toward more vigorous competition not only challenge existing institutions to alter the way they do business, but also present a major opportunity for new and emerging institutions to develop innovative technologies and seize a major share of the market. However, the barriers to entry will grow as the market becomes more crowded and fragmented and institutions are forced to find a niche in the market to survive. Understanding the forces that shape this class of institutions is the focus of this study.

The study is divided into two sections. Section I summarizes the nature and history of public policy research organizations in the United States. It develops a working definition of a public policy research institute. Section II then creates an analytical framework under which public policy research institutions may be categorized into one of seven groups according to the strategy and structure of the organization.

---

[3]The figures presented here were arrived at by reviewing and cross referencing the leading lists and directories of research organizations. These sources included: Gale's Research Centers Directory, 9th ed. and supplement; National Journal, Capital Source, Fall 1989 and Spring 1990; C&P Telephone directory; The Heartland Institute, *List of State-Based Think Tanks*; Grayson's Washington, *A Comprehensive Directory of the Nation's Capital . . . Its People and Institutions*; and Library of Congress, *Public Interest Profiles*. While no comprehensive directory of public policy research institutes exists, *Public Interest Profiles* is the most comprehensive and descriptive.

[4]Strategy is generally viewed as the goals and plans established by an organization, while its structure consists of the organizational design that enables it to execute its plans and achieve its goals.

Methodology

This study will examine the growth and evolution of the public policy research industry in the United States over the last seventy-five years. In particular, the study will focus on the internal and external forces that have shaped the strategies and structures of this class of institutions. A structural analysis of the public policy research industry will provide a clearer picture of the competitive forces acting on the industry.

This study focuses on five basic questions:
1) What are PPRIs and how are they organized?
2) What are the forces that have shaped the industry?
3) What are the major strategies and structures employed by these institutions?
4) Does the strategy and structure of an organization affect its inputs and outputs; and
5) How and under what conditions do policy makers utilize the information generated by PPRIs?

It has been my hope that in answering these questions I would begin to understand how different institutions organize themselves to carry out the same activity and how these differing approaches affect the level of utilization of their products.

Early on in the process, it was suggested that I read business management literature to provide a possible source for the conceptual framework necessary to this study.[5] This research led me to a series of works that examined the interrelationship between the structure and strategy of organizations. Because I was primarily concerned with understanding the differences among the various organizational forms that emerged in the industry, the analytical tools contained in this literature provided an effective framework for the purposes of the study. As the study began to take shape, I saw the utility of viewing the non-profit PPRIs as an industry that has a discernible market for its products and in which firms compete for scarce resources in the marketplace. The firms in this industry have distinguished themselves from other research enterprises through their independent nature, organizational design and focus on public policy research and analysis. By examining PPRIs in this way, it becomes possible to focus on them as a distinct group of firms that have product lines, means of production, distribution mechanisms and marketing strategies that differ among themselves as well as from other research organizations. Approaching this class of institutions as an industry will undoubtedly have certain limitations, especially because they are not for-profit organizations, but the business framework is both compelling and necessary given my interest in examining the competitive forces within the industry.

In an effort to understand the unique nature of these institutions, I reviewed the literature on knowledge utilization. This literature explores the connection between the creation of knowledge and its utilization by policy

---

[5]The works that contributed to my thinking in this area are contained in the bibliography. The seminal work in this area is Alfred D. Chandler, Jr., *Strategy and Structure: Chapters in the History of the American Industrial Enterprise* (Boston: MIT Press, 1962).

makers.[6] Knowledge utilization provides an effective tool for considering the connections between the creation, dissemination and utilization of public policy research. The literature on the economics of knowledge is particularly relevant to the examination of factors that influence the supply and demand for public policy research, as well as its utility. While outside the explicit scope of the study, the literature on both knowledge utilization and economics of knowledge provides an important backdrop to the analysis presented.

The underlying thesis of this study is that changes in the environment have resulted in the creation of new organizational forms in the public policy research industry. The historical frame for the study will extend over seventy-five years but will focus on events that have shaped the industry in the last thirty years. The methodology employs management techniques to develop a structural analysis of the public policy research industry and the competitive forces that shape the strategy and structure of PPRIs. Comparison and contrast of the leading organizational forms will identify the different types of firms that have appeared within the industry. Each major form will be analyzed based on a series of strategic dimensions that influence the strategy and structure of the industry and the firms within it. This analytical construct is intended to highlight the environmental and competitive forces that affect the direction of PPRIs.

The structural analysis is based on data collected from a sample of public policy research institutions. The data were collected through a survey on the financial base, product lines, marketing strategies, staffing patterns, history and purpose of firms in the industry. This information was supplemented by annual reports and publications from each institution. The analysis was further enhanced by interviews with key staff members and by popular and scholarly books and articles that have been written about these institutions. In creating the sample, great care was taken to make sure that a full range of institutions was represented in the initial sample: large and small, generalist and specialist, free standing and university affiliated, liberal and conservative, partisan and non-partisan, academic and policy oriented.

However, the institutions on which this study focuses will be limited to non-profit, non-governmental, non-university affiliated public policy research organizations. Excluded from the study are research and development centers, university based research centers, consulting firms, political action committees, lobbying groups and government supported research centers. This limited the number of institutions to 112. Forty-six of these institutions were surveyed, thirty-four completed the survey. After a preliminary review of the history,

---

[6]The seminal work is the area of knowledge utilization is C.P. Snow, *The Two Cultures and the Scientific Revolution* (Cambridge: Cambridge University Press, 1965). Of particular relevance to my research in the areas of knowledge utilization, social sciences and policy making are the works of Machlup, Weiss, Horowitz, Lynn, Caplan and Yogesh, listed in Section II of the bibliography For a policy maker's stinging critique of the social sciences' contribution to public policy, see Daniel Patrick Moynihan, *Maximum Feasible Misunderstanding, Community Action in the War on Poverty* (New York: Free Press, 1969), pp. 188-89. Additional publications in this area are also listed in Section II of the bibliography. For an excellent reference in this area see the University of Pittsburgh's journal, *Knowledge: Creation, Diffusion and Utilization*, from Sage Publications.

purpose, financial support and staffing patterns of the thirty-four respondents, seven were selected for final use in the study.

The seven institutions will serve as exemplars and demonstrate the possible range of organizations that have emerged in the public policy research industry. Each of these seven institutions represents a major strategic group within the industry. Strategic groups share similar structures and strategies within the public policy industry. A list of these institutions and the strategic groups they represent is provided below:

Table 1.1

Strategic Group	**Institution**
1. Academic Diversified	Brookings Institution
2. Academic Specialized	National Bureau of Economic Research
3. Contract/ Consulting Tank	Rand Corporation
4. Advocacy Tank	Institute for Policy Studies
5. Policy Enterprise	Heritage Foundation
6. Literary Agent/ Publishing House	Manhattan Institute
7. State-Based Think Tank	Commonwealth Foundation

Most, if not all, of the firms within the public policy research industry can be placed into the seven groups listed above. Undoubtedly, questions will be raised about the seven groups and the firms categorized within them. As an analytic device, the strategic groups are not meant to strip away the unique character of PPRIs or to pigeonhole them, but rather to provide a framework for understanding the various organizational forms that have developed. Each of the seven strategic groups provide a snapshot of the products of the PPRI, its organizational culture and its unique staffing patterns, as exemplified by a certain firm. The classification system is meant to create a sensible picture of the industry that is illuminating to industry insiders. It also characterizes all the major firms in a compelling way. Finally, it will provide scholars and others interested in this class of institutions with tools and techniques to help them better understand the industry's operation. Because of the dynamic nature of the public policy research industry, the seven groups and exemplar organizations should be viewed as a starting point for consideration, not an end point.

Each strategic group exhibits a unique set of characteristics that distinguishes it from the other groups within the industry. Product lines, managerial structure, goals, values and technologies vary among strategic groups. Although a firm or group may exhibit some of the characteristics of another strategic group, the strategic groups identified and the exemplar firms have been selected because the characteristics attached to them are sufficiently dominant to determine the strategy and structure of the individual firms within the strategic group. This will become clearer after the characteristics that shape each of the seven groups are described in detail.

CHAPTER 2
THINK TANKS: I KNOW ONE WHEN I SEE ONE

Public policy research grew out of the intellectual and social movements of the late nineteenth century and owes much of its heritage to the social sciences that drove the reform movements of this period. The Brookings Institution, the National Bureau of Economic Research and the Russell Sage Foundation were all established during the early part of this century to help link social science scholars with decision makers in Washington. Much has been written about the role of the social sciences during this period and their impact on public policy, but little attention has been given to the public policy research institutions that arose from these intellectual and social currents.[7] Critical thinking on this class of institutions did not emerge until after World War II when analysts became concerned with one or more (but rarely all) of the following matters:

a. The challenge of free-standing research institutions to the new "research" universities.
b. The organization of interdisciplinary and applied work in a world organized by area of specialization and discipline.
c. The methods, uses and design of applied social research.
d. The methods, uses, limits and design of professionalized public policy research.

These concerns and others focused analysts on different institutions and institutional distinctions than those concentrated on herein. This study will attempt to build on and enrich the existing literature.

Over the last thirty years, a relatively small number of scholarly and a large number of popular authors have written about PPRIs. Since each author wrote for a particular audience or attempted to describe certain characteristics of the industry, a general framework was not important. While these explorations into the nature and design of PPRIs are valuable, they cannot be used to draw generalized conclusions about the industry.

Most published lists of research organizations subsume PPRIs under the more general headings of think tanks, research institutes and research and

---

[7]In addition to the research that has been done in this area, an excellent and voluminous literature exists on universities in the United States and the role they have played in the public policy formulation process. Joseph Ben-David has written extensively on this subject; a sample of his works is listed in Section II of the bibliography. The literature on the sociology of knowledge may also be consulted.

development centers. Over the years, writers on the subject have used these terms interchangeably, which has further blurred the boundaries between such institutions. Unfortunately, previous efforts to define PPRIs as independent institutions that participate in the policy planning and formulation process have had limited utility. This lack of clarity has obscured our understanding of this very important group of institutions.

Confusion about PPRIs that are independent of government may also arise because they are a relatively new type of organization, they have a unique organizational structure and market for their products, and their influence on the public policy process is indirect and informal. These and other factors have prevented scholars from developing a clear conceptual framework to describe this complex set of organizations. Since the definition of PPRIs has been unclear at best, it has been difficult to distinguish them from other organizations that conduct research in the physical and social sciences. This section will build on the existing literature on PPRIs by examining the nature and role of these organizations. Through this process, I hope to develop a working definition of PPRIs by narrowing the field from institutions that engage in research in the physical and social sciences in the United States.

Unfortunately, most of the literature on think tanks has taken the form of magazine and newspaper articles, institutional case histories for organizations like the Rand Corporation and the Brookings Institution, and anecdotal information about the role and influence of these institutions.[8] Because of the narrow focus of

---

[8]The major institutional case histories that have been conducted thus far are as follows: Grace Bassett, *The Urban Institute: A History Of Its Organization* (Washington, DC: Urban Institute, 1969) (unpublished); Donald T. Critchlow, *The Brookings Institution, 1916-1952: Expertise and the Public Interest in a Democratic Society* (DeKalb, Illinois: Northern Illinois University Press, 1985); Peter Duignan, ed., *The Hoover Institution on War, Revolution and Peace: Seventy-Five Years of Its History* (Stanford, CA: Hoover Institution Press, 1989); John S. Friedman, *First Harvest: The Institute for Policy Studies, 1963-83* (New York: Grove Press, 1983); Frederick O. Hayes, et al., *The Urban Institute, 1968-78: An Evaluation of Its Performance, Prospects and Financial Problems* (New York: Ford Foundation, 1978); Charles B. Saunders, Jr., *The Brookings Institute, A Fifty-Year History* (Washington: Brookings Brooks, 1966); Bruce L. Smith, *The Rand Corporation: Case Study of a Nonprofit Advisory Corporation* (Cambridge, MA: Harvard University Press, 1966), *The Rand Corporation: The First Fifteen Years* (Santa Monica, CA: Rand Corporation, 1963), *The Rand Corporation: Its Origins, Evolution and Plans for the Future* (Santa Monica, CA: Rand Corporation, 1971); James A. Smith, *Brookings at Seventy-Five* (Washington, DC: Brookings Books, 1991). Other works and authors such as Donald T. Critchlow, "Think Tanks, Anti-Statism, and Democracy: The Career of the Nonpartisan Ideal in the American Political Order," produced for the Program on American Society and Politics, Woodrow Wilson International Center For Scholars (Washington, DC: Woodrow Wilson Center, 1984), Paul Dickson, *Think Tanks* (New York: Atheneum, 1972), Harold Orlans, *The Non-Profit Research Institute: Its Origins, Operations, Problems and Prospects* (New York: McGraw-Hill Company, 1972), and Joseph G. Peschek, *Policy Planning Organizations, Elite Agendas and American's Rightward Turn* (Philadelphia: Temple University Press, 1987) have included detailed descriptions of the Rand Corporation, Urban Institute, the Brookings Institution, ANSER, Battelle Memorial

their studies, the authors have not found it necessary to build on or consider the existing literature. Furthermore, most of the works written to date do not contain bibliographies or citations. Thus, following the development of the literature on think tanks over the past thirty years is difficult. This chapter primarily organizes the review of literature along chronological lines as the best way of showing its evolution.

Over the years, writers on the subject have attempted to frame an understanding of PPRIs by describing their source of funds, degree of independence, type of research, tax status, organizational structure, affiliation or political orientation. Although each of these elements is important, when taken together they still fail to complete a valid picture of PPRIs.

The first scholarly attempt to define and categorize research institutions was Harold Orlans' The Non-Profit Research Institute: Its Origins, Operations, Problems and Prospects, published in 1972.[9] Orlans' research focuses primarily on the vast number of defense-related research and development centers that came into being after World War II.[10] Writing during a period when students, faculties and administrators at universities throughout the United States were questioning the role of research institutions for political and financial reasons, Orlans attempted to bring order to this seemingly chaotic web of institutions.

Institute, Institute for Policy Studies, Stanford Research Institute and the Hudson Institute to illustrate points in their respective studies of nonprofit research institutes and think tanks.

[9] Orlans, *The Non-Profit Research Institute: Its Origins, Operations, Problems and Prospects* (New York: McGraw-Hill, 1972).

[10] The tensions between academic and policy oriented research merely extend the tensions that exist between applied and basic sciences. While no definition can capture the complexity of these research traditions, it is important to understand the difference between them. Basic research is generally directed toward the creation and expansion of scientific knowledge, while applied research is concerned with the practical application of knowledge. Paul Dickson, in *Think Tanks* (New York: Atheneum, 1972), p. 8, provides an excellent explanation and summary of research and development (R&D) in the opening chapter of his book. According to Dickson, research and development involves three interrelated functions: (1) Basic research is the exploration of the unknown. Sometimes called non-directed research, it is motivated by the desire to pursue knowledge for its own sake. Charles E. Wilson, President Eisenhower's first Secretary of Defense, called it what you do when "you don't know what you're doing." An example would be a chemist working with a compound simply to find what is not known about that compound. The chemist is looking for something but does not know what. (2) Applied research is research directed to satisfying a stated need, such as finding a cure for a disease, or discovering new ways to make aircraft fly faster. It draws on basic research and normally generates additional knowledge. The chemist enters the realm of applied research when attempting to determine whether the compound would curb a specific disease. (3) Development is the systematic use of basic and applied research for the creation and production of tangible objects, systems, methods and materials. It normally includes design and experimentation with a product or process but never production of it. If, for example, the chemist were to find that the compound had potential as an anti-malarial drug, then its development would include the refinement of the compound and its testing and preparation for production in mass quantities.

While Orlans' scope of inquiry extends to all non-profit research institutes, including research and development centers, his general definition of these institutes may provide a useful point of departure. He refers to them as "independent non-profit research institutes administratively independent, often separately incorporated, non-degree granting organizations that devote most of their annual expenditures to the development of new technology and to research in the natural and social sciences, engineering, humanities and professions."[11] Orlans never fully explains this definition, but judging from the period in which he is writing, it appears that his primary interest is research centers that exist independently of the university system and compete directly with colleges and universities for government research grants, contracts and, potentially, students.

The bulk of his analysis focuses on the relative independence of such institutions, their revenue base, their tax status, research agendas and the competition among them, but does not provide any concrete examples. Yet, his work in this area remains ground-breaking because it provides a general framework for understanding all research institutes; however, it is too broad for specific application to PPRIs. Orlans' major contribution to the literature is his attempt to categorize these institutions by funding source. The categories are: federal research and development centers; applied research institutes; operating foundations; endowed institutes; cushioned institutes; and project institutes,[12] but again, Orlans does not fully define these categories or clearly distinguish one from another. Despite these criticisms, Orlans is to be credited for introducing the notion of independent non-profit research institutes into the literature and for attempting to define and categorize this group of institutions.

Other works such as Paul Dickson's *Think Tanks*[13] and David Boorstin's article "Directions of Policy Research"[14] attempt to define what they term "think tanks." Like Orlans, Boorstin and Dickson consider think tanks as a subset of the research and development industry. Boorstin, for example, believes that think tanks are, as he puts it, "a special class of R and D institutions [designed] to act as synthesizers bringing together scholarship and scientific and technological tools for the use of policymakers combining the 'know-how' and the 'know who.'"[15] Both Dickson's and Boorstin's definitions are somewhat imprecise. They agree that the term "think tank" is "broad and subjective"[16] and "ill-defined, subjective, and debated."[17] Certainly, their understanding of the research institute phenomenon was limited because the field had just begun to take shape when they

---

[11] Orlans, *The Non-Profit Research Institute*, p. 3.
[12] Ibid.
[13] Dickson, *Think Tanks* (New York: Atheneum, 1972).
[14] Boorstin, "Directions of Policy Research," *Congressional Quarterly: Editorial Research Reports*, Vol. II, No. 13 (Oct. 10, 1975) pp. 725-44.
[15] Boorstin, "Directions of Policy Research," pp. 726.
[16] Ibid., p. 728
[17] Dickson, *Think Tanks*, p. 27

were writing. Dickson contends that the main characteristic that distinguishes these institutions is their unique role:

> The primary function of a think tank as the term is used here is neither traditional basic research, applied research or development - although all three are commonly performed in think tanks - but to act as a bridge between knowledge and power and between science/technology and policy making in areas of broad interest. They are closer to being agents of new knowledge and discovery than creators of new knowledge.[18]

In general terms, Dickson appears to agree with Boorstin's appraisal of these institutions, but he also makes some useful qualifying remarks about these institutions that clearly separate his analysis from Boorstin's. For example, by excluding centers that do applied or basic research from his definition of research institutes, Dickson makes an important distinction that further helps to shape our understanding of this particular field of think tanks. Dickson also attempts to differentiate think tanks from research and development organizations in the following way:

> [t]here is no set pattern of financial objectives or affiliation. A think tank can be for profit or not for profit, supported by the government or tied to a larger company or university. A think tank must however be a permanent entity as opposed to a study commission or special group with a temporary assignment.[19]

Unfortunately, the characteristics outlined above remain so broad that they could describe almost any institution.

Dickson's discussion of policy research and think tanks is the most compelling aspect of his book. He states that the role of think tanks is to conduct "policy research or research that provides ideas, analysis, and alternatives relevant to people who make policy, in contrast to traditional science and R and D which normally produced scientific knowledge for the scientists and researchers."[20] Dickson's most valuable contribution is this separation of research centers in the applied sciences from those in the social sciences. This view is shared by Robert K. Landers in his article entitled "Think Tanks: The New Partisans?," who writes "that the term think tank is broadly construed to mean simply an organization that does research bearing on public policy."[21]

Like Orlans, Dickson also attempts to classify these institutions by using a system that organizes think tanks by tax status, affiliation and clients served.

---

[18]Ibid., p. 28.
[19]Ibid.
[20]Ibid.
[21]Robert K. Landers, "Think Tanks: The New Partisans?" *Congressional Quarterly: Editorial Research Reports*, vol. I, no. 23, June 20, 1985, pp. 455-72.

Dickson identifies and defines five major categories of think tanks: government research centers; federal contract centers; profit making consulting firms; university-affiliated research centers; and "truly independent, nonprofit self-determining think tanks that exist to explore a single subject or point of view."[22] However, because the two government categories clearly overlap, Dickson has only identified four categories.

The boundaries of Dickson's system are much clearer and his definitions are more precise than Orlans. Dickson's work in this area enables us to begin to distinguish among the various institutions that have become known as think tanks. This will become useful in formulating the definition of PPRIs for this study. Notably, Dickson and Orlans do not include the word "public" in their discussions of research institutes and think tanks, because their concern is policy makers in both the private and public sectors. Confining the focus to public policy will help to further define the role and nature of this type of research organization.

A number of authors – Levien, Baer, Dror, Polsby, Fauriol, Weaver, Durst and Thurber, Wiarda and Gellner – have written articles on the narrower field of institutions described as public policy think tanks. Their observations about these institutions contribute to the field, but there is still considerable overlap and confusion because none of these authors share the same conceptual framework. Consequently, it is not apparent that they are all attempting to describe the same beast.

Roger Levien was the first author to focus on what he terms "the independent public analysis organization."[23] For Levien, these institutions are distinguished from other research organizations by "their role as independent organizations that provide analytic assistance to government agencies in the resolution of public policy issues."[24] Levien further defines these institutions by identifying six characteristics that they must incorporate into their organizational structure to be truly independent policy research organizations: "a policy orientation, influence, breadth of charter, interdisciplinary character, an eye to the future, and a concern with systems."[25] He is the first author to clearly define the role and function of public policy institutes in a way that separates them from university-based think tanks and from for-profit research and development centers. Levien's characteristics for these organizations also give greater shape and meaning to the term "public policy research institutes." The only shortcoming in Levien's definition and characterization of think tanks is that it focuses on a narrow set of institutions and does not include a number of variations that have come into being since he wrote his article in 1969.

---

[22]Ibid., p. 30.
[23]Roger E. Levien, "Independent Public Policy Analysis Organization -- A Major Social Invention," *The Rand Papers Series* (1969) p. 4231, p. 1.
[24]Ibid., p. 28.
[25]Ibid., p. 4.

Most, if not all, of the literature written today is derived from the early works of Orlans, Dickson and Levien. A major advocate of the Levien school of thought is Walter S. Baer, who further defines this set of institutions by focusing on their interdisciplinary nature.[26] Both Baer and Levien contend that PPRIs are the only organizations that are properly designed to conduct policy oriented research. Nelson Polsby introduces the notion of PPRIs in an effort to distinguish this set of institutions from what he terms "true think tanks" that provide scholars the opportunity to think and write free from teaching and administrative duties.[27] Polsby argues that the term "think tank" does not adequately describe centers that are concerned with having "a regular impact on public policy."[28] According to Polsby, think tanks in the humanities and sciences are isolated and "ivory towerish" and have little or no impact on human events. In making this distinction, Polsby isolates for the first time the institutions called PPRIs. Notably, both Dickson and Boorstin voiced similar concerns about the term "think tank" but were unable to make this subtle yet important distinction.

Polsby distinguishes PPRIs from "traditional" think tanks because "public policy research institutes have [research agendas] whereas pure think tanks are designed to allow their researchers to follow their own intellectual agendas."[29] Like Dickson and Boorstin, Polsby believes that PPRIs can be "affiliated with universities or independent, generalized and specific, ideological, eclectic and focused."[30] It seems that the thing they all agree on is that they must be policy oriented. Polsby's work, although lacking in detail, differentiates between think tanks in the social sciences – particularly those engaged in policy research – and those in the basic sciences. However, Polsby's major contribution is the distinction he makes between academic or non-policy-oriented think tanks and PPRIs.

Fauriol classified think tanks along the same lines as Dickson. Fauriol begins by dividing policy-oriented "private voluntary organizations" into three classes of institutions: "leadership groups," "general educational institutions" and "independent research centers."[31] Leadership groups are primarily involved in

---

[26]Walter S. Baer, "Interdisciplinary Policy Research in Independent Research Centers," *The Rand Papers Series*, January 1975, p. 5347, p. 2. Baer examines the relative utility of research conducted by universities, commercial research organizations and policy research centers for decision makers and explains why he thinks universities and commercial enterprises are not properly organized to conduct policy oriented research.

[27]Nelson W. Polsby, "Tanks But No Tanks," *Public Opinion*, vol. VI, (April/May 1983), pp. 14-16, 58-59.

[28]Ibid., p.16.

[29]Ibid., p. 15.

[30]Ibid., p. 58.

[31]George A. Fauriol, "Think Tanks and U.S. Foreign Policy," a paper given at the Fourth Tamkang American Studies Conference, Tamkang University, Taipei, Taiwan, November 25-28, 1984 (Washington: Georgetown University, Center for Strategic and International Studies, 1984), p.7.

educating and networking elites and include organizations such as the Council on Foreign Relations, while general education groups educate the public at large. As an example of the general education class of institutions, Fauriol refers to the Foreign Policy Association, a national organization that works to "increase the understanding of foreign policy issues for all Americans."[32]

Fauriol defines independent research centers as organizations that provide expertise to policy makers. He concludes that "the think tank community may be distinguished from the following set of related organizations: conventional centers of academic research, political education groups and policy think tanks."[33] Conventional centers of academic research are university-affiliated centers with a functional or area specialization that have a joint research/ teaching function and are generally not very concerned with policy issues.[34] Non-profit political education groups are politically motivated organizations that have developed "an overt lobbying function."[35] Fauriol characterizes policy think tanks as follows: "commercial and 'governmental' institutions, closely associated in some way with U.S. government contract research work. These include high technology and management laboratories working in the defense field, many with a high volume of essentially classified activities. The Rand Corporation (RC), often regarded as the archetypal 'think tank,' falls squarely in this category. Characteristic of more commercial ventures is Stanford Research International (SRI)."[36]

Fauriol subdivides the think tank category into commercial and governmental institutions and non-governmental, non-profit research institutes. He then attempts to define non-governmental, non-profit research institutions more by example than by formal definition, citing the Brookings Institution and the Center for Strategic and International Studies. Fauriol comes closest to defining policy think tanks when he concludes that "the foreign policy think tank acts as a conveyor belt of thought...a mid-point between the ivory towers of academia and the hustled atmosphere of the policy-making world of government," where it operates "as a distribution point in the increasingly competitive marketplace of ideas."[37] Here again, the notion arises of think tanks as brokers of ideas or, to use Dickson's phrase, "agents of new knowledge."[38] Fauriol's work further clarifies the differences between university-based research centers and those that are free-standing. His major contribution to the literature, however, is his effort to distinguish PPRIs from political educational organizations.

---

[32]Statement of Purpose for the Foreign Policy Association, 1990 Annual Report.
[33]Fauriol, "Think Tanks and U.S. Foreign Policy," p. 8.
[34]Ibid.
[35]Ibid., p. 9.
[36]Ibid., p. 8.
[37]Ibid., pp. 1, 9.
[38]Dickson, *Think Tanks*, p. 28.

Dror builds on Levien and Baer's work by further defining a think tank as "an island of excellence applying full-time interdisciplinary scientific thinking to the in-depth improvement of policy making, or as a bridge between power and knowledge."[39] Dror attempts to distinguish PPRIs from ad hoc research groups by incorporating the requirement of a full-time staff into his definition. He formulates six interdependent features of a PPRI: "(1) mission; (2) critical mass; (3) methods; (4) research freedom; (5) clientele-dependency; and (6) outputs and impacts."[40] Dror's work seems largely derived from Baer's, Boorstin's and Levien's; for instance, he shares their view that a policy think tank's mission should be focused on "interdisciplinary, science-based contributions to policy making" and that its research staff should have a large degree of freedom in defining the problem and "arriving at their findings."[41] He also posits that five types of interrelated resources – "number of full-time professional staff, quality of staff, scientific diversity and disciplinary range, time, and information" – help constitute a think tank[42] and separate public policy think tanks from "a whole range of advisory organizations" that are ad hoc in nature.[43]

Dror further expands on Levien's definition of think tanks by suggesting that "work methods vary from institution to institution."[44] For example, he contends that "there is quite a difference between...the work methods" at the Rand Corporation and the Brookings Institution because they approach problem analysis differently.[45] This study will further explore Dror's suggestion. Dror's other major contribution is his concept of "outputs and impacts," which focuses on these institutions' products as uniquely defined by their policy orientation and timeliness.[46]

Dror's work provides the first detailed definition and classification system that focuses exclusively on PPRIs yet is broad enough to encompass a whole range of these organizations. Yet, his critical mass requirement of fifteen to twenty professional researchers is too limiting. Adhering to this requirement, only a few large policy research institutes would qualify as PPRIs under his system.

Winard Gellner and Howard J. Wiarda, in their separate works on think tanks, refine Dror's concept of "outputs and impacts." Gellner provides a functional topology for the unique role think tanks play in the American political

---

[39] Yehezkel Dror, "Think Tanks: A New Invention In Government," in Carol H. Weiss & Allen H. Barton, eds., *Making Bureaucracies Work* (Beverly Hills: Sage, 1980) p. 141.
[40] Ibid.
[41] Ibid., p. 145.
[42] Ibid., p. 141.
[43] Ibid., p. 143.
[44] Ibid., p. 142.
[45] Ibid., p. 143.
[46] Ibid., p. 144.

system. He identifies four functions or outputs of public policy think tanks: "generation of ideas and ideologies; convocation [networking]; publication [diffusion]; and transformation [of elites]."[47] These functions differentiate the institutions from what he calls "non-political 'scientific institutions' and non-scientific 'interest groups.'"[48]

Wiarda, on the other hand, identifies nine major think tank outputs: "(1) luncheons, seminars and dinners; (2) television and media appearances; (3) public appearances; (4) contacts with policy makers; (5) congressional testimony; (6) advisory panels; (7) personal contacts; (8) recruitment of government personnel; and (9) studies and publications."[49] Each of these activities sheds some light on the role of think tanks and the impact they have on public policy. Similarly, Fauriol explores the issue of influence and impact when he describes think tanks as a "conveyor-belt of thought."[50] It is important to point out that while each of these authors has identified a series of PPRI "outputs and impacts," none has yet developed a mechanism for effectively measuring their impact. This study will further elaborate on Wiarda and Gellner's output categories.

Samantha Durst and James Thurber attempt to define public policy think tanks by using many of the same characteristics – "organizational purpose, focus of study, intellectual independence and role" – as their predecessors.[51] However, they differ in their attempt to define public policy think tanks by "sources of funding" and "types of expenditures."[52] Durst and Thurber contend that the source of funds, i.e., grants, endowments, contracts, and the nature of the funding, i.e., restricted or unrestricted, public or private, "has an influence on the objectivity, direction, and influence of a think tank."[53] Consequently, they separate government research organizations from those in the private sector. Likewise, Durst and Thurber believe that the manner in which think tanks spend their funds is an important element in defining their character. While they found some variations, Durst and Thurber conclude that "most public policy think tanks and their researchers direct their energies toward the goal of becoming a constant and almost irreplaceable source of knowledge for the public, public officials and the media, through research, consulting, seminars, conferences and publications

---

[47] Winard Gellner, "Political Think Tanks: Functions and Perspectives of a Strategic Elite," prepared for the 1990 Annual Meeting of the American Political Science Association, p. 5.
[48] Ibid., p. 4.
[49] Howard J. Wiarda, *Foreign Policy Without Illusion: How Foreign Policy-Making Works and Fails to Work in the United States* (Glenview, Illinois: Scott, Foresman & Co., 1990), p. 159.
[50] Fauriol, "Think Tanks and U.S. Foreign Policy," p. 4.
[51] Samantha L. Durst & James A. Thurber, "Studying Washington Think Tanks: In Search of Definitions and Data," prepared for delivery at the 1989 Annual Meeting of the American Political Science Association, August 31 - September 3, 1989), pp. 1-38.
[52] Ibid., pp. 13, 17.
[53] Ibid., p. 14.

and impact on public policy."⁵⁴ Through their focus on funding and expenditures, Durst and Thurber have provided two important keys to understanding PPRIs.

Two decades after Levien's article was first published in 1969, R. Kent Weaver concludes that "the think tank universe has become much more diverse...reflecting both new entrants into the marketplace of ideas and changes in these organizations' environment."⁵⁵ Weaver presents three organizational models for all non-profit PPRIs; he intends the models to set such institutions apart from other research enterprises. He divides think tanks into the following categories: "universities without students, contract research organizations and advocacy tanks."⁵⁶

The "universities without students" are obviously characterized by not having students and by "a heavy reliance on academics as researchers, by funding primarily from the private sector, and by book-length studies as the primary research product."⁵⁷ This reflects Orlans' definition of think tanks as "non-degree granting" research institutes. In addition, most of their staff are Ph.D.s in the fields of political science, economics and international affairs.

Weaver's second category is the "contract research organization," which is characterized by a staff of "contract researchers" with advanced degrees who produce "reports for specific government agencies."⁵⁸ Weaver challenges Levien and Dror's assertion that one of the defining characteristics of all think tanks is their research freedom when he states that "the research agenda for contract researchers is set primarily by what the [contracting] agency is willing to pay for."⁵⁹ He gives Rand as the best example of this type of institution.

Weaver contends that the "universities without students" and the contract research organizations have been the dominant models for approximately twenty years. He asserts, however, that a new, third model is redefining how think tanks should be organized. He calls this new breed of PPRI the "advocacy tank," explaining that it "combine[s] a strong policy, partisan or ideological bent with aggressive salesmanship and an effort to influence policy debates."⁶⁰ He believes that this set of institutions "synthesizes and puts a distinctive 'spin' on existing research rather than carrying out original research."⁶¹ It is Weaver's contention that advocacy tanks produce policy briefs which "may be lacking in scholarship"

---

[54] Ibid., p. 22.
[55] R. Kent Weaver, "The Changing World of Think Tanks," *Political Science & Politics*, vol. 22, September 1989, p. 563.
[56] Ibid.
[57] Ibid., p. 568.
[58] Ibid., p. 566.
[59] Ibid.
[60] Ibid., p. 567.
[61] Ibid.

but are effective for legislators who do not have the time to read book-length studies.[62] He maintains that the Heritage Foundation best exemplifies this type of organization.

Weaver also identifies a set of issues – "image, product line, staffing, marketing, and contracting out"[63] – with which think tank managers must struggle in the increasingly competitive market.[64] Analysis of these issues will be used later in the study to compare and contrast the different strategies and structures utilized by public policy research institutes. Weaver's reflections on the changing world of think tanks introduce concepts that distinguish the various types of think tanks by their organizational structure, product lines and marketing strategies.

More recently, authors, such as Robert Landers, Gregg Easterbrook, Patricia Linden, James Smith and Howard Wiarda, have focused on the politicization of PPRIs during the mid-1970s and 1980s. The basic premise surrounding all of these works is that public policy think tanks, once the fountain of reasoned discourse and dictums on public policy, have become armies of ideologues fighting a "war of ideas."[65] For this group of authors, public policy think tanks can be divided into two categories: non-partisan and partisan. The partisan think tanks advocate a particular point of view, while the non-partisan think tanks avoid taking a position on specific pieces of legislation. Commenting on this phenomenon, Robert K. Landers concluded that "in recent years...public policy research organizations that are more overtly ideological have risen to prominence."[66] Gregg Easterbrook similarly finds that "[w]hile the political ascent of conservatism has taken place in full public view, the intellectual transformation has for the most part occurred behind the scenes, in a network of think tanks."[67]

By far the leading proponent of the "politicization of think tanks" school of thought is historian James A. Smith, author of The Idea Brokers: Think Tanks and the Rise of the New Policy Elite. While Smith's book considers the rise and fall of social scientists as a policy elite more than it does the role and influence of think tanks in the United States, he makes the point that these institutions have divided along "philosophical fault lines that traditionally split the American

---

[62]Ibid.
[63]Ibid., pp. 571.
[64]Ibid., p. 563.
[65]Richard Weaver, *Ideas Have Consequences* (Chicago: University of Chicago Press, 1948). The notion of a marketplace of ideas and the competition of ideas has its roots in John Stuart Mill's *On Liberty*, which stresses the importance of liberty in thought and discussion.
[66]Landers, "Think Tanks: The New Partisans," *Congressional Quarterly: Editorial Research Reports*, vol. I, no. 23, June 20, 1985, p. 455.
[67]Gregg Easterbrook, "Ideas Move Nations: How Conservative Think Tanks Have Helped to Transform the Terms of Political Debate," *Atlantic Monthly*, January 1986, p. 66.

policy elite into 'idealist' and 'pragmatist.'"[68] Smith summarized his views as follows:

> If we construe the political debate in this country as a battle of ideas, as a combat, as a marketplace that puts a value on selling ideas, as if they are products competing for attention, and that policies are somehow products that people in government must buy...then we have a very different way of conducting political debate than we had, I think, in the [decade after 1910] and the 1920s, when [there were] the social scientists with their rhetoric of serving the public interest and putting research in the service of policy making. That older conception placed a premium, not on conflict but on consensus building and...making our politics less overtly ideological....And to look broadly at the history of these institutions is to see how they have defined the center of gravity for our policy debate, how they have made discussions much more pragmatic, and at the same time much more technical. And what we've seen over the past 10 or 15 years, I think is a bit of an aberration, as our politics have tended to look more ideological, have tended to look as if there are more fundamental divisions in the body politic than in fact there are.[69]

The emergence of institutions such as the Heritage Foundation and the Institute for Policy Studies is often cited as an illustration of the fundamental change in strategy and structure of public policy research institutes that Smith and others contend has taken place. Weaver describes this class of institutions as "advocacy tanks" because of their overtly partisan and ideological orientation. Smith believes that, for most of their history, think tanks have been pragmatic in their orientation, which has "served to pull our debates toward the center, to narrow the range of policy discourse. They have, by and large, tended to temper and moderate public discussion and to search for compromise and consensus."[70] But, in recent years, think tanks have become more idealistic and ideological, which made them more inclined to argue "explicitly for the primacy of ideas and values" and less inclined to work toward a consensus.[71]

This conflict between the pragmatists and the idealists constitutes the core of Smith's critique of the nature of PPRIs. For Smith the implications of this shift in the nature of public policy formulation and the institutions involved in that process are quite clear:

---

[68] James A. Smith, *The Idea Brokers: Think Tanks and the Rise of the New Policy Elite* (New York: The Free Press, 1991), p. 236.
[69] Smith, quoted *in* Landers, "Think Tanks: The New Partisans," *Congressional Quarterly: Editorial Research Reports*, vol. I, no. 23, June 20, 1985, p. 471.
[70] James A. Smith, "Think Tanks and the Politics of Ideas" *in* David Colander & A.W. Coats, *The Spread of Economic Ideas* (Cambridge: Cambridge University Press, 1989), p. 193.
[71] Ibid., p. 192.

> The pragmatist is committed to the necessity of systematic social inquiry, to policy making as a process of experiment, and to compromise and a search for agreement as the goal of political debate. The idealist begins with a set of values; policies and programs that must reflect those values, and political discourse as a matter of exhortation and moral suasion. 'Ideas' mean different things to pragmatists and idealists. And in the final analysis, the role of ideas in our political life cannot be understood without a grasp of historical tension between these two contending intellectual traditions and the very different implications for our public discourse.[72]

Smith maintains that the war of ideas has served to fragment public debate to such an extent that rational discourse has given way to a "fractious and sectarian disputatiousness."[73] He argues that the intense debate that took place between liberals and conservatives was dysfunctional and that PPRIs should once again embrace relatively value-free research.

Wiarda views the partisan nature of think tanks as a relatively positive force that distinguishes this set of institutions from academic or university based research centers. He concludes that:

> think tank scholars tend to produce concrete analysis and recommendations, not abstract ones; they seldom are preoccupied with general models; they do know the bureaucratic ins and outs; and they keep current on the every day political and bureaucratic changes that their academic counterparts outside of Washington cannot possibly do. Hence the think tank knows how to plug into the system in a way that academic scholars do not.[74]

Wiarda implicitly argues that the general recommendations of academics and some think tanks have little utility for policy makers.

The extent to which public policy think tanks have become politicized and whether they are therefore dysfunctional is likely to become the subject of much debate. I believe that Smith and others have misread the changes in the marketplace and have sounded an alarm that will prove false. PPRIs are only responding to the increased competition between the Democratic and Republican parties that directly resulted from recent Republican political gains and the emergence of the neo-conservative movement in American politics. What Smith and others also fail to see is that the rise of these institutions is a function of the natural maturing process of the field and a sign of healthy competition. I also believe that what has been perceived to be the extreme partisan nature of certain institutions will be reined in by the natural forces of the marketplace, which tend to gravitate toward the center. Despite the advocacy tank theorists' contention

---

[72]Ibid., p. 194.
[73]Smith, *The Idea Brokers*, p. xx.
[74]Wiarda, *Foreign Policy Without Illusion*, pp. 157-58.

that the politicization of think tanks is a recent phenomenon, the facts and literature prove otherwise. I contend that advocacy tanks first appeared in the 1960s as an outgrowth of the social activism of that period. Levien, writing in 1969, concluded that the policy analysis organization must complement its influence with independence: "Indeed, maintaining a proper balance between these complementary and competitive qualities is one of the most difficult tasks that independent policy analysis organizations face. Too much independence and their influence with agencies can be severely reduced; too little independence and their quality and authority can be severely reduced."[75]

The politicization of think tanks only became an issue when conservative thinkers and think tanks entered the marketplace of ideas. Before 1970, the public policy arena was dominated by moderate and liberal research institutions. That public policy think tanks are influenced by politics is self-evident and that some think tanks have become overtly partisan is empirically valid; but to contend, as Smith and others have, that all think tanks have become overtly partisan and therefore dysfunctional is questionable at best. Herein lies the main defect in Smith's critique of these institutions.

One of the more recent works in this field of study is Joseph G. Peschek's Policy Planning Organizations, Elite Agendas and America's Rightward Turn. Drawing on the works of Domhoff and Dye on ruling elites, Peschek contends that the institutions he terms "policy planning organizations" have an undue influence on policy makers in Washington. He concludes that think tanks are controlled by corporate America, which uses them to control the public policy process. Clearly, politics is not that simple. His attempt to use political elite theory to explain PPRIs' role in U.S. politics could have been improved by incorporation of some earlier works on this subject into his analysis.

The literature on PPRIs is a mile wide and an inch deep. Because no clear boundaries have been established, it has been impossible to arrive at a shared definition of them. Most of the attempts are either too broad or too narrow, and many of the writers on this subject confuse PPRIs with research and development centers, planning agencies and government research centers. Moreover, each writer has described PPRIs so as to advance a particular argument, but without fully justifying the definition created or providing adequate examples. Many of the authors have failed to build on the existing literature on the subject, which has resulted in duplication and confusion. Despite these problems, our understanding of these institutions is much clearer than it was fifteen or twenty years ago. These contributions to the scholarship on PPRIs have also provided insights into the independence, tax status, funding base, organizational structure and political orientation of this class of institutions. While I concede that it is not easy to define these complex institutions, we now have enough information to begin.

---

[75]Levien, "Independent Public Policy Analysis Organization," p. 8.

CHAPTER 3
DEVELOPING A WORKING DEFINITION OF PUBLIC POLICY RESEARCH INSTITUTIONS

Determining the exact nature of PPRIs continues to be the source of discussion and debate, and precise and lasting definitions of them may prove elusive. Nonetheless, this chapter seeks to formulate a working definition. Generally speaking, public policy research is research and analysis that relates to current or proposed policies and legislation at the local, state or federal level. PPRIs are designed to study and analyze domestic and international concerns that bear on public policy. PPRIs' orientation toward policy research separates them from most university based research centers and research and development centers.

Policy research is clearly distinguished from basic research in the physical and social sciences that is generally conducted at academic institutions and research and development centers.[76] The primary objective of research institutions that are engaged in basic research is the creation of new knowledge, which also serves as the main means of advancement for the scholars and researchers who work at these institutions. In contrast, policy-oriented research is generally concerned with the production and dissemination of studies that are relevant to public policy. This is not to say that public policy institutions cannot produce new knowledge or that academic institutions are incapable of producing policy-oriented research; it is just to point out that the primary objectives of these institutions are quite different. In fact, some policy-oriented think tanks are affiliated with universities, but these are exceptions to the rule.

While PPRIs' focus on policy is their determining characteristic, a more specific definition will clearly distinguish them from research organizations in other fields. PPRIs are organizations that generate policy-oriented research, ideas, analysis, formulations and recommendations on domestic and international issues. A substantial portion of the financial and human resources of these institutions is devoted to commissioning and publishing research and policy analysis in

---

[76]While it will never be easy to make precise distinctions between policy research organizations and organizations that conduct research in the basic sciences such as biology and physics, there are differences worth noting. For good examinations of the differences between public policy research organizations and universities, commercial research enterprises and between the basic, applied and policy sciences, see J.S. Coleman, *Policy Research in the Social Sciences*, (Morristown, NJ: General Learning Systems, 1972); Harvey A. Averch, "Applied Social Science, Policy Science, and the Federal Government," *Knowledge: Creation, Diffusion, Utilization*, vol. 8, no. 3, March 1987, p. 67; Levien, "Independent Public Policy Analysis Organizations," p. 4231; and Baer, "Interdisciplinary Policy Research," p. 5347.

economics, political science, public administration and international affairs. The major outputs of these organizations are books, monographs, reports, policy briefs, conferences, seminars, briefings and informal discussions with policy makers and government officials. In addition, these institutions often act as a bridge between the academic and policy communities, translating applied and basic research into a language and form that busy policy makers seem to prefer.

This portion of the definition, while still broad and open-ended, begins to narrow the field of institutions that have been lumped under the general heading "think tanks" or "research institutes." By focusing on the policy orientation of these institutions, the definition excludes organizations that also do basic research or research and development. Further characterization of the public policy research industry is necessary to clarify its unique nature.

PPRIs have clearly identifiable organizational forms that make it possible to categorize them. There are ten sets of characteristics that, when taken with the definition outlined above, provide a full description of PPRIs. The following characteristics place further boundaries on these organizations by examining their strategy and structure:

1. affiliated/non-affiliated;
2. diversified/specialized;
3. academic/ policy oriented;
4. partisan/ non-partisan;
5. governmental/ non-governmental;
6. for profit/ not for profit;
7. degree granting/ non-degree granting;
8. multi-disciplinary/ single disciplinary;
9. academic/ policy maker constituency; and
10. contract/independent research.

It is important to keep in mind that drawing precise functional lines across such a large and diverse set of institutions is not easy and inevitably leads to considerable overlap in these characteristics. Despite these limitations, the public policy research community can be defined in a way that will distinguish it from seemingly related, but separate, institutions.

1. Affiliated/ Non-Affiliated

"Affiliated" means that the research institute is administratively, financially and legally connected to another organization. A free-standing institute is administratively, financially and legally independent of any other institution, whether a university or otherwise. University based PPRIs, for instance, are formally affiliated with a university, usually appear as centers or institutes in the social sciences, and are often connected to academic departments such as economics or political science. One example of a university based institute is the Center for International Affairs at Princeton. The Brookings Institution is a good example of a free-standing research institute, because it is completely autonomous.

2. Diversified/ Specialized

Some organizations are highly diversified with a research agenda that covers a wide range of issues and a staff whose expertise includes a number of disciplines. Other organizations choose to focus on a single issue or field of study and are staffed by researchers from a single discipline. The Foundation for Capital Formation assesses tax issues almost exclusively, and therefore is highly specialized. The American Enterprise Institute considers a whole range of economic, social and international issues and therefore is a diversified organization.

3. Academic/ Policy Oriented

PPRIs range from academic institutions whose structure and methods closely resemble universities, to institutions that resemble lobbying organizations. Academically oriented institutions tend to be more scholarly and interested in creating new knowledge, while policy oriented institutions tend to translate ideas into policy. The National Bureau of Economic Research, for example, is primarily interested in conducting applied research in economics that may have relevance for policy makers, while the Heritage Foundation in Washington attempts to influence policy by analyzing policy issues. The staffing patterns of each institution reflects its focus. The National Bureau of Economic Research is staffed entirely by academics with advanced degrees in economics who have solid academic credentials and publication records, while the Heritage Foundation is staffed almost exclusively by young professionals and less well-established scholars and is structured more like a newspaper than a university.

4. Partisan/ Non-Partisan

While all non-profit institutions are supposed to be non-partisan because of their federal tax status, which prohibits them from attempting to influence a specific piece of legislation and from using charitable funds for political activities, the reality is somewhat different.[77] Unlike university based research institutes, which generally do not make appointments on the basis of political philosophy or party affiliation, free-standing institutes take a candidate's philosophical orientation and political persuasion into consideration. Although early think tanks like Brookings were established to promote calm, reasoned, objective analysis of issues of public concern, some recent arrivals seem more adversarial, and polemical in their approach.

Two examples of these different approaches to selecting policy analysts and conducting research are the Cato Institute and the National Bureau of Economic Research (NBER). The Cato Institute is avowedly libertarian, only hires staff that shares its ideology, and as an organization, is dedicated to promoting policies that are consistent with its libertarian philosophy. In contrast,

---

[77]For a good discussion of the limits placed on these institutions by the Internal Revenue Service see John A. Edie, "Influencing Public Policy: The Legal Limits," *Foundation News*, (March /April 1985) and The Council on Foundations, "Foundations and Public Policy," *Resources for Grantmakers Series* (April 1985).

the scholars at NBER are not subjected to ideological tests and are generally discouraged from taking overtly partisan positions in their research. Partisan policy research was taken to an extreme in the period leading up to the 1988 presidential primary, when candidates like Jack Kemp, Gary Hart and Bruce Babbitt established non-profit PPRIs to help further their presidential aspirations.[78]

5. Governmental/Non-Governmental

On the whole, PPRIs are non-governmental, meaning that they are legally and administratively separate from government. While the majority of PPRIs are non-governmental, there are some exceptions. A number of research institutes are formally connected to the U.S. government; some good examples are the Congressional Research Center and the National Institutes for Health, which formulate public policy and are housed within the government. There are also a number of quasi-governmental organizations that are outside government administratively but are formally affiliated with and funded by the U.S. government. An example is the Center for Naval Analysis, which does operational and strategic research for the U.S. Navy.

6. For Profit/Not For Profit

The for profit/ not for profit distinction simply means that the institute is either a commercial research organization that conducts public policy research for a fee, or a tax exempt, publicly supported institution that must rely on individuals, foundations and corporations for its financial support. The profit making firms generally consult, study, conduct surveys, make recommendations, perform applied research and, as Dickson says, "think for a fee."[79] The Planning Research Corporation and Arthur D. Little, Inc., best exemplify this group of research institutes because they conduct policy research under contract for the government for a profit. In contrast, institutions such as the American Enterprise Institute and the Brookings Institution do not seek to make a profit and must rely on the public for their support. Amy Wilentz describes these institutions as "non-profit, tax-exempt foundations dedicated to public policy research"[80] The non-profit, tax exempt status granted by the Internal Revenue Service not only distinguishes these institutions from profit making ventures, but also places real limits on the sources of the financing and the types of activities in which they can engage.[81]

7. Degree Granting/ Non-Degree Granting

Degree granting versus non-degree granting refers to whether the PPRI has a formal educational program and grants degrees as a part of its organizational mission. Most, if not all, free-standing PPRIs are non-degree granting

---

[78] Richard Fly, "What's in for the Presidential Hopefuls: Think Tanks," *Business Week*, May 12, 1986, pp. 60-62.
[79] Ibid., p. 30.
[80] Amy Wilentz, "On the Intellectual Ramparts," *Time*, September 1, 1986, pp. 22-23.
[81] The guidelines for non-profit organizations can be found in the Internal Revenue Service's Tax Code for foundations and public charities, which are commonly known as 501(c)(3) organizations.

institutions. The only current exception is the Rand Corporation, which has a graduate degree program in public policy.[82] Since a large number of PPRIs resemble academic institutions, this is an important means of distinguishing them from universities and university affiliated research centers.

8. Multi-Disciplinary/ Single Disciplinary

Multi-disciplinary/ single disciplinary refers to the composition of the research staff and the nature of the research conducted at PPRIs. This category overlaps with the characteristics of diversification and specialization, as previously discussed. Free-standing PPRIs are generally multi-disciplinary in nature, while those that are affiliated with colleges and universities tend to be dominated by a single discipline. This is because university based PPRIs are usually based in academic departments, while free-standing institutes tend not to be organized by discipline or department. The exceptions are the single issue oriented PPRIs where only a single discipline tends to be represented. An example is the National Bureau of Economic Research, which is almost completely comprised of economists. The Rand Corporation is the best example of a highly diversified organization that takes its staff from a number of disciplines.

9. Academic/ Policy Maker Constituency

This characteristic specifically refers to the market or audience that the institution is organized to serve. PPRIs generally perceive their primary constituency to be policy makers in Washington, while researchers at university affiliated centers and the highly academic oriented think tanks see their primary constituency as students and other academics. For example, the Heritage Foundation views policy makers as its primary constituency in Washington, while the Center for International Studies at Princeton University conducts policy-oriented research primarily for students, professors and other academics.

It is important to isolate this set of characteristics from the academic/ policy-oriented set of characteristics, because while many PPRIs have a policy orientation, the primary market for their publications is academia. As an illustration of this point, I am reminded of a scholar at Brookings who was quoted as saying, "Our books are written for policymakers and read by college students."[83] The difference between the stated policy orientation of these institutions and the actual market they serve is something that will be explored further when the study examines the strategy and structure of these institutions.

---

[82] In addition, the Rand Corporation has developed its own degree granting graduate school and a number of other graduate level programs in conjunction with universities. Rand has also established a series of post-graduate programs at its Santa Monica campus. Brookings established its own graduate school in 1924, but it did not survive for long. Rand's programs are fairly well established and provide an effective mechanism for training students in its brand of policy analysis.

[83] R. Kent Weaver, "The Changing World of Think Tanks," p. 566.

10. Contract/ Independent Research

Contract research is research conducted under contract with the government or another institution. The contracting organization generally establishes the parameters for the research and may even specify the desired conclusions. In addition, the institutions and scholars that conduct contract research often cannot publish their findings because these are for the sole use of the organization that paid for them. Durst and Thurber point out that "think tanks that are forced to rely on the satisfaction of contractors with their research product find it difficult to pursue independent inquiry."[84]

In order for research to be truly independent, the institution and its research staff must be free to set its own research agenda, to set the parameters of its research and to make recommendations without concern for political or economic consequences. Independent research often has a variety of sponsors or is funded through endowment revenues. According to Durst and Thurber, "intellectual independence assumes that the organization extends the privileges of academic freedom to its scholars and that it is to some extent financially independent."[85] As can be seen in the following examples, there is a direct correlation between the degree of research freedom at an institution and its level of financial independence. The Rand Corporation, which receives over seventy percent of its revenues from government research contracts, has far less control over its research agenda and its research findings than the Brookings Institution, which has a sizable endowment and an extremely diversified base of external support.

These ten sets of characteristics provide a tool with which to narrow the field of institutions that would be traditionally included in a study of this sort by selecting those specific qualities that will define a smaller group of think tanks that might be described as independent PPRIs. The study will incorporate the characteristics "non-profit," "non-governmental," "non-affiliated" and "non-degree granting" into its working definition. The focus is now exclusively on those institutions that are legally and administratively separate from government and universities and are not commercial enterprises. In limiting the study in this way, institutions such as university affiliated basic and applied research centers, government research centers, commercial research and development enterprises and commercial public policy research centers are excluded.

---

[84]Durst & Thurber, "Studying Washington Think Tanks," p. 1.
[85]Ibid., p. 11.

Table 3.1
Characteristics & Representative Institutions

	Characteristics	Institutions
1	affiliated/ non-affiliated	Center for International Affairs/ Brookings Institution
2	diversified/ specialized	American Enterprise Institute/ Foundation for Capital Formation
3	academic oriented/ policy oriented	National Bureau of Economic Research/ Heritage Foundation
4	partisan/ non-partisan	Cato Institute/ National Bureau of Economic Research
5	governmental/ non-governmental	Center for Naval Analysis/ Congressional Research Center & National Institutes for Health
6	for profit/ not for profit	Planning Research Corporation & Arthur Little/ American Enterprise Institute & Brookings Institution
7	degree granting/ non-degree granting	Rand Corporation/ most other PPRIs
8	multi-disciplinary/ single disciplinary	Rand Corporation/ National Bureau of Economic Research
9	academic constituency/ policy maker constituency	Center for International Studies/ Heritage Foundation
10	contract research/ independent research	Rand Corporation/ Brookings Institution

I contend that the set of institutions I have defined constitutes an industry and that the firms in this industry have distinguished themselves from other research enterprises through their independent nature, organizational design and focus on public policy research and analysis. In viewing PPRIs in this way, it is possible to focus on them as a unique group of firms that have distinct product lines, means of production, distribution mechanisms and marketing strategies.

Not all of the characteristics identified above have been incorporated into the working definition. The other characteristics will be utilized when I begin discussing the various strategies and structures employed by this group of institutions. The definition that will be used to guide the study and establish its boundaries is as follows:

> Public policy research institutions are non-profit, non-governmental organizations that generate policy-oriented research, ideas, analysis, and formulations and recommendations on domestic and international issues. For the most part, these organizations are not affiliated with academic institutions and do not grant degrees. A substantial portion of the financial and human resources of these institutions is devoted to commissioning and

publishing research and policy analysis in the social sciences, economics, political science, public administration and international affairs. The major outputs of these organizations are books, monographs, reports, policy briefs, conferences, seminars, briefings and informal discussions with policy makers and government officials. In addition, these institutions often act as a bridge between the academic and policy communities, translating applied and basic research into a language and form that meets the needs of busy policymakers.

The PPRIs that fall within these boundaries are listed immediately after this chapter. In addition to providing an overall listing of the institutions, I have attempted to divide them into sub-groups to illustrate the specialization that has taken place in the industry and to point out some of the major market segments served by these firms. The list may not be exhaustive, and is certainly subject to change. Some institutions appear in more than one category.

There are two main classes of institutions: diversified and specialized. The specialized institutions are then divided into two major sub-categories: domestic and international, indicating the broad focus of the policy research conducted by each institution. Domestic focus institutions are concerned with social and economic policies at the federal, state and local levels. The international group includes institutions that are focused primarily but not exclusively on foreign affairs and international economics. These two sub-groups are further divided into a series of sub-specialties. These divisions will contribute to the later discussion of the competitive strategies of these institutions.

Table 3.2
Summary Table of PPRIs by Research Focus

Category	Number of PPRIs
Diversified Research Focus	12
Domestic	57
State and Local	48
Economic	25
Economic and Social	19
Social	10
Defense and National Security	14
Environment	4
Health	1
International	35
Other	6

ALPHABETICAL LISTING OF THINK TANKS BY RESEARCH FOCUS
I.   Diversified Public Policy Research Organizations

American Enterprise Institute for Public Policy Research
Brookings Institution

Cato Institute
Center for National Policy (Republican Party)
Heritage Foundation
Hoover Institution on War, Revolution and Peace
Hudson Institute
Institute for Policy Studies
Institute for Contemporary Studies
Pacific Research Institute for Public Policy
Rand Corporation
Roosevelt Center for American Policy Studies (Closed 6/89)

II. Specialized Public Policy Research Organizations
A. *International Focus*
Atlantic Council of the United States
Carnegie Endowment for International Peace
Center for Applied Research in the Apostolate
Center for Democracy
Center for International Business and Trade
Center for International Policy
Center for Policy Studies
Center for Strategic and International Studies
Center for Women's Policy Studies
Council on Foreign Relations
Council for Social and Economic Studies
Democratic Institute for International Affairs
Ethics and Public Policy Center
Foreign Policy Institute
Human Resources Organization
Indochina Project
Institute for Energy Analysis
Institute for International Economics
Institute for Security and Cooperation in Outer Space
International Center for Research on Women
International Law Institute
Mankind Research Foundation
Middle East Institute
Population Reference Bureau
Resources for the Future
SRI (Stanford Research Institute)
Washington Institute of Foreign Affairs
World Resources Institute
Worldwatch Institute

B. *Domestic Focus*
ANSER
Alan Guttmacher Institute
American Legislative Exchange Council
Battelle Memorial Institute

Bureau for Social Science Research
Center for Congressional & Presidential Studies
Center for Defense Information
Center for National Policy
Center for Naval Analyses
Center for a Responsible Federal Budget
Center for Science in the Public Interest
Center for the Study of Social Policy
Center for the Study of Welfare Policy
Center on Budget and Policy Priorities
Committee for Economic Development
Conference on Economic Progress
Employee Benefit Research Institute
Ethics Resources Center
Governmental Affairs Institute
Hispanic Policy Development Project
Historical Evaluation & Research Organization
Institute for Defense Analyses
Institute for Educational Leadership
Institute for Gas Technology
Institute for Health Analysis
Institute for Policy Studies
Investor Responsibility Research Center
Jefferson Foundation
Joint Center for Political Studies
Lincoln Institute
Logistic Management Institute
Media Institute
National Institute for Public Policy
Northeast-Midwest Institute
Potomac Institute
Progressive Policy Institute
Public Technology
Renewable Energy Institute
Ripon Society
Roosevelt Center for American Policy Studies
Russell Sage Foundation
Sunbelt Institute
Tax Analysts
Tax Foundation
Urban Institute
Washington Center for Public Policy Research
Washington Institute
Washington Journalism Center
Women's Research and Education Institute

  C. *State/ Local/ Regional Focus*
American Studies Institute

American Federation of Small Business
American Legislative Exchange
Atlantic Legal Foundation
The Atlas Economic Research Foundation
The Barry Goldwater Institute for Public Policy Research
California Public Policy Foundation
Capitol Resource Institute
Center for Market Alternatives
Claremont Institute
Competitive Enterprise Institute
The Commonwealth Foundation for Public Policy Alternatives
Free Market Foundation
The Heartland Institute
Heartland Wisconsin
Independence Institute
Institute for Business Ethics
Institute for Policy Innovation
The James Madison Institute
The John Locke Foundation
Landmark Legal Foundation
Lincoln Legal Foundation
The Mackinac Center
The Mid-America Legal Foundation
Mississippi Center for Public Policy Studies
Mountain State Legal Foundation
New Coalition for Economic and Social Change
The New England Center for Political Studies and Research
New England Legal Foundation
Northeast-Midwest Institute
Pacific Legal Foundation
Pacific Research Institute
Pioneer Institute
Political Economy Research Center
Public Affairs Research Institute
Reason Foundation
Rockford Institute
Rose Institute for State and Local Government
Sequoia Institute
South Carolina Policy Council
South Foundation
Southwest Policy Institute
Texans for an Informed Public
Texas Public Policy Foundation
Utah State University
Washington Institute for Policy Studies
Washington Legal Foundation
Wyoming Heritage Society
Yankee Institute

D. Economic Policy Focus

American Council for Capital Formation
ANSER (Analytic Services, Inc.)
Center for Science in the Public Interest
Citizens for a Sound Economy
Committee for a Responsible Federal Budget
Committee for Economic Development
Conference Board
Conference on Economic Progress
Economic Policy Institute
Employee Benefit Research Institute
Institute of Gas Technology
Institute for Energy Analysis
Investor Responsibility Research Center
Logistic Management Institute
Manhattan Institute for Policy
National Center for Appropriate Technology
National Bureau of Economic Research
National Center for Policy Alternatives
Political Economy Research Center
Public Technology
Reason Foundation
Tax Analysts
Tax Foundation
Urban Land Institute
Washington Journalism Center

E. Economic and Social Focus

Bureau of Social Science Research
Center for Women's Policy Studies
Center for the Study of Women's Welfare Policy
Center for the Study of Social Policy
Center on Budget and Policy Priorities
Children's Defense Fund
Council for Social and Economic Studies
Hispanic Policy Development Project
Human Resources Organization
Independence Policy Institute
Jefferson Foundation
Joint Center for Political and Economic Studies
Lincoln Institute
National Center for Policy Analysis
National Institute of Public Affairs
Pacific Research Institute for Public Policy
Potomac Institute
Progressive Policy Institute
Ripon Society

Russell Sage Foundation
Twentieth Century Fund
Urban Institute
Washington Center for Public Policy Research
Washington Institute
Women's Research and Education Institute

    F.   *Defense and National Security Focus*
American Security Council
The Arms Control Association
Center for Strategic and International Studies
Center for Defense Information
Committee for National Security
Foreign Policy Research Institute
Institute for Foreign Policy Analysis
Institute for Security and Cooperation in Outer Space
Institute for Defense Analysis
Foreign Policy Institute (Johns Hopkins University)

    G.   *Environmental Focus*
Renewable Energy Institute
Resources for the Future
World Resources Institute
Worldwatch Institute

    H.   *Health Focus*
Institute for Health Policy Analysis

    I.   *Other*
Alan Guttmacher Institute
Center for Congressional and Presidential Studies
Center for Democracy
Committee for Study of the American Electorate
Ethics and Public Policy Center
Institute for Educational Leadership

An unduplicated count of the organizations listed above reveals that there are 112 institutions that might be considered truly independent non-profit public policy research institutions. The remainder of the study will focus on this class of institutions.

This chapter has attempted to draw together the various strands of knowledge into a coherent picture that focuses on a large but well-defined group of PPRIs. In so doing, I think I have presented an accurate and comprehensive assessment and description of a whole class of organizations – a class of institutions on which Dickson and others did not focus because there were only a "handful of truly independent, nonprofit, self-determining, think tanks."[86] Things have changed, and we now isolate this special class of institutions for further examination. The next chapter will discuss the nature and origin of these institutions.

---

[86]Dickson, *Think Tanks*, p. 265.

CHAPTER 4
ACADEMICS TO IDEOLOGUES: PUBLIC POLICY RESEARCH INSTITUTIONS AND THE AMERICAN DEMOCRATIC EXPERIENCE

An integral part of the American democratic experience has been the proclivity of citizens to form associations or organizations that are independent of government and are designed to influence the political process.[87] This impulse has encouraged the establishment of an array of for profit and not for profit institutions whose main objective is to influence decision makers.[88] Since the turn of the century, PPRIs have partially filled the need for independent analysis and thought. The creation of independent organizations supported by private dollars to conduct policy research and provide a forum for ideas and debate is an overwhelmingly American phenomenon that is deeply rooted in the nation's democratic, pluralistic and philanthropic traditions.

PPRIs occupy a special niche between the academic and policy communities in the American political landscape.[89] As non-profit organizations, they operate independently from the government and do not, for the most part, owe allegiance to any political party or special interest. Because of their unique position in the policy formulation process, they have been able to grow in both in numbers and influence.

The prominence and independence that PPRIs enjoy in America is partially due to the pluralistic (or what some have described as the hyper-pluralistic) character of our political structure. Without multiple decision centers, policy experts would have been largely focused on the executive branch as the dominant or even sole client. Patricia Linden captures the unique aspects of American society and the important role public policy institutes play in the political process when she writes: "Big Pluralistic America. It's the noisiest

---

[87] Alexis de Tocqueville first observed Americans' tendency to form associations in *Democracy in America* (1835).

[88] Easterbrook, "Ideas Move Nations," p. 66. Commenting on the unique role that public policy research institutes play in the policy formulation process he states, "No other country accords such significance to private institutions designed to influence public decisions."

[89] The "two communities" metaphor has been used extensively by researchers concerned with understanding the nature of the relationship between the producers of knowledge (primarily academics) and potential users of social science research (decision makers). Evert Anthony Lindquist argues in *Behind the Myth of Think Tanks: The Organization and Relevance of Canadian Policy Institutes*, (Ph.D. Thesis, University of California at Berkeley) that this approach does not fully consider PPRIs because they are neither policy makers or academic researchers. Lindquist suggest that they are a "third community" that acts as a bridge between the policy and academic communities.

political debating society in the world: a babble of voices airing contrary opinions on how the country should be run. For this democracy, where every view is permissible and each faction seeks to persuade – Republicans, Democrats, left, right and centrist. Lobbyists, journalists, scholars, religionists. And think tanks. Dissonant, protean, cacophonous, they are yeast in the ever-fermenting discussion."[90] While the existence of powerful factions in American society is nothing new – James Madison wrote about them two centuries ago – what is new is the emergence of PPRIs as a central force in the political process. Our open form of government has created a robust debate that has served to catapult think tanks to national and international prominence.

The list of PPRIs provided in the preceding chapter offers evidence that Linden's observations about think tanks are not far off the mark. PPRIs now encompass a wide range of policy concerns and are emerging as a potent force in the policy making process in Washington and throughout the United States. Why is this, and why have they been able to prosper?

Polsby believes that PPRIs "exist and prosper to a very significant degree because American government is so permeable, flexible and pluralistic."[91] The American system is extremely porous, with many political actors and points of access. Polsby contends that, unlike other countries, the United States has allowed institutions such as think tanks to have influence. James Smith asserts that Americans are inclined to embrace outside experts who hold out the promise of providing "a rational, efficient decision-making process."[92] These contentions, taken together, may provide a reason for the dramatic pace of PPRIs' growth.

PPRIs attempt, via independent and somewhat neutral research, to suggest ideas and policy proposals to handle public problems or needs. This rational, value neutral approach to research has served to increase their stature in the policy making community. The unique role these institutions play in the policy process is captured nicely by Polsby when he writes:

> I have thus far avoided enumerating examples of the influence of public policy research on public policy because one would scarcely know where to begin. They have sponsored policy innovations: for example, the idea of having a Council of Economic Advisers was largely the brainchild of a Brookings staff member. They have furnished justifications for all sorts of public policies. They have transformed the terms in which policy have been conceived by government agencies – for example, Rand's Albert Wohlstetter totally reoriented the Air Force thinking about the need for overseas strategic air bases. They have added to the stock of human knowledge by describing the course and effects of public policy making

---

[90] Linden, "Powerhouses of Policy," *Town and Country*, January 1987, p. 99.
[91] Polsby, "Tanks But No Tanks," p. 16.
[92] Smith, *The Idea Brokers*, p. 34.

and administration in a myriad of fields. They have usefully monitored major institutions of government, as in the AEI Vital Statistics on Congress series and its At the Polls series and in the Brooking Setting National Priorities series. They have contributed to public debate and, without question, to public enlightenment.[93]

The unique role that PPRIs occupy in America presents a striking contrast to other democratic societies such as Germany and Japan, where the political parties are the driving force behind the policy planning and formulation process. The differences between the United States and other western democracies are quite evident in this regard. PPRIs in the United States "fulfill four different functions in the political process which, in Western European democracies, are the prerogatives of parties, political foundations and bureaucracies: generation of ideas and ideologies, convocation [networking], publication [diffusion], and transformation [of elites]."[94]

Since the turn of the century the legislative and executive branches of government have turned with greater frequency to outside experts to help solve complex problems and to manage a growing bureaucracy. "The character of our government, increasingly dominated by temporary political executives rather than career bureaucrats, encourages this dependency upon outsiders for intelligence, analysis, and advice."[95] While Polsby attributes this reliance to the permeability of the American system of government, Smith believes that it arises out of the "separation of powers" clause in the Constitution, which set in motion an ongoing conflict between the executive and legislative branches. According to Smith, "Policy research institutes have been able to supply data, analysis, technical help, and political arguments because of inter-branch rivalries."[96] To prove his point, Smith offers the following examples:

> The inspiration for the Brookings Institution came in the 1910s at a time when the federal executive seemed especially weak in relation to Congress. AEI was founded in the 1940s when Congress and conservative supporters outside were trying to redress an imbalance in its powers against a vastly expanded executive bureaucracy. Heritage was set up in the 1970s primarily to assist an ideologically conservative congressional faction in its battles against the Republican Party's then moderate legislative leadership and an Executive Branch that seemed unsympathetic to the conservatism of the hard right.[97]

---

[93]Polsby, "Tanks But No Tanks," p. 59.
[94]Gellner, "Political Think Tanks," p. 5.
[95]Polsby, "Tanks But No Tanks," p. 58.
[96]Smith, "Think Tanks and the Politics of Ideas," pp. 181-83. This assertion has its roots in Hugh Heclo's "Issue Networks and the Executive Establishment," in *The New American Political System*, A. King, ed. (Washington, D.C.: American Enterprise Institute, 1978), pp. 87-124.
[97]Smith, "Think Tanks and the Politics of Ideas," p. 180.

These rivalries have intensified recently and the number of public policy think tanks has mushroomed.

Smith and Polsby also attribute the rise of PPRIs to the special nature of our civil service, the continuing importance of political appointments, the American public's deeply ingrained suspicion of bureaucrats, and governmental agencies' decisions to contract out research and other services normally conducted by government. Each of these factors has served to strengthen and expand the role of the independent organizations in the policy planning an formulation process. Critchlow contends that the role and number of PPRIs expanded as result of the breakdown of the post World War II policy consensus during the Vietnam War.

> While the AEI was emerging to challenge the Brookings Institution, the liberal consensus was coming apart. The first signs of the disintegration began over foreign policy with the crisis precipitated by the war in Vietnam. By the 1970s attacks on the liberal consensus in domestic policy began to come from the Left and Right. Previously such attacks had come primarily from groups isolated from the center of power. In turn, debate within the center had usually focused around incremental increases or decreases of existing programs. Now an increasing polarization in the policy debate allowed previously excluded groups to exert major influence within the policy arena raising questions which challenged the fundamental premises of the liberal state. Under attack from the Left and the Right, confused by their own inability to explain the current economic and social crisis, and America's apparent weakness in international affairs, the liberal center felt a need to find new vitality and to agree if the patient were to survive. Yet with the center falling apart, new policy institutes emerged to represent positions on the Left and the Right of the policy spectrum. On the Left came the Institute for Policy Studies; a decade later the Heritage Foundation was established on the Right. Politics, like nature, seems to abhor a vacuum.[98]

In recent years, the dramatic increase in the size of Congressional staffs along with the fragmented committee and subcommittee structure of Congress, as well as a deeply entrenched bureaucracy, and the media's role in the public policy process have created a greater demand for independent public policy analysis and provided greater opportunities for independent PPRIs.[99] Ironically, most governmental agencies and congressional staffs do very little original research and they turn to governmental research organizations, think tanks and interest groups

---

[98]Critchlow, "Think Tanks, Anti-Statism, and Democracy," pp. 54-55.

[99]For an interesting study of the changes that have taken place in congress in recent years see Richard Fenno, *Homestyle and Washington Work* (Ann Arbor: University of Michigan Press, 1989).

for information and analysis.[100] Additionally, the media's need to present authoritative opposing points of view has increased the demand for policy experts and brought many think tanks into national prominence.[101]

The position these institutions occupy in Washington is quite impressive when one considers their competition. Also producing policy research are legions of scholars and policy analysts at private and public research universities, research and development centers and corporate think tanks. Add to this the now massive governmental research system, which now includes the Congressional Budget Office, the Office of Management and Budget, and the Congressional Research Service, and you have a tremendous policy research apparatus. These individuals and institutions form an impressive group that has the potential to out-person and out-pen the 100 or so independent PPRIs.[102] While it would seem that an increase in the professional staffs of Congress and the executive branch and the establishment of think tanks within government would reduce the demand for independent public policy research, just the opposite has occurred.[103] The independence of PPRIs has enabled them to grow as a sector despite of the development of a large corporate and government based research establishment.

PPRIs have operated in what Hugh Heclo describes as the fringes of government, filling a need created by our governmental structure and political system.[104] Smith and others see PPRIs as contributing to some of the deficiencies that have emerged in our government in recent years. Their growth is viewed as a clear indication of the fragmentation of our policy-making process.

---

[100]Michael Malbin, in *Unelected Representatives* (New York: Basic, 1980), and Harrison W. Fox & Susan Webb Hammond, in *Congressional Staffs: The Invisible Force In American Lawmaking* (New York: Free Press, 1977), examine the growth of congressional staffs and the role they play in the policy planning and formulation process. Fox and Hammond found that congressional staff do not have the time or inclination to do their own research. They tend to rely on sources within the government, independent research organizations and interest groups for most of their information. This assessment has been confirmed by my series of interviews with White House and Congressional staff.

[101]A number of researchers and journalists, including Winard Gellner, Alison Muscatine, and Lawrence C. Soley, have examined the media's increasing use of think tanks and their staffs for expert opinions on public policy questions.

[102]For an interesting comparative study of GAO and OMB, see Frederic C. Mosher, *A Tale of Two Agencies: A Comparative Analysis of the General Accounting Office and the Office of Management and Budget* (Baton Rouge: Louisiana State University Press, 1984).

[103]In a conversation with James Thurber, he described the increases in Congress and the White House as "stafflation". Many observers of the U.S. government are alarmed at how fast congressional staffs have expanded and are concerned about the impact on the policy making process. The Heritage Foundation and the Claremont Institute produced a scathing attack on Congress in *The Imperial Congress: Crisis in the Separation of Powers*, Gordon S. Jones & John A. Marini, eds. (New York: Pharos Books, 1988).

[104]Hugh Heclo, "The In and Outer System: A Critical Assessment," in *The In and Outers: Presidential Appointees and Transient Government*, G. Calvin Mackenzie, ed. (Washington: Johns Hopkins University Press, 1987) p. 310.

Commenting on this problem, Smith suggests that "Woodrow Wilson's feared notion of a 'government of experts'" has come to pass.[105] He contends that Wilson believed "democracy depended on the dedicated amateur who understood the concrete applications of a policy initiative and who could speak the language of the ordinary citizen."[106] What we have now, according to Smith and others, is a tyranny of policy elites that has made "American politics more polarized, short-sighted, and fragmented."[107] In Smith's view "the experts, far from limiting debate and innovation, have created an environment in which so many arguments contend that no consensus is possible. Their never-ending controversies leave even closely attentive citizens in despair of ever coming to agreement on the most important issues."[108] Smith's critique of the role of think tanks and policy elites in America is overly pessimistic. The fragmentation of the policy formulation process has more to do with the short-term orientation of elected officials and the failure of political parties to control their members than it does with the proliferation of think tanks. They are more a symptom than the problem itself. Although they complicate the process, eliminating them in order to limit debate and innovation would be ineffective as well as undesirable.

Fauriol views the situation more optimistically, pointing out that "think tanks [thrive] on the outward chaos of the policy process, [contribute] to its diversity, but also [generate] some of the insights for it to proceed forward."[109] PPRIs are simply responding to the chaos that exists in the political environment, and while they may add to it, they are not responsible for it. In a pluralistic society where power is decentralized and political parties are weak, policy research organizations and other public interest groups play a positive and stabilizing role in the political process.

The 100-plus PPRIs that have come into being in the last seventy-five years have established themselves as an integral part of the policy making framework in Washington and throughout the United States. Their influence has grown with the size of government and the number of domestic and international commitments. Policy makers and media moguls alike have come to rely on them to help make sense of the complexities of modern society and to navigate the political labyrinth. These are some of the political, social and economic forces that have shaped PPRIs.

PPRIs are a twentieth century phenomenon that is in many ways unique to the United States. Rooted in the social sciences and supported by private individual and foundations, they began to appear around the turn of the century as

---

[105]Smith, *The Idea Brokers*, p. 238.
[106]Ibid., pp. 237-39.
[107]Ibid., p. 237.
[108]Ibid., p. 231.
[109]Fauriol, "Think Tanks and U.S. Foreign Policy," p. 26.

a part of a larger effort to bring the expertise of scholars and managers to bear on the economic and social problems of this period[110] According to Linden,

> the early versions [of PPRIs], set up by private capital long before the proliferation of tax-funded social agencies, were organized to alleviate problems of the poor. Two survivors of that era are the National Conference on Social Welfare, formed in 1873, and the Russell Sage Foundation, established in 1907 to help provide housing and better conditions for the elderly, orphaned and indigent.[111]

The history of public policy research industry may be divided into four periods that saw the creation of many of the PPRIs that exist today: 1900-1929, 1930-1959, 1960-1975 and 1976-1990. The chronological list at the end of this chapter illustrates how the industry's expansion is clustered in the last two time periods. A summary table is provided below that indicates the number of institutes that were established during these periods and that have remained in operation. An exhaustive list of institutions would be extremely difficult to develop, because records and lists of institutions that went out of business are not available. Despite this limitation, the data provided help illustrate how the industry has grown.

Table 4.1
Existing Public Policy Research Institutes
(By Period Founded)

Period	Number Founded
1900-1929	10
1930-1959	17
1960-1975	30
1975-1990	55
TOTAL	112

For each of these periods I have selected an institution that reflects the economic and political environment of that time. In the 1920s, it was the Brookings Institution; for the 1940s, Rand Corporation; for the 1960s, the Urban Institute; and for 1970s, it was the Heritage Foundation. The organizations that came into being during these four periods were influenced by the innovations introduced by the four representative institutions. For instance, the majority of the organizations founded in the first period had a strong academic orientation and have similar structure to that of the Brookings Institution.

---

[110]Smith, in *The Idea Brokers*, contends that the history of the policy expert is woven of three intertwined threads. The strongest of these is the mid-nineteenth century attempt to create a "social" science that would be both a method of scholarly investigation and tool for social improvement. The second strand is the ongoing attempt in the United States and elsewhere to incorporate experts' knowledge and analytic techniques into public service through a series of formal and informal mechanisms. The final strand is think tanks.

[111]Linden, "Powerhouses of Policy," p. 99.

Table 4.2
Founding Dates of Selected Organizations

Institution	Date Founded
The Brookings Institution	1916 (1927)[112]
The Rand Corporation	1948
The Urban Institute	1968
The Heritage Foundation	1973

Each of the four periods was marked by a major domestic or international upheaval that sparked the creation of a new generation of public policy research institutes. The major events that influenced the creation of these institutions were wars of one kind or another: World War I, World War II, the War on Poverty and the War of Ideas.

Brookings and the Rise of the Public Policy Research Institute
At the conclusion of World War I, domestic and foreign policy challenges led to the creation of a number of PPRIs in the mid- to late 1920s. On the foreign policy side, the country saw the formation of the Carnegie Endowment for International Peace (1910), the Foreign Policy Association (1918), the Hoover Institution on War, Revolution and Peace (1919), and the Council on Foreign Relations (1921). All of these institutions came into prominence as a result of the United States' emergence as a global power after World War I. Because of the American tendency toward isolationism, some groups wanted to convince political elites and the American public at large that it was in America's interest to play a greater role in international politics.

Fauriol captures the ambivalence that helped shape the nature and character of these early think tanks when he observes that the Carnegie Endowment for International Peace and the Hoover Institution "were clearly the outgrowth of America's domestic economic and overseas diplomatic expansion."[113] Yet,

> [t]he apparent strength of the American economic system and the potential application of its ideals on a global basis generated a certain sense of mission reinforced by frustration with traditional international behavior [exemplified by the catastrophe of World War I] . . . these same frustrations also underline[d] a national feeling of hesitation regarding any deep involvement in world affairs."[114]

Internationally, there appeared to be a clear mandate for greater United States involvement in global affairs, but the American public was not prepared to accept

---

[112] The Institute for Government Research was founded in 1916, but the name Brookings was not used until 1927.
[113] Fauriol, "Think Tanks and U.S. Foreign Policy," p. 11.
[114] Ibid., p. 12.

it. A small but influential elite set out to change this by establishing a series of foreign policy education and foreign policy research organizations.

On the domestic front, a number of public policy research organizations came into being as a result of the social science and scientific management movements popular in the late nineteenth century. Their operating premise was that scientific methods, if properly applied, could solve social problems and improve the efficiency of government. These forces helped shape institutions such as the Russell Sage Foundation (1907), the Brookings Institution (1916), and the National Bureau of Economic Research (1920). Smith concludes that each one of these institutions "owed its origins to different business and professional groups" that were a part of the social reform movements of this period.[115] Individuals like Robert S. Brookings, a successful businessman, and Wesley C. Mitchell, an economist, believed that business and social sciences would improve governmental operations and enlighten public policy. Mitchell's convictions led him to establish the National Bureau of Economic Research (NBER), while Brookings was instrumental in establishing the institution that bears his name. The importance and stature of these institutions, however, was greatly enhanced by the social, political and economic upheaval of the Great Depression. In addition, the New Deal's host of new programs and government agencies created a demand for expert advice that PPRIs like Brookings and NBER could fill.

Robert S. Brookings, a St. Louis industrialist motivated by a desire to bring "economy and efficiency" to government, established three institutions (the Institute for Government Research, the Institute of Economics and the Robert Brookings Graduate School of Economics and Government) that merged to create the Brookings Institution in 1927 at a time when, as Calvin Coolidge explained, the business of America was business, and the principles of science were beginning to be applied to government.[116] Brookings' interest in applying scientific principles to the management of government is reflected in the charter of the institution which states that it will conduct "scientific research" in "the broad fields of economics, government administration and the political and social sciences generally, "in an effort to interpret relevant "economic and political and social facts . . . without regard to and independent of the special interests of any group in the body politic, either political, social or economic."[117] According to Bruce MacLaury, Brookings' current president, Robert Brookings set out to establish a center that would bring social scientists and policy makers together so that a "scientific approach" might be applied to government management, budgeting and spending.[118]

---

[115] Smith, "Think Tanks and the Politics of Ideas," p. 112.

[116] Critchlow, *The Brookings Institution, 1916-1952*, p. 17.

[117] Developed from information provided by the Brookings Institution's Charter, Mission and Statement of Purpose and other historical data, (Washington, D.C.).

[118] Data supplied from the Brookings Institution's Seventy-fifth Anniversary Pamphlet, (Washington, DC, 1991).

The Brookings model, which attempts to bring the knowledge and expertise of academics to bear on public policy, has influenced the nature and design of PPRIs for over fifty years. Brookings has become known for its reliance on recognized scholars that engage in empirical, scholarly and objective analysis of public policy issues in the social sciences. Originally focused on economic analysis, Brookings has since broadened its agenda to include a range of domestic and international concerns. Because its roots are firmly planted in the social sciences and academia, Brookings is without a doubt the best example of the academic-oriented public policy research institute. The Brookings model still, in many ways, dominates the public policy landscape as the preferred model for how think tanks should be organized. It remains unchallenged, in a large measure, because the mystique of the "disinterested social scientist" who conducts "value-free" public policy research is so powerful and alluring.

Rand and the Rise of the Military Intellectual Complex
The next generation of think tanks owes its origins almost entirely to the United States' increased international commitments after World War II. Many of these institutions were also established to help sustain the momentum of the defense efforts generated during the war years. During this period institutions such as the American Enterprise Institute for Public Policy Research (1948), the Rand Corporation (1948) and the Foreign Policy Research Institute (1955) came into being. Fauriol attributes the surge in the number of foreign policy think tanks during this period "to the resurgence of conservatism and also a greater concern for a coherent global vision of U.S. defense and foreign policy."[119] Orlans contends that Rand grew out of "a need to develop a new and more permanent arrangement whereby civilian engineers and scientists could continue the critical technical work begun during the war."[120] These institutes focused on different dimensions of national security and how to maintain it.

While the focus and structure of each is quite different, the political forces that shaped them are quite similar. According to historian Kim McQuaid, business leaders

> had cause for worry by the end of the first full year of the war (1942). The conflict was being won, but there were signs that the liberals were seeking to follow through upon military victories abroad with political victories at home . . . once peace returned, liberal forces would await any favorable opportunities to try to expand the scope of their power. The question, then, was . . . what type of economic and political order would result from the reconversion from a war time to a peace time economy.[121]

---

[119] Fauriol, "Think Tanks and U.S. Foreign Policy," p. 13.
[120] Orlans, *The Nonprofit Research Institute*, pp. 18-23.
[121] Kim McQuaid, *Big Business and Presidential Power: From FDR to Reagan* (New York: William Morrow & Co., 1982) p. 107.

These forces provided the impetus for the creation of conservative think tanks in both the domestic and foreign policy arena. Think tanks like the Foreign Policy Research Institute and the American Enterprise Institute, shared a similar structure with the first generation of academic oriented think tanks, such as Brookings. However, they owe their origins to a more conservative political and philosophical segment of American society and were organized in direct response to the perceived liberal threat created by institutions such as the Carnegie Endowment for International Peace and the Council on Foreign Relations.

The Rand Corporation, however, proved to be a major departure from the academic model. Rand's unique approach to public policy research led Levien to describe Rand as a "major social invention."[122] Rand was based on the research and development center model and was guided by a systems approach to problem solving. It adapted the techniques utilized by the research and development industry to the analysis of public policy problems. Rand not only owes its own research methodologies to the research and development industry, but it is also an acronym for Research ANd Development. It began as Project Rand, which was set up by the Air Force at Douglas Aircraft in Santa Monica, California. Because of the obvious conflict of interest, Rand soon became an independent entity, but it continues to receive nearly two-thirds of its funding from defense contracts. Rand has distinguished itself through its "superb technical competence, originality, depth, breadth and knowledge built up through forty years of work for the Pentagon agencies . . . its thorough, objective methods of analysis and multi-disciplinary approach have been copied by problem solvers in every field, and are paradigms for the Urban and Hudson Institutes."[123] Rand's most distinguishing characteristic, however, has been its extensive use of systems and operations research to examine both military and social problems. The Rand model set the standard for many of the think tanks established during this period.

The Urban Institute and the Rise of the Domestic PPRI

The nature and design of PPRIs took another turn as a result of increased federal involvement in what came to be called War on Poverty. During this period, defense contracts began to dry up as part of a backlash from the Vietnam War, and domestic, specifically urban, social policy research institutions flourished. Dickson, commenting in 1972 on the tremendous impact these changes had on the nature and orientation of such organizations, observed that:

> In 1969 the Urban Institute, a new think tank, reported what it termed to be a trend of 'phenomenal' growth. It was found that while in the 1950s there were only two dozen university-based urban research centers, by 1967 there were about eighty of them – and by late 1969 the total had jumped to nearly two hundred."[124]

---

[122]Levien, "Independent Public Policy Analysis Organizations," p. 1.
[123]Linden, "Powerhouses of Policy," pp. 105-06.
[124]Dickson, Think Tanks, p. 219.

Dickson points out that older institutions influenced this trend because they redirected their resources and staff to "new internal, civil, urban, and environmental matters as quickly as new institutions [were] being created for problem solving in these areas."[125] The shift in research emphasis was especially dramatic "at institutions with a strong military heritage."[126] Defense related think tanks like Rand saw their defense contracts evaporate while the federal domestic policy research portfolio was growing by leaps and bounds. In order to take advantage of this opportunity, Rand and other research organizations developed domestic policy research programs. "Defense contractors, think tanks, and R and D firms [began] creating new divisions applying their skills [and problem solving techniques] to domestic matters."[127] The impact of this shift in research efforts is still being felt today. Almost all major think tanks now have a significant domestic or social policy component.

Two of the major institutions to emerge during this period were The Urban Institute (1968), which was modeled after Rand, and the University of Wisconsin's Institute for Research on Poverty (1966). Both of these institutions were established to examine the social and economic problems that captured the American consciousness during the sixties and early seventies. These institutions and others like them became known as urban think tanks because their research efforts were devoted exclusively to urban and social issues.

The Urban Institute was formed to examine a whole range of domestic issues, but most particularly Johnson's Great Society programs. Once again, this institution was a sign of the times. The Johnson administration, faced with an array of urban problems, encouraged the development of the Urban Institute. According to Dickson, the Urban Institute's incorporators vowed that to avoid Rand's problem of being too identified with one agency of government. "Rather, their plan called for an independent nonprofit think tank supported on a contract basis by a variety of civilian agencies and, to whatever extent, by private foundations."[128] While governmental sources, primarily the Agency for Housing and Urban Development, contributed ninety percent of the initial funding for the institute, they now account for less than half of the its total budget.

The Urban Institute provided a model for a multitude of institutions that focused primarily on social and urban issues. During this period, the number of think tanks mushroomed, as did the number and size of government agencies. This period also saw private foundations and corporations significantly increase their funding of public policy research.

As pointed out previously, foreign policy and defense related think tanks declined during this period. The one exception to this trend, however, was the

---

[125]Ibid., p. 220.
[126]Ibid., p. .219.
[127]Ibid., p. 219.
[128]Ibid., p. 223.

Overseas Development Council (1969), established to conduct research on developing countries and U.S. aid programs to those countries. This institution was created as a direct response to the substantial foreign aid programs launched during the Truman, Kennedy and Johnson administrations.

The Heritage Foundation and the Rise of the Specialty PPRI

In the last thirty years, six interrelated trends have emerged to influence the development of sub-groups among the PPRIs. First and foremost, the number of institutions conducting public policy research has proliferated. Not since the 1940s' dramatic increase in the number of research and development centers and defense-related think tanks has there been such an explosion in the number of research institutes. The increased number of policy-related institutes has intensified the competition for dollars, scholars, and influence and has brought about some fundamental changes in how these institutions operate. The second major trend has been the tilt toward Washington as the center of influence. Many of the West Coast and New York-based think tanks were forced to relocate to Washington or open branch offices in order to remain competitive. The third major trend involved the emergence of specialized think tanks. In an effort to distinguish themselves from the vast array of think tanks already in existence, the newer public policy organizations chose to focus on a narrow audience or adopted a single issue orientation. This trend was in direct response to the increased influence of special interest groups in Washington and to private foundations' shifting their grant funds from institutional support to project-specific grants. The fourth major trend to emerge during this period was the politicization of think tanks. The fifth trend to surface during this period was the increase in the number of professional staff in the executive and legislative branches of government and the creation of governmental policy reseach organizations, all of which rely on the independent PPRIs for research, data and analysis. The sixth trend was the increasing influence of the media on the public policy process.

A number of multi-purpose (diversified) and single issue (specialized) think tanks can now be found working on every domestic and international concern. The intense rivalry among these institutions has been characterized as a "war of ideas."[129] According to Weaver, the competition has forced PPRIs to become more image conscious, to improve the quality and diversity of their product lines, and to consider alternative means of staffing and financing.[130] The two institutions that best exemplify the fundamental changes that have taken place in the field are the Heritage Foundation and the Institute for International Economics.

The growing tendency of PPRIs to specialize has gone relatively unnoticed in the literature and, to a large extent, has been overshadowed by what some scholars see as the politicization of think tanks. I contend, however, that the politicization of PPRIs is just another form of specialization. PPRIs not only

---

[129]Richard Weaver, *Ideas Have Consequences*.
[130]R. Kent Weaver, "The Changing World of Think Tanks," p. 571.

specialize by policy issue or program; they now specialize by ideology and political orientation. Commenting on the general trend toward specialization, Weaver concludes that "another set of organizations – mostly newer, smaller and Washington based – which focus on a narrow range of issues, but with the same stress on rigorous research and (in most cases) reliance on academic research," have grown up alongside the more diversified research institutions in Washington.[131] The Institute for International Economics, as well as the Center for Budget Priorities which examines the U.S. federal budget, and Resources for the Future and the Worldwatch Institute, which consider environmental issues, exemplify this trend toward specialization.

The Institute for International Economics (IIE), for instance, is focused almost entirely on international economic issues. It was created by the German Marshall Fund and "devoted solely to analyzing important international issues and developing and communicating potential new approaches for dealing with them."[132] The above quote, taken from IIE's mission statement, clearly indicates the specialized nature of this organization and the specific niche it has carved out for itself.

The politicization of public policy research created a new breed of institution that challenged the conventional wisdom about how think tanks should be organized and operated. Commenting on this phenomenon, Linden writes that:

> As the new, well-funded political movement embodied by the Reagan administration became entrenched in the mid-seventies, two things happened. First, a new breed of think tank sprang up: politically purposeful bodies whose mission is to back the new conservative movement or fight it. At the same time, the established tanks broadened the scope of their studies and joined the swelling debate over government's national and foreign policies. Increasingly, amid the roar of contention and cries of dissent, public policy research centers became centers for the politics of public policy research.[133]

The organization that best exemplifies this new brand of think tank is the Heritage Foundation. Established in 1973, this institute, as Linden describes it, is "less a think tank than a priori ideology factory, avowedly a marketing agency for the neoconservative movement."[134] This point is confirmed by Burton Yale Pines, senior vice president at Heritage, when he states: "The goal is a conservative nation. Our role is to provide...public policy-makers with arguments to bolster

---

[131]Ibid., p. 565.
[132]Taken from the Institute for International Economics' mission statement (Washington, DC, 1990).
[133]Linden, "Powerhouses of Policy," p. 100.
[134]Ibid. p. 103.

our side."[135] This is a far cry from Robert Brookings' call for the objective analysis of public policy problems. The Heritage Foundation's objectives and design remain at odds with Brookings, Rand and the Urban Institute, whose studies remain more or less objective assessments of critical policy concerns. However, these institutions have been forced to become more market oriented and ideological in their approach to policy analysis in order to keep pace with the conservative onslaught.

The newest specialization in the industry is state-based think tanks, located in state capitals throughout the United States and focused on state and local issues. The devolution of federal programs and power to the states sparked this latest movement. Since the early 1980s, over thirty institutions have come into being, most of them with the backing of conservative foundations and corporations.

Growth and Survival in the Public Policy Research Industry

The nature and rate of growth in the public policy research industry is not unique. In fact, the industry has followed a pattern of growth that resembles the population ecology model established by the organizational theorists R.L. Daft and H.E. Aldrich.[136] Daft's work in this area is particularly illuminating, for he divides the evolution of a population of institutions into three phases: (1) variation; (2) selection; and (3) retention.[137] In the variation phase, a large number of variations appear and the population of organizations begins to compete for scarce resources. A natural selection process takes place in phase two where the weak organizations wither away and the strong survive. In the retention phase, a few of the surviving organizations grow large and become entrenched in the environment. Over the past seventy-five years, the growth and development of the public policy industry has closely paralleled the population ecology model. In each of the four periods the industry has seen a surge in the number of new organizations. From each period of increased growth, a select group of institutions grew and prospered while other institutions went out of business.

This recent trend toward specialization and vigorous competition not only challenges existing institutions to alter the ways they do business but also presents a major opportunity for new or emerging institutions to develop innovative technologies and seize a major share of the market. To survive, institutions have been forced to seek out specialized niches. Clearly, this has affected the nature and composition of the industry. The differences in Brookings, Rand and

---

[135]Burton Yale Pines, *Back to Basics. The Traditionalist Movement That Is Sweeping Grass-Roots America* (New York: William Morrow & Co., 1982), p. 21.

[136]R. L. Daft, *Organization Theory and Design* (New York: West Publishing Co., 1963) and H. E. Aldrich, *Organizations and Environment* (New York: Prentice-Hall, 1979) provide good insights into the population ecology model. This school of thought focuses on the characteristics of organizational populations rather than on management strategies and individual organizations. This model assumes that the environment is always in a state of flux and new organizational forms are continuously being established and dying.

[137]Daft, *Organization Theory and Design*, p. 76.

Heritage's approaches to both method and product illustrate this specialization. Brookings employs an academic/ scientific approach to its research that produces book-length studies marketed to policy makers and academics. In contrast, Rand focuses on policy analysis more than scholarly research, producing technical reports for government agencies. Heritage produces non-technical policy analysis and prepares digests and recommendations for policy makers. The dramatic increase in the degree of differentiation in the industry is underscored by the fact that of the fifty-eight institutes established between 1975 and 1989, over two-thirds are specialty research organizations. Institutions have also created a demand for new enterprises by creating new areas of policy analysis or defining problems in a new ways.[138]

Dickson's observations about the growth of the research industry in 1973 have even greater relevance in the 1990s: "Today, think tanks represent a wide variety of institutionalized thought. The phenomenon has grown quickly and in all directions. It seems that almost every conceivable interest group in the nation has or has had at least one think tank working for it."[139] This brief survey of the evolution of public policy research institutes is designed to give a sense of how these organizations have evolved over the last seventy-five years. The institutional examples presented continue to influence and shape the field. The dramatic increase in the number of these institutions, when coupled with the decline in government funding and the narrowing interests of foundations, is likely to intensify the competition among them in the coming years. While these institutions are organized to shape public policy, it is the public policy environment that has influenced and continues to influence the nature and direction of these institutions.

Chronological Listing of Existing Policy Research Institutions

1907	The Russell Sage Foundation
1910	Carnegie Endowment for International Peace
1927	Brookings Institution
1916	Institute for Government Research
1916	Conference Board
1919	Hoover Institution on War, Revolution and Peace
1919	Twentieth Century Fund
1920	National Bureau of Economic Research
1921	Council on Foreign Relations
1925	Battelle Memorial Institute
1936	Urban Land Institute

---

[138]Daniel Patrick Moynihan's conceptualization of poverty, in *On Understanding Poverty* (New York: Basic Books, 1969) and George Gilder's *Wealth and Poverty* which helped set the stage for the Reagan tax cuts, both served to create demand for new organizations to advance these causes.
[139]Dickson, *Think Tanks*, p. 31.

1937	Tax Foundation
1941	Institute of Gas Technology
1942	Center for Naval Analysis
1942	Committee for Economic Development
1943	American Enterprise Institute for Public Policy Research
1946	Middle East Institute
1946	SRI International [Stanford Research Institute]
1948	Rand Corporation
1950	Bureau of Social Science Research
1951	Human Resources Research Organization
1952	Resources for the Future
1954	Conference on Economic Progress
1955	Foreign Policy Research Institute
1955	International Law Institute
1956	Institute for Defense Analysis
1958	ANSER (Analytic Services, Inc.)
1961	Atlantic Council of the U.S.
1961	Hudson Institute
1961	Logistic Management Institute
1961	Potomac Institute
1962	Center for Strategic and International Studies
1962	National Institute of Public Affairs
1963	Institute for Policy Studies
1963	Ripon Society
1965	Center for Applied Research in the Apostolate
1965	Washington Journalism Center
1968	Urban Institute
1970	Joint Center for Political and Economic Studies
1970	Tax Analysts
1970	Center for Science in the Public Interest
1970	Center for the Study of Welfare Policy
1971	Public Technology
1972	Center for Defense Information
1972	Center for Women's Policy Studies
1972	Investor Responsibility Research Center
1973	American Council for Capital Formation
1973	American Legislative Exchange Council
1973	Children's Defense Fund
1973	Mankind Research Foundation
1973	Heritage Foundation
1974	Institute for Contemporary Studies
1974	Institute for Energy Analysis
1974	Worldwatch Institute
1975	Center for International Policy

1975	Council for Social and Economic Studies
1975	National Center for Policy Alternatives
1976	Committee for the Study of the American Electorate
1976	Ethics and Public Policy Center
1976	International Center for Research on Women
1976	Institute for Foreign Policy Analysis
1976	Media Institute
1976	National Center for Appropriate Technology
1976	Northeast-Midwest Institute
1976	The Rockford Institute
1977	Alan Guttmacher Institute
1977	Cato Institute
1977	Ethics Resource Center
1977	Free Congress Research and Education Foundation
1977	Manhattan Institute for Policy
1977	Women's Research and Education Institute
1978	Employee Benefit Research Institute
1978	Reason Foundation
1978	Lincoln Institute
1979	Pacific Research Institute for Public Policy
1979	Center for the Study of Social Policy
1979	Indochina Project
1980	Foreign Policy Institute (Johns Hopkins University)
1980	Renewable Energy Institute
1981	Center on Budget and Policy Priorities
1981	Center for International Business and Trade (Georgetown Univ.)
1981	Center for National Policy (Republican Party)
1981	Committee for a Responsible Federal Budget
1981	Democracy Project
1981	Institute for Educational Leadership
1981	Institute for International Economics
1981	Political Economy Research Center
1981	Roosevelt Center for American Policy Studies(Closed 6/89)
1981	Washington Center for Public Policy Research (Duke University–Closed 7/30/89)
1982	Hispanic Policy Development Project
1982	Washington Institute
1982	World Resources Institute
1983	Democratic Institute for International Affairs (Democratic Party)
1983	Institute for Health Policy Analysis
1983	Institute for Security and Cooperation in Outer Space
1983	Jefferson Foundation
1983	National Center for Policy Analysis
1983	National Institute for Public Policy
1983	Capital Research Center
1984	Citizens for a Sound Economy
1984	Committee for Economic Development

1984	Economic Policy Institute
1985	Center for Democracy
1985	The Citizens' Network for Foreign Affairs
1986	Economic Policy Institute
1986	Independence Policy Institute
1986	Sunbelt Institute
1986	The Independent Institute
1986	United States Institutes of Peace
1986	Progressive Policy Institute
1986	Washington Institute of Foreign Affairs

Section II
Competition and Organizational Innovation

Section II will attempt to answer the following questions:

- What are some of the leading strategies and structures in the public policy research industry?
- How do the strategy and structure of an organization affect its inputs and outputs?
- How do the strategic choices made by an organization affect its competitive position?

CHAPTER 5
AN ANALYTICAL FRAMEWORK FOR STUDYING THE PUBLIC POLICY RESEARCH INDUSTRY

In constructing an analytic framework for my analysis of PPRIs, I have attempted to integrate the works of political theorists such as David Easton, organizational theorists such as Kast and Rosenzweig, and management theorists such as Chandler and Porter in a way that will help improve our understanding of these institutions.

In the field of political science, systems analysis has been proven a valid analytical tool for understanding the complexities of the policy making process. Easton and others view public policy as a response to forces in the environment that place demands on the political system. Inputs consist of demands made and supportive actions taken by individuals, institutions and groups that affect the political system. Demands include the public's call for a response to problems such as poverty or homelessness while their support involves the willingness of individuals and groups to obey laws, pay taxes and accept policy decisions.

The environment is comprised of all those conditions and circumstances – physical, social, economic and psycho-social – that are outside the boundaries of the political system. The political system is the mechanism by which values are allocated within society. This is achieved through a series of inter-related structures and activities that transform policy inputs into policy outputs. Outputs are generally viewed as laws, rules and judicial actions that constitute public policy. The transformation process has an impact on the environment which creates new demands (feedback) which in turn creates additional policy outputs. This process affects the overall character of the political system. This systems approach to understanding politics and public policy is captured in figure 5.1.

62   THE COMPETITION FOR DOLLARS, SCHOLARS AND INFLUENCE

**Figure 5.1
The Public Policy Research Environment**

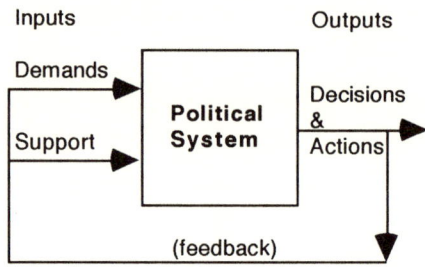

By placing PPRIs into this context, we begin to understand how the political and social forces identified in the previous chapters can have an impact on the nature and direction of these institutions. The value of this model will be further illustrated when I discuss the specific inputs and outputs of PPRIs.

The work of organizational theorists Fremont Kast and James Rosenzweig in general is also instructive. Kast and Rosenzweig believe that "open systems theory recognizes that the biological or social system is in a dynamic relationship with its environment and receives various inputs, which it transforms in some way, and exports [as] outputs."[140] They explain that "[t]hese systems are open not only in relation to their environment but also in relation to themselves, or 'internally' in that interaction between components affects the system as a whole. The open system adapts to its environment by changing the structure and processes of its internal components."[141] This model provides an integrative framework that will enable us to understand how PPRIs influence actors in their system and how they are, in turn, influenced by their environment. Specifically, it will provide the necessary tools to examine the structure, tasks and formal relationships of PPRIs and how these variables are influenced by their operating environment.

Kast and Rosenzweig's description of an organization as a structured socio-technical system[142] also provides a useful model. First proposed by Trist and his associates at Tavistock Institute in England, the socio-technical model

---

[140]Kast & Rosenzweig, "The Modern View: A Systems Approach, p. 19.
[141]Ibid.
[142]Ibid., p. 20.

recognizes that any organization is composed of a technological component, which includes equipment, process and layout, and a social component, which includes the relationships among the people who carry out the work.[143] The technology used affects an organization's inputs and outputs. The socio-technical analysis is particularly relevant for the analysis of PPRIs because it "views the organization as a structured sociotechnical system and considers each of the primary subsystems and their interactions."[144] According to Kast and Rosenzweig, there are goals and values, technology, structure, psychosocial, and managerial subsystems. Using this approach, we will be able to examine how the organizational design of PPRIs enhances or impedes their ability to influence public policy.

Inputs and Outputs of PPRIs

Using an open sociotechnical framework of organizations to identify and define the major inputs and outputs of PPRIs indicates that these organizations receive inputs from society in the form of people, money, and ideas and values. They transform these into outputs through their main technology – policy analysis and research – which takes the form of ideas, books, articles, position papers and policy recommendations. These outputs are then consumed by the policy community and the general public. The outputs, in turn, alter the environment, and are recycled to become new inputs.[145]

Figure 5.2
The Policy Formulation Process

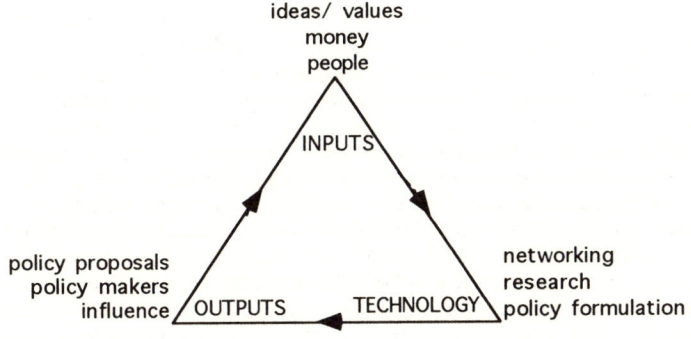

---

[143]Ibid.
[144]Ibid.
[145]Ibid.

Inputs

People

The "people" input category includes the scholars, policy analysts, research assistants, board members, advisors, current and former members of the legislative and executive branches of government, support personnel and administrators, whose ideas, values, work and intelligence help shape the fabric of the institution. In public policy research, it takes individuals with a special orientation and set of skills to conceive, create, package and market policy proposals and programs to policy makers, academics and the media.[146]

Money

This category includes gifts, grants and contracts from sources such as individuals, corporations, foundations, and local, state and federal governments. Often the mix of these inputs will determine the nature of the organization. For instance, a PPRI that does a large amount of contract research tends to be organized more like a consulting firm than an academic institution. In addition, an institution with more unrestricted funds will have greater freedom to determine its research agenda.

Ideas and Values

Often called "the idea industry," PPRIs are defined by the ideas, values or philosophies that serve as their organizing principles. Supply side economics, the Great Society, free enterprise, efficient government, international peace and security, privatization, libertarianism, and democracy have each been the core principle of one or more institutions. This short list of examples demonstrates that the idea can be quite narrow or quite broad. Ideas, to use a cliché, are what makes these organizations tick. Similarly, the new ideas generated as outputs enable these institutions to achieve a dynamic equilibrium.

Subsystems

Goals and Values

The goals of a particular organization are shaped by its ideas, values and philosophy. The goals guide the establishment of the organizational structure and the technologies employed. These ideas, values and philosophy are often expressed in the mission statement of an organization, such as: to provide non-partisan research on policy issues that promote a limited form of government and a free enterprise system.

Technology

Kast and Rosenzweig point out that the "technical subsystems are determined by the task requirements of the organization and vary widely."[147]

---

[146] Smith, *The Idea Brokers*, pp. 224-27. Smith contends that there are four types of policy experts that inhabit public policy research institutes: "scholar-statesmen," "policy specialists," "government expert" and "policy entrepreneurs." According to Smith, each type is determined by the institutions in which they work, the career path they have chosen and their approach to policy analysis.

[147] Kast & Rosenzweig, "The Modern View," p. 20.

This is also true for PPRIs, where the focus might be on one or more of the following activities: public policy research training, public education, or advocacy. This is important because "technology is the prime factor in determining structure and the relationship between jobs."[148] I hope to demonstrate that a PPRI's technological makeup determines its structure, staffing patterns and output.

Structure
As indicated above, the structure of a PPRI is greatly influenced by its particular tasks and technology requirements. Because the major activity of most PPRIs is research, their organizational structures often resemble those of academic institutions with flexible organizations, non-routine activities, and adaptive planning and control processes. Like universities, PPRIs are often organized into departments or functional specialties. However, the technologies employed by the new entrants to the public policy research industry vary, which has an impact on their structure.

Psychosocial
Kast and Rosenzweig state that the "psychosocial subsystem consists of the interactions, expectations and aspirations, sentiments, and values of the participants."[149] In PPRIs, these factors are most influenced by the particular research interests and philosophy of the scholars and analysts who make up these institutions.

Managerial
The managerial subsystem "spans the entire organization by directing the technology, organizing people and other resources, and relating the organization to its environment."[150] This integrative role is particularly important in PPRIs, where changes in the environment often directly affect personnel and research agendas. The longevity of these organizations is therefore determined by their ability to adapt to change. This requires effective internal and external coordination.

Outputs
The major outputs of PPRIs are people and ideas. Ideas make their way into books, monographs, journals, magazines, newsletters, and films, and ultimately into governmental policies and laws. The other major output is people, who frequently enter government positions in which they can attempt to transform their ideas into policy. When combined, these two outputs often translate into influence. A PPRI's effectiveness is often measured more by the degree of its influence than by the number of its conferences and publications.

---

[148]Ibid.
[149]Ibid.
[150]Ibid., p. 24.

While Kast and Rosenzweig's ideas have provided a broad integrative framework for understanding how PPRIs interact with their environment, another specific set of techniques is needed for examining how these institutions interact with one another. Michael Porter's general discussion of the forces that shape industries and competitors provides tools to effectively analyze PPRIs. Porter's structural analysis within industries has been a valuable organizing principle for this study.[151]

Porter believes that the threat of new entrants, the rivalry among existing firms, the bargaining power of suppliers and buyers, and the threat of substitute products and services jointly influence the nature and intensity of competition in a given industry.[152] These forces are seen as an effective basis for examining how all firms in an industry compete. But as Porter points out, "We must explain why some firms are persistently more profitable than others and how this relates to their strategic postures."[153]

Porter uses a structural analysis to explain the differences in the performance of firms in the same industry. Employing Porter's concept of strategic groups and his dimensions of a competitive strategy, this study will describe the various competitive strategies that have been applied by firms in the public policy research industry. Porter uses thirteen strategic dimensions to capture a company's strategic options in a given industry. This study will employ eleven of his dimensions:

1) *Specialization*: the degree to which an organization focuses its efforts in terms of the width of its line, the target customer segments, and the geographic markets served.

2) *Brand identification*: the degree to which it seeks brand identification rather than competition based mainly on price or other variables. This can be achieved through advertising, a sales force, or a variety of other means.

3) *Push versus pull*: the degree to which it seeks to develop brand identification directly with the ultimate consumer, as opposed to gaining the support of distribution channels in selling its product.

4) *Channel selection*: the choice of distribution channels, ranging from company-owned channels, to specialty outlets, to broad-line outlets.

5) *Product quality*: its level of product quality, in terms of raw materials, specifications, adherence to tolerances, features, etc.

---

[151] Michael E. Porter, *Competitive Strategy: Techniques for Analyzing Industries and Competitions* (New York: The Free Press, 1980), p. 4.
[152] Ibid., p. 127.
[153] Ibid., p. 129.

6) *Technological leadership*: the degree to which it seeks technological leadership as opposed to following or imitation.

7) *Vertical integration*: the extent of value added as reflected in the level of forward and backward integration adopted, including whether the firm has captive distribution, exclusive or owned retail outlets, an in-house service network, etc.

8) *Cost position*: the extent to which it seeks the low cost position in manufacturing and distribution through investment in cost minimizing facilities and equipment.

9) *Service*: the degree to which it provides ancillary services with its product line, such as engineering assistance, an in-house service network, credit, and so forth. This aspect of strategy could be viewed as part of vertical integration but is separated for analytical purposes.

10) *Price policy*: its relative price position in the market. Price position will usually be related to such other variables as cost position and product quality, but price is a distinct strategic variable that must be treated separately.

11) *Leverage*: the amount of financial and operating leverage it has.[154]

I have omitted his dimensions of relationship to parent company and relationship to host or home government, which I replace with three new dimensions:

1) *Relationship to policy community*: the nature of the relationship between the organization and the elected officials, bureaucrats and appointed officials who make up the policy community influences the policy orientation of a firm, which in turn determines its objectives and how it is managed. The exact nature and quality of this relationship will also affect the inputs and outputs of an organization. The degree of influence a firm has in the policy community is often the best measure of its success.

2) *Relationship to academic community*: likewise, the nature of the relationship between the organization and the academic community will influence and reflect both its strategy and structure. The degree of acceptance within the academic community is often used to measure the quality of the outputs produced by these organizations.

---

[154]Ibid.

3) *Relationship to the funding community*: the funding community is composed of private and corporate foundations, corporations, government contractors, granting agencies and individuals. The relative strength or weakness of an organization's relationship to its principal financial supporters often determines whether the organization will succeed or fail. Also, the mix of support from this community will influence the nature and direction of an institution. Over-reliance on a single source of funds can leave an institution vulnerable in the same way that a for profit corporation would be vulnerable if it relied on a single buyer.

These new dimensions will contribute to an overall understanding of the competition among PPRIs. Other characteristics identified earlier, such as the degree of diversification and specialization in a PPRI and the nature and type of its activities (contract vs. independent research and partisan vs. nonpartisan research), will be incorporated into the appropriate dimensions provided by Porter.

These strategic dimensions interact in much the same way that Kast and Rosenzweig's variables – managerial structure, goals and values, technology, organizational structure, and psychosocial makeup – do. According to Porter,

a firm with a low relative price (such as Texas Instruments in semiconductors) usually has a low-cost position and good, though not superior, product quality. To achieve its low costs, such a firm probably has a high degree of vertical integration. The strategic dimensions for a particular firm usually form an internally consistent set, as in this example. An industry normally has firms with a number of different, though internally consistent, combinations of dimensions.[155]

Applying this to the public policy research industry shows that, for example, an academically oriented institution's reliance on highly trained scholars will affect its cost position in the industry.

Once I have characterized the strategies of some of the major firms along these dimensions and described the organizational and environmental context in which they operate, I will attempt to organize the field into strategic groups. Porter's concept of strategic groups and Kast and Rosenzweig's open systems theory will become the central organizing principles behind my research. According to Porter, "A strategic group is the group of firms in an industry along the strategic dimensions."[156] It is my hope that by effectively tracing these firms along strategic dimensions outlined above, I will be able to organize the divergent approaches taken in marketing, management and organization into meaningful groups.

---

[155]Ibid.
[156]Ibid., p. 131.

Porter states that "strategic groups are present for a wide variety of reasons, such as firms' differing initial strengths and weaknesses, differing times of entry into the business and historical accidents."[157] This observation is borne out in my study of PPRIs. Porter concludes that the firms in the same strategic group generally resemble one another closely in many ways besides their strategies. They tend to have similar market segments and also to be affected and respond similarly to external threats.[158] Understanding and effectively mapping these characteristics becomes an important key to using the Porter techniques as an analytic tool.

Porter's strategic groups and strategic dimensions of a competitive strategy are best illustrated by the map of inter-group rivalry provided below.

Figure 5.3
Competition Among Strategic Groups

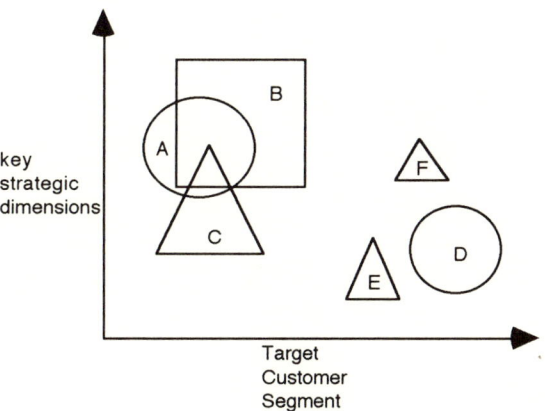

In this map, as Porter calls it, the horizontal axis is the largest customer segment of the strategic group and the vertical axis is one of the other key dimensions of strategy in the industry. Each figure represents a strategic group's market size and is directly proportional to its market share. The shape of a group represents its overall strategic configuration in the industry. The distance between figures indicates level of competition between each group represented.

Porter provides this analysis of the strategic groups found in the map: "It is clear that Group D will be much less affected by industry rivalry than Group A. Group A competes with similarly large groups B and C, who use very different

---

[157]Ibid., p. 141.
[158]Ibid., p. 137.

strategies to reach the same basic customer segment. Firms in these three groups are in constant warfare. Group D, on the other hand, competes for a different segment and interacts most strongly in searching this segment with Groups E and F, who are smaller and follow similar strategies (they could be viewed as 'specialist' producers following the ['triangle'] strategy....)" [159]

The underlying thesis of this study is that changes in the environment have resulted in the creation of new organizational forms in the public policy research industry. The tools and techniques described this chapter for analyzing the strategy and structure of industries and firms will be adapted for the analysis of the public policy research industry. This approach involves a structural analysis of the industry and the competitive forces that shape the strategy and structure of PPRIs. Comparing and contrasting the leading organizational forms will make it possible to identify the different types of firms within the industry. The following chapters will distinguish the major strategic groups that exist in the public policy industry and map them along the strategic dimensions previously discussed, and will also provide an overall picture of the competitive environment in which PPRIs operate.

---

[159]Ibid.

CHAPTER 6
STRATEGIC GROUPS AND THE STRATEGY AND STRUCTURE OF THE PUBLIC POLICY RESEARCH INDUSTRY

This chapter undertakes a structural analysis of the public policy research industry, based on data collected from thirty-four PPRIs. A twelve page survey gathered information on the financial base, product lines, marketing strategies, staffing patterns, history and purpose of firms in the industry. Annual reports and publications from each institution supplemented this information. The analysis was further enhanced by interviews with key staff members and by popular and scholarly books and articles written about these institutions. The five and a half years I spent at the Pew Charitable Trusts as a program officer responsible for analyzing and critiquing PPRIs further contributed to my analysis and final selections.

The PPRIs that participated in the study were carefully selected to ensure a representative sample. A full range of institutions were surveyed: large and small, generalist and specialist, free-standing and university affiliated, liberal and conservative, partisan and non-partisan, academic and policy oriented. After a review of the history, purpose, financial support and staffing patterns of these institutions, seven of the thirty-nine institutions were chosen for further analysis. I plan to demonstrate that each of these institutions has become deeply rooted within its environment and represents a major strategic group within the industry. The list of these institutions and the strategic groups they represent is repeated below:

Table 6.1

	Strategic Group	Institution
1.	Academic Diversified	Brookings Institution
2.	Academic Specialized	National Bureau of Economic Research
3.	Contract/ Consulting Tank	Rand Corporation
4.	Advocacy Tank	Institute for Policy Studies
5.	Policy Enterprise	Heritage Foundation
6.	Literary Agent/ Publishing House	Manhattan Institute
7.	State-Based Think Tank	Commonwealth Foundation

Most, if not all, PPRIs can be placed into one of the seven groups listed above. The strategic groups are not meant to strip away the unique characteristics of each firm, but rather to provide a framework for understanding the various organizational forms that have developed over the last seventy-five years.

Because the industry is dynamic, the seven groups should be viewed as a starting point for analysis, and not as a fixed definition.

Each group exhibits a unique set of characteristics that distinguishes it from the other groups in the industry. As I hope to demonstrate, the product lines, managerial structure, goals and values, and technologies vary from one strategic group to another. A firm or entire group may exhibit some of the characteristics of another strategic group, but the groups identified and the representative firms exhibit dominant characteristics that exemplify the strategy and structure of the firms within the various strategic groups. This will become clearer as I describe the characteristics that shape each of the seven groups.

1.   Academic Diversified

As previously explained, the public policy industry owes its origin less to policy makers in Washington than it does to the social science movement of the latter part of the nineteenth century. The scholars and academic institutions of that period provided both the workforce and organizational model for the budding public policy research industry. Consequently, most of the early PPRIs closely resemble academic institutions. The reason for this group's continued dominance in the industry has more to do with the power of academic culture than with market forces. The institutions in this group will at times ignore the primary market for their policy research, policy makers, in order to serve another master, academic traditions.

In order to gain credibility, the academic oriented institutions are often directed and staffed by academics and organized around established academic disciplines. In addition, these institutions tend to have organized research programs to conduct research that takes a longer view than the analysis conducted by their more policy oriented counter-parts. The mission and purpose of these organizations embody the basic tenets of academic research: that it be objective and independent and that it meet rigorous scholarly standards. The output and reward systems are also closely modeled after those of colleges and universities. Researchers are hired and rewarded based on their scholarly output, which often takes the form of book-length studies, journal articles, and conferences and seminars. The only aspects of the university model not adopted by these institutions are teaching and granting degrees.

Although the structure of these institutions closely resembles that of academic institutions, the primary focus of their activities is policy oriented research. Ironically, the research, in some cases, is utilized more by professors and students than by policy makers. The difference between the stated goals of the organization and its actual products and customers has caused problems for these institutions in recent years. Institutions such as the American Enterprise Institute and the Brookings Institution have, in the face of criticism from some of their supporters and from policy makers, introduced new product lines to be more responsive to the needs of the policy making community. Both of these institutions now produce summaries of studies by their scholars and develop them into policy briefs for policy makers. Many of the scholars within these two and at other academic oriented institutions have resisted these innovations because they are viewed as diminishing the scholarly content of the research product.

Built into the structure is a healthy tension that is played out on a daily basis in these real world ivory towers that seek to influence public policy while serving the goals of academia. It is a major challenge for independent PPRIs to maintain a proper balance between policy relevance and independent analysis. With too much independence their products may be viewed as having limited utility, yet with too little, their quality and objectivity may be called into question.

Despite these tensions, the academic model has remained one of the dominant PPRI models, because it provides an accepted method for selecting staff, i.e., requiring academic credentials, a publication record and professional research standards. Moreover, the notion of the scholar who conducts objective research remains attractive to policy makers who prefer non-partisan research. Consequently, the diversified and specialized academic groups contains most of the PPRIs.

The Brookings Institution is the best example of a diversified academic oriented institution. It is known for highly respected scholars with solid academic credentials and publication records. This approach to public policy analysis has earned Brookings a reputation for producing empirically based research that is scholarly and non-partisan.

2.   Academic Specialized

The general orientation of the academic specialized institutions is the same as the academic diversified; they differ only in their degree of specialization. The terms "diversified" and "specialized" refers to an institution's research agenda and client base. The degree of specialization in an institution's research topics is reflected in the range of clients it serves. All of the institutions that fall into the specialized and diversified strategic groups, however, share an academic heritage and are modeled after colleges and universities. Over the last twenty years, the issue or discipline specific academic oriented institutes have emerged as a major trend in the field. It is no surprise that the field of economics dominated this recent trend. Institutes that are directed and staffed by economists and focused exclusively on economic issues are one of the largest segments of the public policy research industry. More recently, organizations focused on environmental concerns have exhibited this strategy and structure.

The National Bureau of Economic Research is a good example of the specialized academic oriented institution because of its specialization in the field of economics and production of highly technical, scholarly publications that are devoid of policy recommendations. A senior NBER staff member told me that NBER has a formal policy that discourages policy recommendations of any kind. This, however, has limited its impact on policy since NBER's staff are frequently tapped for key posts in Washington. It is also no accident that this institution is located in Cambridge, Massachusetts and finds many of its scholars at Harvard.

3. Public Policy Contract/ Consulting Firm

Starting in the late 1940s, another group of firms emerged in the marketplace. These institutions are characterized by their policy orientation, close working relationship with various government agencies, role as program/policy consultants, and reliance on government contracts. These institutions are more likely to produce reports and memos than book-length studies, and while they are staffed by academics, they are less bound by academic standards and traditions than the two previous groups. Research is often conducted according to the specifications of the commissioning agency or department, and therefore, researchers do not have the same degree of independence as those in the other strategic groups. For the same reason, these institutions conduct more interdisciplinary research.

Because of the close working relationship between these institutions and their clients, the institutions are more likely to reflect the methodologies, goals and values of the client. The Rand Corporation, for instance, is known for its systems approach to research, which it adopted from its major contractor, the Defense Department (via the defense industry). Similarly, the Urban Institute's approach to urban problems was shaped by Johnson's Great Society Programs, which it was created to serve. These firms differ markedly from the academic oriented PPRIs in that the reward system, production schedule, degree of independence and final product are all determined, in a large measure, by the contracting agency. In academic research, the production schedule is set by the scholar; in the consulting institution, it is largely determined by the needs of the client. A researcher in this type of institution is more likely to be promoted for having agency contacts and an ability to produce reports on schedule than for academic publications and standing. All of these factors limit the degree of freedom that researchers have at these institutions. The tensions, therefore, are just the reverse of the academic oriented firms because the academics whom these institutions employ strive for the same rewards and degree of freedom found in academic institutions, but which are not consonant with the needs of clients. The strategy and structure of the consulting/ contracting group focus on clients' demands.

The Rand Corporation is the best example of this strategic group, which has extensive contracts to conduct highly specialized research for the federal government. Researching and managing defense-related projects constitutes the core of Rand's research program.

4. Advocacy Tank

In recent years, another major strategic group has emerged. The firms in this group have chosen to advance a particular cause, constituency or ideology. Unlike the academic and consulting organizations that depend on academic disciplines and contracting agencies for ideas, people and resources, the advocacy PPRIs are driven by the issues, philosophies or constituencies that they have been organized to promote. These PPRIs may reject research techniques employed by academics and technocrats in favor of their attempts to promote a particular agenda.

The best example of this group is the Institute for Policy Studies (IPS), which has a long history of liberal political activism and describes itself as "an independent center of thought, action and social invention in the nation's capital."[160] In comparison, the avowedly libertarian Cato Institute dedicates itself to introducing libertarian policies into the national agenda. Other institutions such as the Public Policy Institute, an arm of the American Association of Retired Persons (AARP), and the Economic Policy Institute, established by a group of labor leaders and funded by a coalition of labor unions, are bound to the constituency they serve. Because they exist to promote an agenda that fosters their cause, they tend not to approach their research with either the scholarly or methodological bent exhibited at Brookings and Rand, respectively. Since ideology and constituency define the culture of these firms, the program staff are rewarded for their ability to advance the desired cause. Although these institutions do not ignore their funding sources or totally reject academic approaches to research and publications, those elements are far less important. They are far more likely to evaluate prospective staff members based on ideological responses than on publications lists. Similarly, the outputs of this group are judged on their attractiveness to the constituency or adherence to the particular ideology, not on whether they will stand up to academic criticism. Clearly, the product will be more effective if it does both, but this is not absolutely required.

5. Policy Enterprise

Another important strategic group to emerge in recent years is the PPRI that operates with the effectiveness and efficiency of a corporation. The firms in this group have effectively employed the principles of management, marketing and sales to the public policy research industry. They have carefully studied the market and the other firms in the industry and concluded that paying scholars to write books for policy makers that only college professors and students will read is all wrong. Driven by an entrepreneurial spirit and guided by business principles, these firms began to turn the orientation of the industry on its head. They have developed new product lines and innovative marketing techniques directed at and, more importantly, actually reaching Washington policy makers. This new approach challenged the traditional academic oriented PPRIs and sent shock waves through the industry.

The institutions in this strategic group are characterized by a strong business and marketing mind set that strongly influences their goals, values, technology, structure, and managerial culture. They recruit researchers who can digest and formulate existing ideas and research into a form that meets the needs of busy bureaucrats, politicians and policy makers who lack time to read detailed studies or books. The major products of these institutions are short, timely studies that focus on current legislation or policy concerns. These studies are packaged into aggressively marketed policy briefs and memoranda.

---

[160]This quotation is taken from IPS' brochure: Purpose and Structure.

Because they are in the business of marketing and selling ideas, they are organized much like newspapers or weekly magazines and are driven by tight production schedules and readerships that requires concise, no-nonsense publications. Their staff must exhibit the skill of journalists at distilling information into compelling articles and briefs. Rewards and promotions then go to those who meet tight deadlines and produce effective policy briefs. The goal is to influence policy, and these well-oiled machines are structured to do just that. The Heritage Foundation best exemplifies this strategic group of firms because of its focus on producing short, pithy policy briefs that are filled with recommendations on how to change Washington and America.

6. Literary Agent/ Publishing House

The sixth group consists of firms that utilize an organizational structure and production and marketing strategy resembling that of a literary agent or publishing house. The most distinctive feature of these firms is that they do not have a permanent research staff. Scholars are hired on a short-term basis to write a book or conduct a study. Once the study is completed they move on to another institution or assignment. Like a literary agent, the role of the executive director in these institutions is to identify hot prospects whose ideas will sell. Conversely, a new public policy idea or problem will set in motion a search for someone to develop it. The staff of these institutions act as idea-brokers in the area of public policy. They identify the hot issues of the day, select writers, secure funding, identify publishers and organize an array of promotional activities. The success of this type of institution obviously depends on the careful selection of winners: books that will be funded by corporations and foundations and that will have a wide readership in the policy and academic communities.

These institutions tend to be thinly staffed and directed by an individual who, as a scholar, can see the potential of an idea and then market it to funders and publishers. It is a high-risk business that keeps these institutions always teetering on the edge. The staff are recruited and rewarded on the same basis as the staff of literary agencies. They are judged not so much on what they know, but on whom they know. They must be well-versed in a range of policy issues, and well-connected to policy makers inside and outside the Beltway. It is important to note that while the staff of these institutions tend to be generalists and their focus is usually broad, the technologies employed and the target markets are highly specialized. The best example of this strategic group is the Manhattan Institute, which is located in New York, and has helped publish and promote a number of major books in the field of public policy.

7. State-Based Think Tank

The latest entrants into the public policy research industry are state-based PPRIs. These institutions constitute the fastest growing segment of the industry, with some twenty being created in the last fifteen years. They exhibit a variety of technologies, managerial structures and organizational cultures, but roughly follow the model of one of the six previous strategic groups. The two characteristics that distinguish these firms are highly specialized customer segment (states and local policy makers) and limited geographical focus on a single state.

Notably, the Rand Corporation experimented with a similar approach in the 1960s when it established what has became known as an "urban Rand" in New York City. Unfortunately the effort fell victim to changing political and budgetary priorities. They were reborn due to the initiative of conservative foundations and policy organizations. The impetus for this movement was the realization that the transfer of federal programs and funding to state and local governments would lead to a tremendous shift in power. Conservative founders and supporters viewed these institutions as important catalysts for change at the state and local level.

It is not surprising then, that the staffs and products of these institutions resemble their national counterparts. The best example of this type of PPRI is the Commonwealth Foundation, which is located in Pennsylvania and focuses on that state's public policy issues. Commonwealth is modeled after the Heritage Foundation and therefore has a strong policy orientation.

Table 6.2
Historical Framework for the Emergence of Strategic Groups

Institution	Date Founded	Strategic Group
Brookings Institution	1916	Academic Diversified
National Bureau of Economic Research	1920	Academic Specialized
Rand Corporation	1948	Contract/ Consulting Tank
Institute for Policy Studies	1963	Advocacy Tank
Heritage Foundation	1973	Policy Enterprise
Manhattan Institute	1977	Literary Agent/ Publishing House
Commonwealth Foundation	1988	State-Based Think Tank

Sample List of Firms by Strategic Group

1.   Academic Diversified
American Enterprise Institute for Public Policy Research
Brookings Institute
Bureau of Social Science Research
Hoover Institution on War, Revolution and Peace
Pacific Research Institute for Public Policy

2.   Academic Specialized
Atlantic Council of the United States
Carnegie Endowment for International Peace

Center for International Policy
Center for Strategic and International Studies
Center for the Study of Social Policy
Committee for Economic Development
Committee for the Study of the American Electorate
Council on Foreign Relations
Ethics and Public Policy Center
Foreign Policy Institute (Johns Hopkins University)
Foreign Policy Research Institute
Hispanic Policy Development Project
Institute for Foreign Policy Analysis
Institute for Health Policy Analysis
Institute for International Economics
Institute for Security and Cooperation in Outer Space
International Center for Research on Women
Lincoln Institute
Media Institute
National Bureau of Economic Research
Renewable Energy Institute
Resources for the Future
The Rockford Institute
Washington Journalism Center
Worldwatch Institute
World Resources Institute

3.   Contract/Consulting Tank
Battelle Memorial Institute
Center for Defense Information
Center for Naval Analyses
Hudson Institute
Institute of Gas Technology
Rand Corporation
SRI International
Urban Institute

4.   Advocacy Tank
American Council for Capital Formation
American Legislative Exchange Council
Capital Research Center
Cato Institute
Center for National Policy (Republican Party)
Center on Budget Policy and Priorities
Children's Defense Fund
Citizens for a Sound Economy
Economic Policy Institute
Ethics Research Institute
Institute for Policy Studies
Jefferson Foundation

National Center for Policy Analysis
Progressive Policy Institute
Public Policy Institute (AARP)

5.   *Policy Enterprise*
Heritage Foundation

6.   *Literary Agent/Publishing House*
Institute for Contemporary Studies
Manhattan Institute
Twentieth-Century Fund

7.   *State Based Think Tank*
Commonwealth Foundation
Heartland Institute
Independence Policy Institute
The Independent Institute
Sunbelt Institute

Chapter 7
Analyzing the Competition for Dollars, Scholars and Influence

The competition for dollars, scholars and influence has intensified in recent years because of the proliferation in the number of PPRIs. This dramatic increase occurred at a time of major shifts in the funding patterns of private and public supporters of policy research. These two changes left many organizations scrambling for support and created a fiercely competitive environment. In order to survive, PPRIs have been forced to develop new markets and product lines. The examples presented in the preceding chapter illustrate how firms in the public policy industry employ very different strategies in order to achieve a competitive advantage in the marketplace. Understanding the nature of these changes and how each strategic group struggles to achieve a competitive advantage in the marketplace of ideas is the focus of this chapter.

As explained in the previous chapter, this study will clarify the differences among the seven strategic PPRI groups utilizing Porter's strategic dimensions; the latter three of these are based on my modifications. The dimensions utilized in this study are as follows:

1) *Specialization*
2) *Brand identification*
3) *Push versus pull*
4) *Channel selection*
5) *Product quality*
6) *Technological leadership*
7) *Vertical integration*
8) *Cost position*
9) *Service*
10) *Price policy*
11) *Leverage*
12) *Relationship to policy community*
13) *Relationship to academic community*
14) *Relationship to the funding community*

The seven firms that have been selected to represent the strategic groups will be assigned a rating (low, medium, high) for each of the fourteen characteristics listed above. The assignment of a particular rating will be based on the background data collected and an assessment of the firm and its position in the industry.

For each firm, an institutional profile is provided, which includes an assessment of the people, values, goals, managerial structure, sources of revenue, resource allocation, and the strategies and technologies it employs. The profiles are based on data that was collected from published directories, annual reports, the survey conducted for the study, and other published material. The strategic dimensions were then employed to analyze each firm in relation to its competitors.

The resulting institutional assessments are not meant to be the definitive word on these institutions, but merely to improve our understanding of them and to demonstrate the utility of the analytical framework presented herein. The purpose of this exercise is to illustrate how the techniques for analyzing industries and competitors in the for profit world might be successfully applied to the not for profit public policy research industry. It is my hope that the techniques and the findings presented will enable a response to the major changes that are taking place in the public policy research industry.

1. Academic Diversified – The Brookings Institution
Institutional Profile

The Brookings Institution is a private non-profit organization devoted to research, education, and publication in economics, government, foreign policy, and the social sciences. According to its charter, its principal purpose is to bring knowledge to bear on current and emerging public policy issues. Brookings sees itself functioning as "an independent analyst and critic, committed to publishing its findings for the information of the public."[161] In its conferences and other activities, it attempts to serve "as a bridge between scholarship and public policy, bringing new knowledge to the attention of decision makers and affording scholars a better insight into public policy issues."[162] It carries out its activities through three research programs (Economic Studies, Governmental Studies, Foreign Policy Studies), a Center for Public Policy Education, a Publications Program, and a Social Science Computation Center.

Brookings traces its origins to 1916, with the founding of the Institute for Government Research, the first private organization devoted to public policy issues at the national level. In 1922 and 1924, the Institute was joined by two sister organizations, the Institute of Economics and the Robert Brookings Graduate School. In 1927, these three groups were consolidated into one institution, named in honor of Robert Somers Brookings (1850-1932), a St. Louis businessman whose leadership had shaped the earlier organizations.

Brookings is financed largely by its endowment and by the support of philanthropic foundations, corporations, and private individuals. Its funds are devoted to carrying out independent research and educational activities. It also undertakes some unclassified government contract studies, reserving the right to

---

[161]This quotation is taken from Brookings' brochure, p. 1.
[162]Ibid.

publish its findings. It has tax-exempt status under the federal income tax code, section 501(c)(3).[163]

In 1989, Brookings' operating expenditures were $ 16,063,000, and its total income for that year was $ 15,897,000. Brookings has one of the industry's largest endowments, with a market value in 1989 of $ 88,100,000.

In 1989, Brookings reported having 245 staff members (ninety-two administration, seventy-eight program and seventy-five support). Over sixty-eight percent of the staff have Ph.D.s. This staff produced approximately thirty books, three journals and eighty seminars in 1989. Since the late 1970s, Brookings has attempted to position itself as a centrist organization in an effort to broaden its financial base and avoid being labeled "the think tank of the Democratic party."[164]

A board of trustees is responsible for general supervision of Brookings, approval of fields of investigation, and safeguarding the independence of the its work. The president is the chief administrative officer and is responsible for formulating and coordinating policies, recommending projects, approving publications, and selecting staff.

Bruce K. MacLaury, president of the Brookings Institution, joined the organization in 1977. Previously, he had served as president of the Minneapolis Federal Reserve Bank (1971-1977); Deputy Undersecretary of the U.S. Treasury for Monetary Affairs (1969-1971); and staff member of the Organization for Economic Cooperation and Development, among other positions. Presently, MacLaury is a member of the board of trustees of the Joint Council on Economic Education, the Committee for Economic Development, the Council on Foreign Relations, and the Trilateral Commission, in addition to being director of several corporate boards. He received his undergraduate degree from Princeton and graduate degrees in economics from Harvard.

The Brookings Institution is located at 1775 Massachusetts Avenue, NW, Washington, DC 20036.

---

[163] Section 501(c)(3) lists the following as tax exempt organizations: "corporations, and any community chest, fund, or foundation, organized and operated exclusively for religious, charitable, scientific, testing for public safety, literary or educational purposes, or to foster national or international amateur sports competition..., or for the prevention of cruelty to animals, no part of the net earnings of which inures to the benefit of any private shareholder or individual, no substantial part of the operations of which is carrying on propaganda, or otherwise attempting, to influence legislation,...and which does not participate in, or intervene in (including the publishing or distributing of statements), any political campaign on behalf or (or in opposition to) any candidate for public office."

[164] This was the response of a senior member of the Reagan administration when I asked him when he thought about the work of the Brookings Institution.

Analysis of Strategic Dimensions
Specialization

The Brookings Institution and the other members of this strategic group exhibit a *low* degree of specialization because of their diversified research agenda and product line. They also serve a broad geographic and customer market segment. They are national in focus and serve the academic, policy and corporate communities.

Brand Identification

Its name says it all. The Brookings Institution has the *highest* level of brand recognition among all the PPRIs in Washington. Its nationally and internationally known scholars and publications have provided Brookings with extensive recognition. Without doubt, it is the leading PPRI in the industry.

Push versus Pull

Brookings has, for the most part, chosen to develop brand recognition directly with its two primary customer groups, academics and policy makers, through its publications, seminars and briefings. *High* push/*Low* pull.

Channel Selection

Unlike most of the other firms in the industry, Brookings has chosen a *direct* method to produce and distribute its major product, books, through its own publishing company.

Product Quality

Brookings generally receives very *high* ratings from its major consumers for all of its products. In the 1960s and 1970s, however, its ratings from its corporate customers were unfavorable, but a major change in strategy enabled Brookings to regain its share of the corporate customer market.

Technological Leadership

Brookings has been the standard-bearer in the industry and receives a *high* rating for its technological leadership. It has set the standard for the structure and strategies employed by a majority of the firms in the business; its model is the most widely imitated today. Recent technological innovations in product lines, introduced by the Heritage Foundation, have eroded Brookings' leadership position in the industry but have not cut too deeply into its market or financial support.

Vertical Integration

Brookings has exhibited a *high* degree of vertical integration, adding publications and data processing operations into its organizational structure. Its size has enabled it to attain this integration.

Cost Position

Brookings is on the *high* end of the scale of production and distribution. Brookings' reliance on researchers with advanced degrees, and on books as the primary means of getting its message across, has driven up its costs of production and distribution.

Service
Brookings provides a greater range of services for its three primary customers (business, corporations and government) than is provided by most other firms in the industry. Its size and longevity in the business enables it to offer services, such as a directory of its scholars, computer services and conference facilities, that most of its competitors cannot provide. Brookings receives a *high* rating for service.

Price Policy
Because Brookings does not charge for its products or services, it is difficult to establish an exact rating for this variable. It may be assumed that because the costs of the production and distribution of its products is high, the price would be *high* relative to its competitors if Brookings had to charge for its products. Another indicator is book sales and publishing contracts. Because of its reputation, scholars at Brookings are able to command higher prices for their books and secure lucrative publishing contracts.

Leverage
Brookings has a *high* degree of financial and operating leverage. Its position in this regard is strengthened by the fact that it owns its building and publishing operation and has significant capital reserves in the form of an endowment.

Relationship to Policy Community
Brookings commands a *high* degree of respect in the policy community for its scholarly publications. This is evidenced by its role as the leading producer of scholarly, policy oriented, book-length studies of key policy questions.

Relationship to Academic Community
Brookings has the *highest* rating among academics for the scholarly nature of its research and publications. Brookings books are used extensively in colleges and universities throughout the United States This relationship has paid off for Brookings, in that its book sales generate a healthy revenue stream for the organization.

Relationship to Funding Community
Brookings has improved its products and services for corporate customers, but still receives a *medium* rating relative to the other firms in the industry. It has always had an excellent relationship with the foundation community, as reflected by the generous and diverse support it receives. The absence of advisory committees has, until recently, hurt Brookings with corporate and individual supporters.

Summary
The Brookings Institution is the leading firm in the industry and enjoys a large share of the market. It enjoys a reputation for producing research and publications that are of the highest quality. It is a highly diversified organization that has an excellent product line and diversified base of support. Its relationship to the academic and policy communities is excellent, but its relationship with the business community remains mixed. Brookings is in a strong competitive position relative to its competitors.

2. Academic Specialized – National Bureau of Economic Research
Institutional Profile

The National Bureau of Economic Research, Inc., (NBER), a private, nonprofit research organization, was founded in 1920. According to NBER, its purpose is to improve economic understanding by providing measures and objective analyses of economic activity. This organization contributed greatly to the early scientific research on business cycles and on measures of the gross national product. Simon Kuznets, Milton Friedman, George Stigler and Theodore Schultz, who received Nobel prizes in economics, performed much of this work.

While NBER competes with Brookings, American Enterprise Institute, and other Washington PPRIs, it considers its program focus (conferences and publications) to be different in that its products are more technical, and are directed solely to economists, government agencies and officials working with economic policy questions. NBER also distinguishes itself by consciously avoiding political overtones, such as policy recommendations, in its presentations.

NBER also views universities as competitors. NBER researchers may submit their papers both to university "working papers" series and to NBER. Despite this competition, NBER's Working Papers remains one of the largest and most widely read economic series in the country. NBER believes that this factor, as well as its reputation for well-organized conferences and collaborative research projects, will enable it to maintain its position as the centrist front leader in economic analysis and research.

The major users of the NBER's products and services are academic economists, business journalists, and business and government economists.

NBER receives funding from private and corporate contributions as well as from government grants. In 1989, its total income was $ 12,419,904, while expenditures were $ 9,533,000. Thirty-six percent of NBER's total revenue is derived from government grants. To address issues of funding patterns that affect its mode of operation, NBER has stated that it is committed to a policy of reducing costs because of its rising staff and overhead costs, but not at the expense of quality. It is a tax-exempt organization.

Unlike many other PPRIs, NBER does not have a permanent research staff. Rather, its 275 research associates (tenured faculty members) and ninety-eight faculty research fellows (untenured), are professors who teach at universities in the United States and abroad. Directors, who are responsible for organizing meetings, are legally employees, and usually receive fifteen to twenty percent of their university salary for NBER work. Other NBER researchers may become employees for the summer months; however, they are paid through National Science Foundation grants that they have obtained themselves. Student research assistants are often employed on a part-time basis during the academic year and may work full or part time during the summer. NBER has six economists who receive one-year fellowships, and occasionally, it provides fellowships to economists for less than one year. (Most economists who attend NBER meetings receive no compensation from NBER.) NBER has a small staff that provides the intellectual core and administrative support for the much larger and variable group of scholars who conduct research under NBER's auspices. There are approximately thirty-five permanent staff members.

NBER directs its research at eight major issues: economic fluctuations; financial markets and monetary economics; international economics; labor economics; taxation; productivity; health economics; and the American economy (economic history). Additionally, NBER conducts twenty-five to thirty other temporary projects on narrower topics. Research on temporary projects generally lasts from one to three years; while the majority of researchers engaged on these projects are NBER members, a few non-members also participate.

A percentage breakdown of research activities indicates that individual specialists conduct seventy-five percent of all research work at NBER. Interdisciplinary teams carry out five percent of the work, and teams of economists perform an additional twenty percent of NBER's research programs.

During the 1988-1989 period, as part of its media-related outreach activities, NBER participated in approximately eight press briefings, seven television/radio interviews and six newspaper editorials. Publications during this period included 400 Working Papers, four journals, twelve NBER Digests (NBER's newsletter), and four NBER Reporters (NBER's magazine). Its list of publications for 1990 includes more than 132 reprints, over 340 Working Papers and fifteen new books. During 1990, NBER reported that it organized and conducted more than seventy national and international conferences on various economic issues.

Martin S. Feldstein, who has been president of the Bureau almost continuously since 1977, is a widely respected economist who moves comfortably in academic, business and government circles. Feldstein also serves as the George Baker Professor of Economics at Harvard University. Feldstein served as chairman of the President's Council of Economic Advisors from 1982-1984. He graduated summa cum laude from Harvard University in 1961, and received his M.A. (1964) and Ph.D. (1967) from Oxford University.

NBER is located at 1050 Massachusetts Avenue, Cambridge, MA 02138.

Analysis of Strategic Dimensions
Specialization
NBER and the other firms in this strategic group exhibit a *high* degree of specialization. NBER is a specialized organization, focusing exclusively on highly technical economic policy studies.

Brand Identification
NBER has a *medium* degree of brand identification among policy makers but a *high* degree of brand identification among academic economists and policy makers who deal with economic matters, including Treasury, Commerce and Budget officials. Its brand recognition is improved because Martin Feldstein, a former chairman of the President's Council of Economic Advisors, is its president. Its extensive network of economists helps create greater recognition and credibility within the academic community.

Push versus Pull
NBER uses a well-established network of economists at universities and research organizations to produce and promote its monographs and books. Additionally, it relies upon a variety of publishing companies to produce and distribute its products. Because NBER uses distribution channels, rather than dealing directly with customers, it exhibits a *low* degree of push and a *high* degree of pull to achieve brand identification.

Channel Selection
Because of the highly specialized nature of its publications, NBER uses the *indirect* channel of specialty outlets, such as academic publishers that specialize in books for economists. It also relies upon its network of economists to teach classes using NBER books and reports.

Product Quality
NBER has a reputation for producing high quality products that serve a narrow customer segment, i.e., academic and policy oriented economists. Because of the rigorous review process for each study, NBER products receive a *high* rating for product quality.

Technological Leadership
While NBER is known for the quality of its work, its scholars' approach to economic questions and the research it produces are perceived as being quite traditional. It therefore receives a *low* rating for this dimension.

Vertical Integration
NBER exhibits a *low* degree of vertical integration because it is entirely dependent upon other companies for the production and distribution of its products.

Cost Position
Because of the relatively low cost involved in the production and distribution of its research products, NBER maintains a *low* cost position.

Service
   Once again, the strategy and structure of NBER limits the degree of ancillary services provided to its customers. NBER receives a *low* service rating for this reason.

Price Policy
   Because of the high quality of its products and its low overhead, NBER's price position in the market is on the *low* end of the scale.

Leverage
   For the above reasons, in addition to its longevity in the business, NBER has obtained significant political and financial leverage in the marketplace. It receives a *high* leverage rating.

Relationship to Policy Community
   NBER has an excellent working relationship with policy makers who consider with economic issues and consistently receives *high* ratings from this group. Some policy makers, however, view its work as being too technical and academic to have relevance for the policy making process.

Relationship to Academic Community
   Because of its close working relationship with the academic community, NBER receives *high* ratings from this group. NBER is viewed by academics as one of the leading independent economic research centers in the world.

Relationship to Funding Community
   NBER receives a mixed rating from the business community, which is reflected in the fact that NBER received only eleven percent of its funding from corporate contributors in 1989. However, NBER has a good relationship with the foundation community, from which it received thirty-eight percent of its support. NBER also enjoys healthy support from the U.S. government through major grants from the National Science Foundation. NBER receives almost no funding from individuals. Its overall rating in this area is *medium* because it lacks diversity.

Summary
   NBER has been producing a highly specialized, high-quality product for about seventy-five years. It is well-established in the marketplace and has effectively capitalized on its role as an independent research center that does scholarly, but policy oriented, economic research. This is a narrow niche in which to succeed, but NBER has done it. NBER also benefits from a structure that allows it to enjoy a highly trained staff without incurring related overhead costs. This combination of effective strategy and structure helps insulate NBER from the competition in the industry.

3. Contract/ Consulting Institute – The Rand Corporation
Institutional Profile

The Rand Corporation grew out of Project RAND, which was launched in 1946 when the Air Force (then the U.S. Army Air Force) contracted with the Douglas Aircraft Company to research the future of air power and national security. To avoid an obvious conflict of interest, the Rand Corporation was formed two years later as an independent, private, non-profit corporation. Rand was chartered "to further and promote scientific, educational and charitable purposes, all for the public welfare and security of the United States of America."[165] The Ford Foundation provided the funding that enabled Rand to become independent.

Today, Rand's research ranges over many dimensions of national security and domestic policy issues, but the majority of its programs and funding are still for defense-related projects. Programs include long-term efforts on new aspects of major national problems, together with individual, separately sponsored projects, that investigate issues of policy, technology, program assessment and operations analysis. Rand has approximately 480 projects underway for forty-eight sponsors in the federal government, state and local governments, and foundations. Several hundred private sector companies have contributed additional support. All research is non-proprietary.

Rand operates three federally-funded research and development centers (FFRDCs) in defense research that provide ongoing technical and policy analyses to the federal government under special oversight arrangements. The oldest is Project Air Force, formerly Project RAND, which has been in continuous existence since 1946. An Air Force-wide program, it works primarily on long-term cross-cutting problems. The Arroyo Center 1, The Army's FFRDC for studies and analysis, conducts research on major policy and management concerns, emphasizing mid- and long-range problems. It also provides a limited amount of short-term assistance on urgent problems. Rand's third FFRDC is the National Defense Research Institute, housed in the National Security Research Division; it is sponsored by components of the Office of the Secretary of Defense, defense agencies, and the Joint Chiefs of Staff. Defense research for non-FFRDC sponsors is managed within the National Security Research Division.

The decision to develop a substantial domestic policy research program was made in the late 1960s, although Rand has conducted research on problems unrelated to defense dates from the outset. It now conducts research in six major areas within its Domestic Research Division (criminal justice, education and human resources, health services, international economic studies, labor and population studies, and regulatory policies). Rand also operates an Institute for Civil Justice, which was established in 1979 to perform independent, objective policy analysis and research on the American civil justice system. It is supported by grants from foundations and more than 300 corporations, trade and

---

[165]Rand Brochure, p. 3.

professional associations, and individuals. Additionally, under the auspices of the Rand Graduate School, it conducts a number of educational programs that provide advanced study for students in the social sciences. Rand also has post-doctoral programs in Population and Aging Studies and Regulatory Policy.

According to Rand, it employs 1,132 people (149 administration, 606 program and 377 support), of which 522 are full-time researchers. Forty-four percent of the research staff have Ph.D.s. In addition to its full time staff, Rand employs nearly 500 consultant researchers. In 1989, Rand's staff produced eight books, 210 reports, one journal and twenty newsletters.

In 1988, Rand generated $ 84,977,180 in revenues, of which $ 62,846,619 were contract revenues; in 1989, its revenues reached $ 93,707,319. Seventy-nine percent of Rand's revenue is derived from government grants and contracts, a level of support that is unparalleled in the industry. The market value of Rand's endowment in 1989 was $41,828,113. Earnings from its endowment fund, leverage contracts and grant-funded research fill gaps in externally sponsored research programs, support development of innovative ideas, increase the flow of published results into the public domain, support corporate research chairs, fund education and training, and support public service and dissemination activities.

James A. Thomson is president and CEO of the Rand Corporation. A member of the Rand staff since 1981, he has held a number of positions, including Director of the National Security Research Division (1981-1985), Vice President in charge of Project AIR FORCE Division (1984-1988), and Executive Vice President (1989). Thomson was a member of the National Security Council at the White House from 1977 to 1981, where he was responsible for European and NATO defense and arms control issues. He is a physicist by training, holding a B.S. from the University of New Hampshire (1967), M.S. and Ph.D. from Purdue University, and completed post-doctoral work at the University of Wisconsin (1972-1974). Thomson is currently conducting research on nuclear deterrence and European security.

The Rand Corporation is located at 1700 Main Street, Santa Monica, CA 90407-2138.

Analysis of Strategic Dimensions
Specialization
Rand and the other firms in this strategic group exhibit a *low* degree of specialization. Its research program is highly diversified, covering the entire spectrum of domestic, international and security-related policy issues.

Brand Identification
Rand has achieved brand recognition, primarily through its application of systems analysis, which has become a trademark of sorts for the organization. Rand successfully demonstrated the utility of systems analysis to the military in the late 1940s. Rand capitalized on the early successes of its unique brand of policy analysis and has marketed it to customers ever since. Rand's success with

this methodology for the analysis of military questions has enabled it to expand into other areas. While Rand continues to expand into non-defense related areas, its success in these areas is limited, as is its brand recognition. The institution has *high* brand recognition within its market segment.

Push versus Pull
Rand relies on an aggressive push strategy to market its products to its customers. To assure that its highly specialized customer segment is properly served, Rand works directly with clients and does not distribute through other channels. Rand's major source of support is defense-related contracts, which requires *high* push and *low* pull.

Channel Selection
Because Rand produces its policy analysis and reports for a specific client, and generally according to that client's specifications, Rand does not rely on independent distribution channels. Reports are produced in-house and distributed *directly* to the customer. Since Rand carries out a considerable amount of classified research for the government, its distribution channels are quite limited.

Product Quality
Rand has a reputation for producing *high* quality, specialized products for its clients. Rand has a formal technical review process for all products. According to Rand, all reviews assess the technical quality of the report, including the assumptions, matters of fact, logic of development, quality of analysis, and soundness of conclusions. At least two reviewers evaluate each report. Rand has by far the best procedures for assuring the quality of its products.

Technological Leadership
In the 1950s and 1960s, Rand was viewed as a "major social invention"[166] because of its innovative approach to analyzing policy problems. Since then, Rand's systems approach to policy analysis has been called into question, but through diversification and a shift in strategies, it has been able to maintain its market position. It exhibits a *medium* degree of technological leadership.

Vertical Integration
Rand exhibits a *high* degree of vertical integration. Its size and specialization have enabled it to achieve considerable economies of scale in the production and distribution of its products. Rand has its own computer facilities and has the capacity to print all of its publications and reports in house. In addition, Rand's graduate school helps to ensure that it has a ready supply of analysts trained to its own standards.

Cost Position
Rand has not been able to achieve a low cost position in the industry because of its high overhead. Rand's immense staff makes it the largest of the

---

[166]Baer, "Interdisciplinary Policy Research in Independent Research Centers," p. 5347, p. 2.

PPRIs. This tends to drive up the cost of its products, but does not seem to affect its competitive position within its defense-related market segment. This is because Rand has no real competitors in its specialty market. Barriers to entry in this area are considerable because of high start-up costs, the specialized nature of the research, and the security requirements needed for classified research. These costs are reflected in the high prices of its other products (domestic studies and privately supported projects), which are consequently less competitive in other markets. It has a *high* cost position.

Service
Rand provides a number of ancillary services for its customers, that other firms in the industry generally do not offer. These services include individualized briefings, customized reports, and staff consultation and training. Thus, it has a *high* service rating.

Price Policy
Rand has a *high* price position in the market because of the absence of competitors in its primary market segment. Moreover, the vagaries of government contracts, such as high overhead charges and red tape, tend to inflate its costs and therefore its prices.

Leverage
Rand's size and specialized markets and products give it *high* financial and operational leverage. In addition, Rand owns prime real estate in Santa Monica, California, and has a large endowment.

Relationship to Policy Community
Rand has a *high* rating for its relationship to the policy community. The Defense Department would give it *high* ratings, while other policy makers would give it *medium* ratings because of the highly specialized nature of its work.

Relationship to Academic Community
Rand has a *high* rating from academics, who generally respect the rigor of its methodology.

Relationship to Funding Community
Rand receives a *low* rating in this area because its products and programs are highly specialized, which limits its financial base. Because most of its funding comes from government contracts, its networks and influence in the foundation and corporate communities are somewhat limited. The exception to this is the defense industry, which closely follows and generously funds Rand's research programs.

Summary
Rand's greatest strengths are its size and specialization, but those are also its greatest weaknesses. Should its defense contracts suddenly dry up, Rand would be put in great jeopardy. Its size and its lack of diversification in the funding area would make it difficult for the firm to recover. It is still unclear if

Rand's recent attempts to increase its private contributions will prove successful in insulating the organization from this problem. Despite Rand's highly diversified program, it has not been able to dispel the widely held belief that it just does consulting and contract research for the Pentagon.

4.   Advocacy Institute – Institute For Policy Studies
Institutional Profile

The Institute for Policy Studies (IPS), was founded in 1963 by Richard Barnet and Marcus Raskin. IPS considers itself "an independent center of thought, action, and social invention in the nation's capital."[167] IPS states that its purpose is to challenge "the political pieties of the day, to explore alternative directions for achieving security, economic justice, and protection for environmental balance, and to promote grassroots political participation of citizens in the life of the nation."[168]

Since its inception twenty-eight years ago, IPS' associates have included scholar-activists, film makers, and creative writers, people like Saul Landau, John Berger, Barbara Ehrenreich and Roger Wilkins. George McGovern has served as both a fellow and as a member of the board of directors. IPS' "public scholars" produce writings, films and videotapes, and teach in adult education programs carried out through the IPS Washington School, as part of IPS' efforts to educate and encourage greater citizen participation in public affairs.

IPS points to its Third World Women's Project as an example of the breadth of its programs. This project is dedicated to increasing international understanding of third world women's struggle for justice and social change. Joint program activities include IPS's affiliation with the Transnational Institute in Amsterdam, participation in the Rose and Erwin Wolfson Center on Public Policy, the Luke and Ruth Wilson Center on Health, and the Luke Wilson lectures and seminars on public policy.

IPS employs eight resident researchers, of whom six are full-time, and two are part-time. Individual specialists conduct sixty percent of IPS' research activities, and interdisciplinary teams the remaining forty percent. IPS also employs three research scholars, two project assistants, eight executive administrative support staff and four associate directors. Three staff members are responsible for fund raising programs and three staff members conduct outreach activities. During the 1990-1991 program year, four visiting scholars joined the regular staff.

IPS reports that its financial support comes from over 5,000 individuals and nearly fifty foundations. A review of its 1989 budget revealed a total income of $1.5 million and expenditures of $2 million. It is a tax-exempt organization.

---

[167]IPS Brochure, p. 1.
[168]Ibid., p. 2.

During 1989, IPS participated in twelve issue/ policy briefings and produced five books. As part of its media-related outreach activities conducted during 1988-1989, IPS estimates that it conducted four press briefings, participated in thirty television/radio interviews, and wrote forty newspaper editorials. According to IPS, the major consumers of its products and services are scholars, politicians, activists and students.

In the fall of 1990, IPS began an affiliation with the New School for Social Research in New York in an effort to greatly expand opportunities for research, public education and outreach. A few of the nineteen broad themes and issues on which its 1990-1991 projects focused are: the impact of the global economy on the United States; the political impact of the ethnic revolution in the United States; the special role of women in developing societies; the changing meaning and possibilities of democracy in the United States; Cold War institutions in the post-Cold War world; the uses of force in the post-Cold War world; racial justice and affirmative action; the troubled U.S. banking system; nuclear weapons after Hiroshima; and the collapse of socialism and the theory of the good society.

Director Marcus Raskin, along with other "action intellectuals" like Richard Barnet, a fellow lawyer-activist, came to Washington, D.C., in 1959 to enter government service. In 1963, both Raskin and Barnet became disillusioned with the Washington establishment and joined together to form IPS. Both have remained actively involved, serving for the last eighteen years as co-directors (1963-1977), distinguished fellows (1978-1990), and co-directors (1990- present). Raskin's former positions include advisor to the Congressional Liberal Project Group, 1959-1961; a staff position on the National Security Council during the Kennedy administration, 1961-1963; and a brief period as advisor to the Bureau of the Budget. Raskin received his B.A. from the University of Chicago in 1954 and his J.D. in 1957. Despite his law degree, IPS describes Barnet as an "historian, political analyst and former State Department Official." He is the author of a number of books, including Who Wants Disarmament?, Global Reach, Roots of War, Real Security, and Global Dreams: Imperial Corporations and the New World Order. Barnet earned his B.A. and L.L.B. from Harvard.

Raskin's personal philosophy, presented in his book Being and Doing, is based on his belief that knowledge and ideas can only be tested through action. This activist philosophy continues to play a major role in shaping the purpose and programs of the Institute.

The Institute for Policy Studies is located at 1601 Connecticut Avenue, NW, Washington, DC 20009.

Analysis of Strategic Dimensions
Specialization
For the most part, IPS and the other firms in this strategic group can be characterized as exhibiting a *high* degree of specialization because their customer segment is quite narrow. Like other members of this strategic group, IPS

specializes in the promotion and service of a particular philosophy, idea, or constituency.

Brand Identification
　　IPS has achieved significant brand identification among its narrow customer segment. It has done so by effectively positioning itself as the only ultra-liberal public policy think tank in Washington. It does, however, have a *low* brand identification rating relative to the other strategic groups.

Push versus Pull
　　Since IPS does not have its own distribution channels, it relies upon established ultra-liberal publishers and distribution companies to link it to its highly specialized target customers. IPS exhibits a *low* degree of push and a *high* degree of pull in its marketing and distribution strategies.

Channel Selection
　　Because it is a highly specialized organization, IPS relies almost exclusively on *indirect* specialty outlets to effectively reach its target customers. Its position out of the political mainstream limits the market for its products. Moreover, IPS also targets customers, such as activists, who are not traditionally served by public policy research.

Product Quality
　　Because IPS is viewed as biased, its product quality is often questioned. Because IPS is perceived as not living up to the academic standards of objective and dispassionate analysis that are widely applied to public policy research, it receives a *low* product quality rating from its competitors. IPS has attempted to deal with this problem by establishing close working relationships with universities and colleges and, as previously mentioned, recently announced an affiliation with the New School for Social Research.

Technological Leadership
　　IPS' highly specialized approach to public policy research prevents it from providing technological leadership to the industry. Even its work with video and films has not proven to be terribly innovative. Consequently, it receives a *low* rating.

Vertical Integration
　　Once again, IPS' high specialization has limited its ability to introduce vertical integration into its operations. It receives a *low* rating.

Cost Position
　　IPS's high overhead and its high production and distribution costs have adversely affected its cost position in the market. The limited market for its products has also increased costs. IPS is on the *high* end of the cost scale.

Service
IPS makes limited use of ancillary and in-house services to promote its product line, choosing, rather, to rely upon specialty distributors. IPS receives a *low* service rating for this reason.

Price Policy
IPS's price position in the market is at the *high* end of the scale because of its production and distribution costs.

Leverage
IPS has *low* financial and operational leverage, due to its highly specialized products and target market. IPS has been able to survive thanks to a solid core of devoted customers who fund its programs and purchase its books.

Relationship to Policy Community
IPS has limited exposure to the policy community. Its products appeal to the extreme left, which is quite small. Since most elected politicians tend to be centrist, IPS has *low* appeal for them.

Relationship to Academic Community
IPS's primary audience is the academic community, where its ideas and publications are best received. IPS was most successful in the 1960s and 1970s when its ultra-liberal policies were more likely to be taught and debated on U.S. college campuses. However, the nation's shift towards the center during the last two decades is beginning to erode IPS' support in the academic community. Thus, IPS receives a *high to medium* rating here.

Relationship to Funding Community
IPS' relationship to the corporate community can best be described as non-existent. Its publications and research agenda are viewed by most corporations as being at odds with corporate interests. However, the heirs to large fortunes have been some of its greatest supporters. IPS receives substantial support from a narrow band of the more liberal foundations. An astonishing thirty-eight percent of its support comes from individuals, which is extremely high for the public policy research industry.

Summary

For almost thirty years, IPS has successfully produced highly specialized products for a small niche in the market. It remains to be seen how the rightward shift in America will ultimately affect IPS' share of the market. Early signs, however, are not good. Recent years have been particularly bad for the firm. Its budget has been declining, and in 1989, it reported running $ 500,000 over budget. Obviously, IPS' lack of diversification has hurt it in recent years, and the institution has failed to respond effectively to major changes in the marketplace.

5. Policy Enterprise – The Heritage Foundation
Institutional Profile

The Heritage Foundation was established in 1973 and describes itself as a nonpartisan, tax-exempt policy research institute dedicated to the principles of free competitive enterprise, limited government, individual liberty, and a strong national defense. Heritage's research and studies programs are "designed to make the voices of responsible conservatism heard in Washington, D.C., throughout the United States, and in the capitals of the world."[169]

The keys to the success of Heritage's research efforts in the last two decades have been their brevity and timeliness. Heritage prides itself on its ability to provide the policy making community with topical research on current issues. Heritage publishes its findings in a variety of formats for the benefit of decision makers, the media, the academic community, business people, and the public at large. During a recent six year period, the Heritage Foundation reported publishing some 1,000 books, monographs and studies, ranging in size from the 927-page government blueprint, Mandate for Leadership III: Policy Strategies for the 1990s, to more frequent Critical Issues monographs and the topical Backgrounders and Issue Bulletins of a dozen pages. Heritage's other regular publications include Education Update, The SDI Report, U.S.S.R. Monitor, The Heritage Foundation Federal Budget Reporter, and Policy Review, a quarterly journal of analysis and opinion. Heritage issued its first book-length publications in 1989; previously, it produced only monographs, policy briefs and newsletters.

In 1989, the Heritage Foundation reported that it had a staff of 141 (thirty-two administration, seventy-six program and thirty-three support). Forty of the program staff are full-time researchers, several of whom are internationally recognized scholars and former government officials. Heritage's research program concentrates on four areas of general study: domestic and economic policy; foreign policy and defense; the United Nations; and Asian studies. Only thirty percent of the Foundation's research staff have Ph.D.s. Heritage has linked together 1,900 individual scholars and research organizations working with its Resource Bank to provide U.S. policy makers with "the intellectual resources needed to guide America into the 21st century."[170]

In addition to its publication program, Heritage regularly brings together national and international opinion leaders and policy makers to discuss issues and ideas in a variety of formal and informal settings. Through a continuing series of seminars, lectures, debates and briefings, it provides a forum for the exchange of ideas and a laboratory for developing these ideas into practical public policy proposals. Heritage reported that it conducted fifty seminars and three major conferences in 1989.

---

[169] Heritage Foundation Brochure.
[170] Ibid.

While Heritage is seen as innovative, questions have been raised about the thoroughness and overall quality of its research. Relative to its competitors and for an institution of its size, Heritage has a small research staff and a very small number of Ph.D.s. Rand and Brookings, for instance, have researcher/program staff ratios of 522/606 and 69/78 respectively, while Heritage's ratio is much lower at 40/76. The percentage of Ph.D.s per institution is forty-four percent at Rand, sixty-eight percent at Brookings and thirty percent at Heritage. These factors have enabled Heritage's competitors to undercut its credibility by questioning the quality of its staff and products. Heritage has also been criticized for the strident nature of its direct mail campaigns.

Individuals, corporations, companies, associations, and foundations support the work of The Heritage Foundation through tax-deductible gifts. In 1989, Heritage reported that it received $ 17,916,781 in total revenues, of which twenty-six percent came from foundations; thirteen percent from corporations, and forty-five percent from individuals. The remainder of its funds came from its endowment, fees and sales. Heritage owns its building and has a solid endowment of $ 14,262,471.

Edwin J. Feulner, Jr., president of the Heritage Foundation since 1973, previously was executive director of the House Republican Study Committee and an administrative assistant to Rep. Philip M. Crane (R-IL). He also serves as chairman of the U.S. Advisory Commission on Public Diplomacy and writes a national newspaper column. Feulner received a B.S. from Regis College in Denver and an M.B.A. from the Wharton School of the University of Pennsylvania. He earned his Ph.D. at the University of Edinburgh.

The Heritage Foundation is located at 214 Massachusetts Avenue, SE, Washington, DC 20002.

Analysis of Strategic Dimensions
Specialization
Heritage and the other members of this strategic group exhibit a *low* degree of specialization in terms of its target customer segment. However, Heritage exhibits a *high* degree of specialization in its product line.

Brand Identification
Heritage developed a successful marketing strategy and an innovative product line, which give it almost instant recognition among policy makers and policy elites inside and outside of Washington. It has a *high* brand identification.

Push versus Pull
Heritage owes much of its success to its efforts to market its products directly to consumers. Because of this, it has a very *high* push rating for its effective approaches to creating significant brand identification by aggressively marketing its products. It has a *low* pull.

Channel Selection
Heritage has made a substantial investment in its own distribution channels. It is known throughout the industry for the *direct* and timely distribution of its products.

Product Quality
Heritage has been criticized for producing research products that are not up to the standards of its peers. Only thirty percent of Heritage's staff have Ph.D.s, which is consistent with its innovative strategy, but detrimental when it comes to questions of product quality. Heritage products have a *low* quality rating.

Technological Leadership
Heritage receives a very *high* rating for introducing a number of innovative strategies into the industry. Porter points out that an inverse relationship often exists in areas of product quality and technological leadership; high technological leadership frequently comes at the expense of product quality. This is particularly true in the early stages of product innovation.[171] Heritage's highly successful short policy briefs have challenged the traditional method of producing book-length studies for policy makers. In addition, as a means of generating significant unrestricted revenues for its operations, Heritage introduced direct mail fundraising that operates with an efficiency and effectiveness that is unmatched in the industry.

Vertical Integration
Heritage has a *high* degree of vertical integration in the marketing, production and distribution of its products. It emphasizes serving the customers' needs, as evidenced by the significant financial commitment it has made to outreach activities. Heritage spends more on outreach then any of its competitors.

Cost Position
Heritage has achieved a *low* cost position by not hiring expensive scholars and public policy specialists. Rather, it has chosen to focus on less established scholars and analysts who have a journalistic flair and the ability to condense immense amounts of information into meaningful policy briefs. This strategy has enabled Heritage to reduce costs in this area and to shift resources to marketing and outreach activities.

Service
Heritage provides a number of ancillary services in connection with its product line, including hand delivering policy briefs to members of Congress before voting on an issue takes place, and linking legislators with specialists on a particular issue. It receives a *high* rating.

---

[171]The example of the Japanese role in the electronics industry in the 1950s and 1960s is a clear illustration of this point.

Price Policy
Heritage's ability to produce shorter and cheaper policy research products, relative to its competitors, has enabled it to achieve a commanding *low* price position in the market. It tends to be on the *low* end of the price scale.

Leverage
Relative to its competitors, Heritage enjoys a *high* degree of financial and operational leverage. For an institution that only became a major player in the last ten years, it has achieved a remarkable degree of success. Heritage has effectively leveraged this success through careful management and expansion, which has enabled it to buy and renovate its headquarters in Washington and build a very respectable endowment. More importantly, Heritage has capitalized on its success by establishing strong ties to the policy and funding communities that surpass those of most of its competitors.

Relationship to Policy Community
Heritage has a variable rating when it comes to the policy community. Heritage is praised by most policy makers for creating products that are user-friendly and that recognize the importance of brevity for busy officials. Its rating becomes mixed because of its conservative orientation. Among conservative policy makers, it has a very *high* rating, but moderates and liberals have generally given Heritage a *low* rating. This aside, it has developed the most effective strategy for reaching policy makers with its products, and for this reason it receives an overall *high* rating.

Relationship to Academic Community
Despite the fact that Heritage has established a network of 1,900 scholars at universities and colleges throughout the United States, it has a *low* rating among academics because its studies are perceived to be biased and not rigorous in their examination of policy issues.

Relationship to Funding Community
Heritage receives *high* ratings from the business community because the corporate community is comfortable with both its medium and its message. Its highly effective direct mail campaigns have enabled it to raise substantial funds from individuals, which has led to tremendous flexibility since these funds tend to be unrestricted. Corporate foundations have responded well to Heritage's programs, while private foundations have, for the most part, been lukewarm to requests for funds.

Summary
Heritage has in a very short time established itself as one of the leading firms in the business by introducing new products and innovative marketing techniques. While some disagree with its political orientation or its approach to policy analysis, most agree that it has developed a highly effective medium for conveying its message. Heritage has continued to be successful in the post-Reagan era and has begun to tone down its rhetoric and improve the quality of its staff and products.

6. Literary Agent/Publishing House – Manhattan Institute
Institutional Profile

The Manhattan Institute for Policy Research (MI) was founded in New York in 1977. Originally the International Center for Economic Policy Studies, MI was renamed in 1981 to reflect an expanded policy agenda. MI was a moving force behind the book Wealth and Poverty, by George Gilder, its program director at the time. The book was widely credited with laying the basis for what has since become known as supply-side economics. In 1984, MI sponsored Charles Murray's critique of contemporary welfare policy, Losing Ground: American Social Policy 1950-1980. In 1988, Senior Fellow Peter Huber's book, Liability, helped initiate a broad-based "counterrevolution" in judicial thinking. MI produces two to three books and conducts between twenty and thirty conferences and seminars a year. In recent years, MI has attempted to focus its publishing efforts by establishing a Center for New York Policy Studies, a Center for Educational Innovation and a Judicial Studies Program. It also publishes the quarterly City Journal.

Since its inception, MI's fellowship program has supported and promoted the works of market-oriented scholars and policy analysts writing on a diverse set of policy questions. MI also plays an important role as one of the leading literary agents for promising ideas and talent in the fields of economics, philosophy, law and public policy. It helps raise funding for an author's work, provides a home base for writing, secures a publisher, and then aggressively markets the book. MI's success in this area led The New Republic to conclude that "the Brookings Institution, the Ford Foundation, the prominent New York publishing houses and the like, are hardly as tuned-in to the way political ideas get into circulation as are organizations like the Manhattan Institute."[172] The current chairman of MI, Richard Gilder, has referred to its president William Hammet as "'the greatest intellectual stock picker of our time.'"[173]

MI has a staff of twenty-one (eight administrative, nine program staff members and four support staff), of whom six are research fellows. Sixty percent of MI's research staff have Ph.Ds.

Over the last twelve years, MI has seen dramatic growth for an organization of its size, reporting revenues of $ 109,059 and expenditures of $ 76,211 in 1977, and revenues of $ 2,407,360 and expenditures of $ 2,054,725 in 1989. The majority of MI's support in 1989 came from foundations (forty-three percent) and corporations (thirty percent) with twenty-five percent contributed by individuals. Fees and sales constituted two percent of its revenues. MI has not, however, been able to build an endowment, reporting capital reserves of only $ 157,072 in 1989. It has tax-exempt status. Still more recently, its annual budget has neared five million dollars "and it has received large grants not only from the

---

[172]Chuck Lane, "The Manhattan Project," *New Republic*, March 25, 1985, p. 14.
[173]James Traub, "Intellectual Stock Picking," *New Yorker*, February 7, 1994, p. 38.

usual roster of right-wing foundations but also from the liberal and apolitical groups...even so the bult of its individual contributions still comes from conservative Wall Street figures."[174]

William M.H. Hammett, president of MI, directs its affairs. Before becoming its president in 1980, Hammett was president of the Center for Libertarian Studies. He has held positions in investments and marketing, attended Southern Illinois University, and earned an M.A. in economics from the University of Chicago.

The Manhattan Institute for Policy Research is located at 52 Vanderbilt Ave., Second Floor, New York, NY 10017.

Analysis of Strategic Dimensions
Specialization

MI and the other firms in this strategic group exhibit a variable degree of specialization. MI has a relatively narrow product line, focusing almost exclusively on the publication of books, which indicates a *high* degree of specialization. Conversely, it has a diverse set of customer targets, i.e., policy makers, academics, business leaders and the general public, which would suggest a *low* degree of specialization.

Brand Identification

Since MI does not have a permanent staff or a research agenda, it has *low* brand recognition. MI's customers tend to identify more with the scholars who write its books than with the institution itself. MI's brand recognition is also limited by the fact that it can only publish a few specialized books a year. In addition, since so much in the publishing business depends on luck and timing, these books cannot be relied upon to build a firm customer base. MI has attempted to deal with its brand recognition and service problems in recent years by dramatically increasing the number of seminars it conducts to promote its products, going from one in 1980 to thirty-five in 1989.

Push versus Pull

MI relies on distribution channels for the bulk of its products. However, it handles the majority of the promotional and sales work for its products through the many conferences and seminars it produces. Relative to its competitors, MI is a *low* push/*high* pull organization.

Channel Selection

Because MI tries to reach a broad audience with its books, it uses both broad-line and specialty outlets to distribute its products. The choice of indirect distribution channel is largely dependent on the author and the subject matter of the books. For example, Charles Murray's Losing Ground had a wide appeal and

---

[174]Ibid., p. 39.

was marketed broadly, while Peter Huber's Liability had a much more limited audience.

Product Quality
MI's reliance on scholars who are not permanent members of its staff lessens its control over product quality. Scholars come and go, and the quality and timeliness of their products vary. While MI products are generally viewed in a positive light, they do not exhibit the continuity and quality of their competitors' products. MI's strategy and structure inhibit its ability to transcend the individual scholar to project a clear picture of the institution and its mission and, more importantly, to establish effective quality controls. It is for these reasons that MI receives a *low* product quality rating

Technological Leadership
MI, like Heritage, has developed a *highly* innovative strategy and structure to deliver its products, but again, this has come at the expense of product quality.

Vertical Integration
Relative to the other strategic groups, MI has achieved a *low* degree of vertical integration. Most, if not all, of MI's production and service distribution mechanisms are external to the organization. MI depends heavily upon its production and distribution channels.

Cost Position
MI's structure has given it a very *low* cost position when it comes to manufacturing and distributing its products. In this area, MI does not have any expensive in-house scholars, and its distribution channels work in its favor. It is able to retain its competitive edge through low operational costs and careful selection of scholars and books.

Service
MI has a *low* service rating because it has no service staff.

Price Policy
Because of its low overhead, MI is quite competitive on price. The quality is variable, but generally, customers receive their money's worth. It remains to be seen if MI can maintain this position as it increases its permanent research staff and the number of conferences and seminars it produces. MI receives a *low* rating for pricing.

Leverage
MI's overall strategy does not allow it to have significant financial leverage. This, in turn, limits its operational leverage to a *low* level, both with its buyers and suppliers. MI is, in the final analysis, captive to the scholars it hires to write its books and to the big publishing houses, such Random House and Simon and Schuster that publish its studies.

Relationship to Policy Community
MI has a good relationship to the policy community, but is limited by its narrow product line and geographical remoteness from Washington. It receives a *medium* rating.

Relationship to Academic Community
MI also has a *medium* rating among academics. The scholars who produce MI's books and studies are generally respected in the academic community for the thoroughness of their work, but MI does not command the overall respect that its competitors do. By not having a permanent staff of recognized scholars or an established network of college and university scholars, MI has limited its access to this market.

Relationship to Funding Community
MI is located in New York City, which gives it greater access to the numerous corporations and foundations based there. It has capitalized on its location through a series of programs that are specifically designed to serve this customer segment. But, its size and other structural impediments limit its ability to exploit these advantages. Since 1977, MI has steadily diversified its funding base, increasing individual contributions from six percent in that year to twenty-five percent in 1989. Overall, it receives a *high* rating for this dimension.

Summary
While MI's strategy and structure allow it to respond more readily to current policy concerns and to achieve tremendous savings on staff and production costs, its method of operation limits the control it has over its scholars and their research products. Consequently, MI does not have the reputation for continuity and quality that its competitors have been able to achieve. In addition, its over-dependence on a single product – books – makes it highly vulnerable to changes in the marketplace. It is hard to predict what issues will be hot, and since MI can only afford to buy a few books each year, its fortunes can rise or fall very quickly. Yet, its establishment of the City Journal in 1990 represents its attempt to diversify its activities and explore ideas that can be disseminated more rapidly than the book publication process will allow.

7. State Based Tanks – The Commonwealth Foundation for Public Policy Alternatives
Institutional Profile
The Commonwealth Foundation for Public Policy Alternatives, founded in 1988, describes itself as an independent, nonpartisan public policy think tank committed to furthering the goals of economic growth and individual opportunity. It seeks to "generate new ideas and policy change"[175] at the state and local level in Pennsylvania. According to Commonwealth, it is committed to affirming the belief that market competition enhances the public interest by creating growth

---
[175]Commonwealth Foundation Brochure.

and prosperity for all. Commonwealth's programs attempt to foster an economic climate where entrepreneurship and private initiative can flourish.

Since its inception in 1988, Commonwealth has published over thirty reports, issue briefs, and editorials that are designed to reach policy makers in Harrisburg. Publications cover a wide range of state and local issues, including educational reform, reapportionment, privatization, government regulations, tort reform, and tax reform. Most are done in-house or copied from another source; Commonwealth does very little contracted research. Most of its publications and strategies for reaching policy makers are modeled after those of the Heritage Foundation.

Commonwealth also brings together state and national scholars, opinion leaders, and policy makers to address issues and ideas through a series of conferences, seminars, and policy briefings. Commonwealth's research is disseminated to policy makers, opinion leaders, the communications media, the academic, business and financial communities, and the interested public in Pennsylvania.

Commonwealth has a full-time staff of five. Most of Commonwealth's research is conducted by non-resident scholars since it has no real in-house research capacity.

Commonwealth is a tax exempt educational organization. It is supported by private foundations, corporations and 200 private individuals. In 1989, its revenues were $ 320,000 and its expenditures were $ 271,000. Its budget for 1990 was $ 275,000. Commonwealth received a major start-up grant from the Katherine Mabis McKenna Foundation in 1988 and has expanded its funding to include some of the other major foundations in Pennsylvania, such as the Pew Charitable Trusts and the Sarah Scaife Foundation.

A study of state-based think tanks conducted by the Roe Foundation concluded that Commonwealth is "a high quality organization that probably is a model for how to do it – but then money up front changes the way you have to go about things. They were very fortunate to have both the Sarah Scaife and McKenna Foundations in their state and to have their strong financial backing."[176]

Don Eberly is the founder and president of the Commonwealth Foundation. He spent eight years in Washington in various key positions in Congress, the White House, and with presidential candidate Jack Kemp. He is editor of the book Leading Pennsylvania into the 21st Century: Policy Strategies for the Future, and has written on numerous economic policy subjects. He holds masters degrees from George Washington University and Harvard University, and has done doctoral studies at Penn State University. He is a native of Lancaster, Pennsylvania, where he lives with his wife and three children.

---

[176] The 1989 Roe Foundation Report on Twelve State Policy Institutes (Greenville, SC: December 31, 1990).

The Commonwealth Foundation for Public Policy Alternatives is located at 600 North Second Street, Suite 400, Harrisburg, PA 17101.

Analysis of Strategic Dimensions
Specialization
Commonwealth and the other members of this strategic group exhibit a very *high* degree of specialization. As the name implies, state-based think tanks are limited to state policy issues and therefore have a narrow product line, a highly restricted customer base, and a small geographic market.

Brand Identification
Commonwealth has limited brand identification on the national market, but has achieved significant brand recognition in its own state through aggressive sales and marketing efforts directed at policy makers in Pennsylvania. Commonwealth has a *low* brand identification rating overall.

Push versus Pull
Since Commonwealth uses the same aggressive marketing techniques as Heritage, and distributes its products directly to its customers, it receives a *high* push/ *low* pull rating.

Channel Selection
Because of the extremely specialized market segment it serves, Commonwealth must use its own *direct* distribution channels to reach its customers. No existing channels fit its needs.

Product Quality
Commonwealth receives a *high* quality rating because its products meet the highly specialized needs of its customers. No other major producers compete with Commonwealth in this market segment. Commonwealth's products, however, do not reach the same quality as those of the national strategic groups. Commonwealth's rating would be less if it competed with these strategic groups.

Technological Leadership
Since most of the technologies employed by Commonwealth are borrowed from the national PPRIs, it is not viewed as a major innovator in the industry. It receives a *low* technological leadership rating.

Vertical Integration
Commonwealth has achieved a *medium* degree of vertical integration in the production and distribution of its products. Unlike the Institute for Policy Studies, for example, Commonwealth has been forced to vertically integrate because of its specialization. Because Commonwealth serves a market segment that has no real suppliers, it has added value to its products by developing its own in-house service network and distribution channels.

Cost Position

Commonwealth has sought to contain its costs by keeping the scale of its operations proportional to the market it serves. Commonwealth and the other firms in this segment of the industry tend to be small but highly efficient in the production and distribution of their products. The highly specialized nature of their products and limited revenue sources require that they be cost competitive in order to survive. Commonwealth receives a *low* rating for this category.

Service

Despite its small size, Commonwealth and other organizations like it have placed a premium on service. Most state legislators have little or no staff, so in order to effectively reach them, Commonwealth has adapted the products and marketing strategies developed by the Heritage Foundation for its customers. Commonwealth's extensive use of policy briefs and its publication of Leading Pennsylvania into the 21st Century, which is modeled after Heritage's Mandate for Leadership, are just a few examples of the close connection between these two institutions. Like Heritage, it has a *high* service rating.

Price Policy

Because of its "lean and mean" mode of operation, Commonwealth has a highly competitive price policy. It keeps prices *low* by contracting research out to scholars at other research organizations, colleges and universities.

Leverage

Commonwealth has limited leverage because its financial base is so narrow; the sources of funding for state-based PPRIs are quite limited. This simple fact gives these institutions a *low* leverage rating.

Relationship to Policy Community

Commonwealth receives a *high* rating for its relationship to the policy community in its state. It has carefully selected a set of issues that are of concern to state policy makers and has successfully developed products that meet their needs.

Relationship to Academic Community

Commonwealth, unlike Heritage, has from its inception attempted to link itself with the academic community in Pennsylvania. It speaks proudly of the fact that thirteen professors contributed to Leading Pennsylvania into the 21st Century, which is Commonwealth's blueprint for Pennsylvania and one of its major publications. It receives a *high* rating for this relationship.

Relationship to Funding Community

Commonwealth receives a *high* rating in this category. It has done exceptionally well for an institution that has only been in business since 1988. It is supported by twenty foundations, 218 corporations and 200 individuals, which shows both depth and diversity. The major problem that faces this institution and the others in its class is that individual contributions tend to be small, and the labor involved in generating them is quite extensive. In addition, state-based

PPRIs can generally seek funds only in their home state. National foundations and national and international corporations tend not to fund state and local organizations (unless those potential funders are focused on state and local issues or have an operation that happens to be located in the state.) Thus, while Commonwealth's funding appears to be quite diverse, almost all of the contributors listed in its annual report are from Pennsylvania.

Summary
Commonwealth has successfully found a niche in a market where there is little or no competition and a strong demand for its services and products exists. Its degree of specialization, however, puts serious limits on its growth. Its products have little or no utility outside of the state, so expansion into other markets is not an option. It is yet to be seen whether or not Commonwealth's high degree of specialization will benefit it in the long term.

Overall Findings
The ratings for the seven firms are provided in the table presented below. Brookings, Rand and Heritage received the high ratings for most of the strategic dimensions while the other four firms received variable ratings. It comes as no surprise then, that these three institutions were cited most frequently as both peers and competitors by the thirty-nine institutions originally surveyed. However, there are some important exceptions. It should be pointed out that Heritage's role as an innovator within the industry seems to have come at the expense of product quality, and that Rand's over-reliance on government contracts has made it difficult for the institution to truly diversify its funding base. Brookings, Rand and Heritage are also the most vertically integrated firms within the industry, as a result of their size. They are the only firms that have the capacity to do their own computer processing, printing and publishing. Rand has become the most vertically integrated, with its graduate programs that provide a continuing supply of policy analysts

The major advantage that the lesser known firms such as the Manhattan Institute, Commonwealth Foundation and the Institute for Policy Studies enjoy over the larger firms is their size and specialization. The degree of specialization they have achieved both in their products and market and their relatively low cost of operation has enabled them to effectively compete with the larger, more vertically integrated firms. In addition, the specialized firms tend to rely on their specialized networks to distribute their products for them (low push/high pull) while the diversified firms are forced to distribute their products directly to the customers (high push/low pull), which increases their cost of operation.

With the exception of the Heritage Foundation there seems to be a direct connection between a firm's high service rating and high cost position. Heritage has been able to effectively serve it customers while maintaining its relatively low cost position.

All of this might be viewed as idle speculation on my part if the empirical data did not support it. Tables 7.1 - 7.9 are intended to help validate the analysis of the strategic dimensions conducted in this chapter and to further highlight the differences among these seven institutions.

Table 7.3 illustrates the variation of strategies by product lines among institutions. Brookings and NBER, both of which resemble academic institutions, produce academically oriented books and working papers, while the more policy oriented institutions, such as Rand, Heritage and Commonwealth produce monographs and policy briefs.

Table 7.6 demonstrates how the nature and composition of an institution's funding base plays a major role in determining the strategy and structure of an organization. The level of restricted and unrestricted revenues, for instance, or the level and mix of support from corporations, foundations, government and individuals are important keys to understanding the nature and direction of these institutions. These factors help determine what is produced, what staff are hired and what management structure is employed. As we have seen, an institution like Rand that does mostly contract research will have a centralized decision making process that enables it to control research outputs. In addition, it will hire policy analysts who are willing to produce reports to meet the basic requirements set by the contracting agency. The impact this has on an institution is that

> Think tanks that are forced to rely on the satisfaction of contractors with their research product find it difficult to pursue independent inquiry. They are driven by the marketplace and availability of contract funds. The search for funding often encourages would-be think tanks to mold their research agenda into one that is appealing to prospective clients and not around issues that are of scholarly or public interest. In the extreme, think tanks that are not financially independent may receive pressure (either explicitly or implicitly) from clients who are interested in "acceptable" results. These situations limit the think tank's enterprise.[177]

What once could only be said about contract research can now be said about most corporate and foundation grants. In recent years, foundations and an increasing number of corporations have stopped making general, unrestricted grants and begun to make project-specific grants that are as restricted as some contracts.

Heritage and Brookings have the most diversified and balanced sources of revenue, which affords them considerable stability and independence. Both receive significant revenues from all the major funding streams except government grants and contracts. Brookings' endowment income (27%) and Heritage's support from individuals (35-45%) provide these two institutions with a greater degree of control over their products and operations because these revenue sources are unrestricted. In recent years, Brookings' executive training and publishing and data processing operations have provides significant additional support, which has served to further diversify its funding base.

---

[177]Durst & Thurber, "Studying Washington Think Tanks," p. 13.

The other five institutions have much narrower funding bases because they rely heavily on public and private grants and contracts. NBER receives in excess of thirty-five percent of its funding from the National Science Foundation in the form of research grants, while the majority of Rand's financial support comes from government grants and contracts, most of which are defense-related. IPS and Commonwealth derive an extremely high level of support from foundation grants, at seventy (approximately) and seventy-two percent respectively. The lack of diversification in the funding sources and the restrictions on the money they do receive makes these institutions more dependent and vulnerable.

Table 7.7 illustrates the sustained growth these institutions have experienced since 1970. Rand and Heritage have seen their total income double or triple in the last ten years. Heritage's ability to capture a significant share of the market in a relatively short time is underscored by its dramatic increase in revenues. In 1989 Heritage's total revenue exceeded Brookings' by two million dollars, making it the largest PPRI in Washington.

It has been my contention that such strategic choices as what to produce and who to hire are directly related to the structure of an institution. Tables 7.2 and 7.3 dramatically illustrate the relationship between the outputs of these institutions and their staffing patterns. The academic oriented institutions have the highest percentage of Ph.D.s, while the policy oriented ones have the lowest. Heritage, which has been criticized for the poor quality of some of its products, has only thirty percent Ph.Ds, while Brookings' staff is sixty-eight percent Ph.Ds. Notably, Brookings and Heritage have almost the same number of program staff, seventy-eight and seventy-six respectively.

Brookings' reliance on the high credentials of its staff and its varied research portfolio explains its characterization as an academic diversified policy research organization. Similarly, Heritage's significant financial commitment to outreach and fundraising (36%) helps explain its business orientation. Rand's large number of government grants and contracts (79%) help explain the dominance of contract/consulting culture at this institution. Clearly, the choices an institution makes greatly affect its structure. While further data and analysis are needed to prove the validity of the seven groups identified in this study, the data collected thus far seem to indicate that the seven firms represent compelling examples of the differing strategies and structures adopted by most PPRIs.

Table 7.1
Strategic Dimension Ratings for Each Exemplar Firm

	Brookings Institution	National Bureau of Economic Research	Rand Corporation	Institute for Policy Studies	Heritage Foundation	Manhattan Institute	Commonwealth Foundation
Specialization	low	high	high/low*	high	high/low	high/low*	high
Brand Identification	highest	medium	high	low	high	low	low (outside PA)
Push/Pull	high/low	low/high	high/low	low/high	high/low	low/high	high/low
Channel Selection	direct	indirect	direct	indirect	direct	variable/indirect	direct
Product Quality	high	high	high	low	low	low	high
Technological Leadership	high	low	medium	low	high	high	low
Vertical Integration	high	low	high	medium	high	low	medium
Cost Position	high	low	high	high	low	low	low
Service	high	low	high	low	high	low	high
Price Policy	high	low	high	high	low	low	low
Leverage	high	high	high	low	high	low	low
Relationship to Policy Community	high	high	high	low	high	medium	high
Relationship to Academic Community	highest	high	high	high > medium	low	medium	high
Relationship to Funding Community	medium	medium	low	low	high	high	high

* Has a highly specialized product line but deals with a diverse range of customers

Table 7.2
Product Lines for 1989

Product—Organization	Books	Journals	Monographs	ISS/Policy Briefs	Newsletters	Magazines	Seminars	Major Conferences	Films	Other
Brookings Institution	30	3				1	80	4		
National Bureau of Economic Research	8	4	400		12	4	31	29		
Rand Corporation	8	1	210	20	2					
Institute for Policy Studies	5			12						
Heritage Foundation	4	4	3	138	30	4	50	3		
Manhattan Institute	1			12			35	3		
Commonwealth Foundation	1			8	2			2		

Table 7.3
Staff Compositions for 1989

Organization	Staff Size			Researchers				
	Admin.	Program	Support	Full Time	Part Time	Resident	Non-Resident	Researchers with Ph.Ds
Brookings Institution	92	78	75	69	3	70	2	68%
National Bureau of Economic Research	30	373	5	0	373	373	0	100%
Rand Corporation	149	606	377	86	522	NA	NA	44%
Institute for Policy Studies	5	5	8	6	2	8	–	50%
Heritage Foundation	32	76	33	40	–	40	–	30%
Manhattan Institute	8	9	4	5	1	–	6	60%
Commonwealth Foundation	1	3	1	1	–	1	–	0%

Table 7.4
Expenditures for 1989

Organization	Research	Printing Publications	Salaries & Related	Conferences & Seminars	Fund Raising	Outreach Activities	Overhead	Other (Specify)
Brookings Institution	66%	included in admin.	NA	NA	included in admin.	19%	14%	1% fellowships
National Bureau of Economic Research	93%	2%	NA	9%	1%	–	20%	–
Rand Corporation	NA	NA	NA	NA	NA	NA	NA	NA
Institute for Policy Studies	–	–	70%	5%	–	10%	15%	–
Heritage Foundation	15.3%	1.6%	38.7%	4.4%	13.5%	22.1%	1.7%	–
Manhattan Institute	35%	7%	41%	4%	3%	3%	7%	–
Commonwealth Foundation	30%	10%	20%	5%	10%	15%	10%	–

Table 7.5
Sources of Revenue for 1988 & 1989

Organization	Years	Govt. Grants & Contracts	Endowments & Similar	Fees & Sales	Foundations	Corporations	Individuals
Brookings Institution	1988	1%	27%	32%	*40%		
	1989	1%	27%	32%	40%		
National Bureau of Economic Research	1988	34%	14%	–	39%	13%	–
	1989	37%	14%	–	38%	11%	–
Rand Corporation	1988	79%	0.4%	0.6%	20%	–	–
	1989	79%	1.0%	0.2%	19%	–	–
Institute for Policy Studies	1988	–	2%	11%	87%	NA	NA
	1989	–	9%	2%	**89%	NA	NA
Heritage Foundation	1988	–	3%	4%	40%	18%	35%
	1989	–	10%	6%	26%	13%	45%
Manhattan Institute	1988	–	–	2%	48%	28%	22%
	1989	–	–	3%	43%	30%	25%
Commonwealth Foundation	1988	–	–	–	58%	25%	17%
	1989	–	–	–	72%	20%	8%

* Unrestricted and restricted grants and contributions constituted 40% of Brookings' revenues in 1988 and 1989. (1988: foundations 83%, corporate 16%, and individuals 1%; 1989: foundations 65%, corporate 33%, and individuals 2%.)
** Revenue from foundations, corporations, and individuals for 1988 and 1989 are not available. Figures reported above are all private grants and contributions, of which approximately 70% are foundation grants.

Table 7.6
Areas of Specialization

Organization	Domestic Econ.	Int'l Econ.	Political Science	Security Studies	Reg'l Studies	Social Policy	Education Policy	Int'l Relations	Other (specify)
Brookings Institution	x	x	x	x		x	x		
National Bureau of Economic Research	x								
Rand Corporation		x		x		x			
Institute for Policy Studies									public policy studies
Heritage Foundation	x			x					
Manhattan Institute	x	x				x	x		legal reform
Commonwealth Foundation						state public policy issues			

Table 7.7
Total Income

Organization	1970	1980	1988	1989
Brookings Institution	$ 5,476,000	$ 9,426,000	$ 15,381,000	$ 15,897,000
National Bureau of Economic Research	$ 2,242,000	$ 5,688,828	$ 7,573,078	$ 12,419,904
Rand Corporation	$ 25,097,028	$ 48,017,419	$ 84,977,180	$ 93,731,875
Institute for Policy Studies	$ 150,000	$400,000	$1,300,000	$1,500,000
Heritage Foundation	*$ 413,497	$ 5,329,117	$ 15,003,930	$ 17,916,781
Manhattan Institute	–	$ 473,106	$ 1,833,344	$ 2,407,360
Commonwealth Foundation	–	–	$ 168,000	$ 320,738

* Heritage's first year of actual operations was 1974.

Table 7.8
Media-Related Outreach Activities for 1988 & 1989

Organization	Press Briefings	Television & Radio Interviews	Newspaper Editorials
Brookings Institution	80	NA	NA
National Bureau of Economic Research	8	7	6
Rand Corporation	2	7	6
Institute for Policy Studies	4	30	40
Heritage Foundation	25	1,100	300
Manhattan Institute	55	20	100
Commonwealth Foundation	8	50	150

Table 7.9
Constituency Ranking

Organization	Congress	Executive Branch	Corporate Community	Academic/ Scholarly Community	Media	General Public	Other (specify)
Brookings Institution	8	8	5	8	8	5	5 foundations
National Bureau of Economic Research	7	7	7	10	8	6	
Rand Corporation	9	10	5	8	6	7	
Institute for Policy Studies	10	9	1	7	6	8	
Heritage Foundation	10	10	8	6	9	7	
Manhattan Institute	6	6	8	9	10	5	8*
Commonwealth Foundation	3	3	5	6	7	9	

*Foundation, community professionals in the area of research, educators, judges, etc.

Organizations were asked to rank each constituency on a scale of 1-10. 1 = least important (to organization), 10 = most important (to organization.)

CHAPTER 8
CONCLUSIONS AND IMPLICATIONS FOR THE INDUSTRY

I believe that the competitive analysis of the seven strategic groups clearly demonstrates how the strategy and structure of a firm influences its selection of staff, product lines, and customer and funding targets. These fundamental differences in how PPRIs organize themselves determine how the institutions compete for scholars, dollars and influence. The strategic choices made by an organization ultimately determine a firm's competitive position in the marketplace. By using Porter's strategic dimensions, we see that a firm's rating on each of these dimensions is directly influenced by its organizational structure and the marketing and production strategies it employs. I have also attempted to demonstrate the tremendous variations in the institutional capacity of the firms discussed. These firms have taken quite divergent approaches to producing and marketing their products, cutting costs, and managing their internal and external environments. We have also seen that the technologies employed determine the sphere of influence of the institution and, more specifically, the market it serves. The rate of change that has taken place over the past twenty to twenty-five years has been dramatic and has created an industry that is quite diverse and complex. I will now attempt to show how the seven strategic groups influence the overall nature and direction of the industry through a series of case studies.

The reason that the level and intensity of the competition vary from one segment of the industry to the other has good deal to with nature and composition of the strategic groups in an industry. According to Porter, four factors determine how strongly the strategic groups in an industry will interact when competing for customers:
1) the market interdependence among groups, or the extent to which their customer targets overlap;
2) the product differentiation achieved by the groups;
3) the number of strategic groups and their relative sizes;
4) the strategic distance among the groups or the extent to which strategies diverge.[178]

I will discuss each of these factors in turn and will provide some case examples to further demonstrate how the strategies and structures vary from one group to the next. A schematic illustration of the competition in the industry will be presented at the end of the chapter. The illustration will show the great variance in the nature and size of the groups and that increased competition has affected certain segments of the industry more adversely than others.

---

[178]Porter, *Competitive Strategy*, p. 138.

Market Interdependence

There is considerable overlap in the two primary customer targets (academics and policy makers) served by PPRIs. The overlap in the customer targets and the increase in the number of PPRIs have forced firms to target customer segments, such as Democrats and Republicans, state and local policy makers, international organizations and defense agencies, so that they can distance themselves from their competitors. As we shall see, institutions that have failed to effectively adapt to this new reality have experienced considerable erosion of their market share.

What we have seen in the industry in recent years is that, in order to survive and to effectively insulate themselves from the competition, institutions have begun to target specific segments of the market. It is no surprise, then, that Brookings identified the group of specialized PPRIs as one of its major competitors. More important, a majority of the new entrants to the industry surveyed for this study viewed Brookings and, to a lesser degree, the American Enterprise Institute as their major competitors. The impact of these changes was captured in a December 27, 1985 New York Times article which stated that "Until recent years, the world of Washington think tanks revolved around a scholarly rivalry between American Enterprise Institute and the venerable Brookings Institution, both of whom are known for their academic, long term studies on issues. Today, the two no longer have the field to themselves."

The survey results seem to confirm Porter's assertion that "the existence of multiple strategic groups usually means that the forces of competitive rivalry are not faced equally by all firms in the industry."[179] This is further underscored by the fact that the majority of the new entrants to the field have been specialized PPRIs. In the case of the public policy research industry, the numerous specialized research organizations are attacking the diversified research organizations on all fronts, and seriously eroding the diversified firms' share of the market. In general terms, the specialized firms place the diversified firms at a distinct disadvantage because they tend to be smaller, more efficient operations. Their operating costs are much lower and they are better equipped to tailor their products to meet the special interests and needs of their customers. And while the fortunes of the specialized firms may change as policies, politics and funding patterns shift, their specialization tends to insulate them from their competitors.

A Funny Thing Happened on the Way to the War of Ideas

An illustration of this competition and market interdependence is the case of the American Enterprise Institute (AEI), one of the leading conservative public policy research firms in Washington. It is ironic that the institution that many fiscal conservatives looked to for ideas in the late seventies and early eighties nearly went out of business when it failed to respond to the competition presented by the Heritage Foundation and the Brookings Institution. This unfortunate irony

---

[179]Ibid.

is magnified by AEI's own purpose statement: "The primary role for AEI is to insure sufficient competition of ideas in the public policy formation process." The case of AEI provides a dramatic illustration of the competition for dollars, scholars and influence and how much the marketplace of ideas has changed.

Founded in 1943 by Lewis Brown, president of the Manville Corporation, the institute lacked focus and leadership for the first eleven years until William Baroody, Sr. was recruited from the U.S. Chamber of Commerce to whip the organization into shape. Baroody led the institute for the next twenty-two years and during that time effectively carved out a niche for AEI as a small independent economic policy research center that became known for its economic analysis, conservative orientation and close ties to the Republican party. AEI achieved modest growth during the sixties but grew at a dramatic rate during the early seventies. It was at this time that Baroody Sr. anointed his son, William Baroody, Jr. as his successor. Under his leadership, AEI transformed again from a specialized economic institute into a multi-purpose policy research organization conducting research and analysis on a whole host of domestic and foreign policy issues. As a means of attracting more funding and media attention, AEI recruited leading conservative scholars and former government officials to give greater clout to its policy proposals. During this period, AEI became a hotbed of conservative ideas and its scholars and senior fellows seemed to be everywhere in Washington promoting AEI and its policy proposals.

AEI's remarkable accomplishment can be attributed to its unique position in the market. Its strong market position was assured in part by the fact that it was the only conservative voice in Washington for the first three decades of its existence. As the leading conservative PPRI, it enjoyed great success with its products in the business and policy making communities. The breakup of the post World War II policy consensus that occurred in the late sixties and the growing perception that Brookings was allied with the Democratic party helped AEI establish itself as a clear alternative to liberal oriented think tanks in Washington. During this period AEI's brand of economic analysis, specifically in the areas of government spending and government regulation, began to take root and the institute was heralded as the new policy powerhouse in Washington.

AEI's ability to distinguish itself from other PPRIs enabled it to rapidly expand its base of financial support and influence with decision makers. According to Donald Critchlow and others, AEI was so successful at "disseminating its product" that "by 1977, [it] had emerged as a clear rival to the Brookings Institution."[180] AEI's rising fortunes were closely associated with William Baroody Sr., who served as its president from 1954 to 1976 and effectively built a research program that appealed to conservative business interests and policy makers. James A. Smith points out that in addition to building "an academically respectable institution," Baroody introduced a number of "marketing and promotional strategies that set it [AEI] apart from the more

---

[180]Critchlow, "Think Tanks, Anti-Statism, and Democracy," p. 50.

established policy research centers."[181] The success strategies and the transformation of AEI from the policy arm of a business association in 1943 to a powerhouse of policy is chronicled by Robert K. Landers in "Think Tanks The New Partisans?":

> It [AEI] had been an $ 80,000-a-year operation with five full-time employees; by 1961 the budget had increased to only $ 303,000 and the staff to only 12. By 1970, the budget was still under $ 1 million and the staff was under 20....But a decade later, in 1980, AEI had grown into an organization with a budget of $ 10.4 million and a staff of 135.[182]

By 1980, AEI had achieved its goal of being in the mainstream of American politics.

Many credit AEI for being the intellectual and personnel wellspring of the Reagan administration, in which more than twenty AEI scholars and associates served.

> In 1981, a writer for the New York Times declared that 'AEI was probably the leading source of conservative intellectual firepower in the country today....The ideas that AEI had been carefully cultivating for the last decade – curbing federal regulations, slashing the budget and corporate taxes, raising defense spending – had blossomed with Ronald Reagan's election.'[183]

But, just as AEI started to savor the fruits of its success, other institutions emerged as formidable rivals for the same scholars, dollars and influence. This newly blossomed conservative rose would soon wilt under the intense heat of competition.

AEI's rapid growth and weak management structure made it difficult for it to prepare for the intense competition it would face in the eighties. In its rise to the top of Washington's Tower of Babel, AEI failed to see some of the fundamental changes taking place in the marketplace of ideas, particularly among the growing number of conservative PPRIs in Washington. It is important to remember that AEI achieved mainstream status during the Ford administration and often distanced itself from the hard line positions taken by the New Right. This served to alienate AEI from the fundamentalist and right wing of the Republican party which increasingly viewed AEI with suspicion. Commenting on the problem of competition and its implications for AEI, Robert K. Landers concludes that:

---

[181]Smith, *The Idea Brokers*, p. 182.
[182]Landers, "Think Tanks: The New Partisans," p. 662.
[183]Ibid.

> The "conservative" AEI has remained ideologically moderate and has come to be widely regarded as an institution of the political center, especially as that center has shifted to the right, and as AEI has been outflanked on the right by the Heritage Foundation [and, as this study posits, on the left by Brookings]... And there are now many more think tanks in existence all competing for the presumably limited dollars available.[184]

Many observers believed that AEI lost it programmatic focus and became too middle of the road, making it indistinguishable from its centrist competitors. Since consensus is the mainstay of American politics, most politicians and the majority of PPRI strive for their place in the mushy middle. AEI's emergence as the new centrist think tank in Washington was the worst thing that could happen to this venerable institution. Writing in 1987, AEI Resident Scholar Norman J. Ornstein commented:

> I think what's happened in the last five years, is that the center has moved and its moved, in effect, toward AEI, so that AEI is now seen as an organization of the center. And there's no question that some money that would go to think tanks is going to go to think tanks [that] have the more defined ideological position. It's not going to go to organizations of the 'mushy middle.'[185]

AEI's success at becoming a part of the establishment came with a high price because it began to lose its distinctive qualities, making it an easy target for its competitors on the left and right.

The significance of 1980 election and the fundamental shifts taking place in the political mainstream were not lost on AEI's competitors. The impact of these political currents on Brookings was profound:

> There's been a major metamorphosis [taking place in the institutions and political climate in Washington] over the last fifteen years, and after a second Reagan administration, it would be a lot further along. In the think tank orbit, for example, the once-dominant Brookings Institution has lost its leadership [position], swinging to the right [by enlisting big name Republicans] to recoup.[186]

The most dramatic shifts, however, occurred on the right where traditional institutions like AEI were under assault by a new group of PPRIs that became known as advocacy tanks because they put a premium on aggressively selling their policy proposals. Commenting on this dimension of the competitive problem, Amy Wilentz noted:

---

[184]Ibid.
[185]Ibid., p. 665 (quoting Ornstein).
[186]*Business & Public Affairs*, September 15, 1984.

Traditional think tanks like the American Enterprise Institute are finding it harder to maintain their public influence and attract funds from corporations and private foundations. AEI, once Washington's most influential citadel of mainstream conservative policy research has been the most seriously injured by the rise of the advocacy tanks.[187]

The Brookings Institution and the Heritage Foundation, along with a host of new competitors, stood ready to capitalize on AEI's shifting fortunes. As early as the mid-seventies, Brookings and Heritage had begun implementing strategies to capture a share of AEI's supporters, placing AEI in the competitive cross fire. Heritage attacked it on the right as not being conservative enough in order to lure away its more conservative supporters, while Brookings denounced it from the left in an attempt to capture some of it more centrist supporters. Heritage introduced new products and marketing techniques that cut deeply into AEI's traditional customer base and Brookings successfully repositioned itself to attract some of AEI's centrist supporters.

Without a doubt, Heritage did the greatest amount of damage by effectively targeting conservative academics, funders and policy makers. "Heritage has captured the hearts and pocketbooks of some conservatives who prefer its succinct, action-oriented studies to the often weighty analysis of the more scholarly and moderate AEI."[188] Heritage sent AEI into a tailspin from which it has been unable to recover.[189] Heritage's specialization and innovative marketing techniques enabled it to seriously erode AEI's position as one of the leading firms in the industry.

AEI did not feel the impact of these changes until the mid-eighties when large numbers of its contributors reduced or cut their funding. Long time supporters such as Reader's Digest and the Olin Foundation withdrew their support while others actively lobbied other foundations to do the same in an effort to oust Baroody. The results were devastating. In the short span of two years, it saw its budget drop from $ 13.9 million in 1985 to $ 7.7 million in 1987, and racked up a $ 4 million short term debt. In a highly publicized blood-letting, AEI fired Baroody, Jr., let almost seventy of its staff members go, and eliminated whole programs.

---

[187] Amy Wilentz, "On the Intellectual Ramparts," *Time*, September 1, 1986, p. 22.

[188] Alvin P. Sanoff, "Matters over Minds," *Regardie's*, January 1987, p. 51.

[189] For a good discussion of the problems at AEI and the market forces that brought them to a head, see Sidney Blumenthal's "Hard Times at the Think Tank," *Washington Post*, June 26, 1986, p. D1 and "Think Tank a Drift in the Center," *Washington Post*, June 26, 1986, p. D3. Also see Michael Balzano's " The Sacking of a Centrist," *Washington Post*, July 6, 1986 p. D3; Boorstin's "Directions of Policy Research"; Weaver's "The Changing World of Think Tanks;" and Morton Kondracke's "The Heritage Model," *New Republic*, December 20, 1980, p. 54.

While many blamed Bill Baroody, Jr. for AEI's financial troubles, clearly AEI's problems are rooted in more than the failure of one man and can be traced to the late sixties and early seventies when its fortunes started to rise. Bill Baroody, Sr.'s autocratic management style, failure to create an endowment for the institution and unwillingness to recruit a management team that could support this growing policy enterprise contributed to the institution's demise. Needless to say, the sins of the father were visited upon the son, who became a lightning rod for all that was wrong with the institute. However, many PPRI observers tend to overlook the contributions William Baroody, Jr. made to AEI's success. The younger Baroody catapulted AEI into national prominence and made it a power to be reckoned with in Washington.

AEI was also a victim of its own success, suffering the same fate as Brookings did in the 1960s when it was captured by the Kennedy and Johnson Administrations and lost its competitive edge. A convergence of factors such as increased competition, poor management, lack of endowment, changes in the political climate and the brain drain brought on by the Reagan Administration's recruiting away some of AEI's well known scholars and associates, all contributed to AEI's downward spiral.

AEI is unlikely to regain its position in the industry because the "more specialized and ideological think tanks such as the Heritage Foundation and the Ethics and Public Policy Center are now in vogue and all purpose institutions face hard times without a substantial endowment."[190] In its struggle to stay alive, AEI will have to narrow the focus of its research agenda and may well emerge as a specialty tank in the not too distant future.

It is no small irony that an institution that promoted the value of the free enterprise system and the competition of ideas was mortally wounded by the same competition. The lessons of the AEI case are quite clear: in a segment of the industry where there is significant market interdependence, a firm must tend its market carefully and not lose its distinctive qualities.

Product Differentiation
In the mid-seventies policy makers, scholars and policy analysts began to challenge the tradition of producing book length studies for policy makers. "Concern that policymakers will not read book-length studies...prompted many think tanks to develop new product lines."[191] PPRIs have begun to differentiate their products by offering a range of research and analysis products; they now produce reports, journals, monographs, policy briefs, editorials, position papers and seminars and briefings for the White House, Congress and opinion leaders in Washington. This change in the industry has served to further distinguish the academic oriented policy institutes such as Brookings and AEI from the more

---

[190]Unnamed analyst quoted in Sanoff's "Matters Over Minds," p. 60.
[191]Weaver, "The Changing World of Think Tanks," p. 572.

policy oriented institutions such as Rand, Urban Institute, Center for Budget and Policy Priorities, Progressive Policy Institute and Heritage Foundation.

PPRIs now cover the entire political spectrum. Clearly, the two dominant types to emerge during the 1970s were the liberal and conservative policy research organizations. During this period, the press and Brookings' major competitors, AEI and Heritage, branded it as the Democrats' think tank. "When William Baroody Sr. was 'selling' AEI during the 1970s, he argued, to the annoyance of Brookings, that there was a need for a conservative counterpart to the 'liberal' Brookings, an institution that would do solid research but from a conservative perspective"[192] This and other assaults on Brookings enabled AEI and Heritage to achieve a greater share of the market and attract corporate dollars to their coffers.

Other excellent examples of the level of diversity and high degree of specialization in the industry are the Joint Center For Political and Economic Studies, a liberal research organization that considers on issues affecting African Americans, and the Lincoln Institute, which is the Center's conservative counterpart. These two organizations focus on a very small customer segment (relative to their competitors) and have developed a highly specialized product line to serve this segment of the
market.
The patterns within the industry reveal that, despite the movement toward greater product differentiation, the majority of the firms seem to fall into four groups (academic diversified, academic specialized, policy entrepreneur and advocacy tank). The lack of significant strategic distance among the major groups within the industry has served to intensify competition. As previously explained earlier, the level and intensity of the competition tends to vary from one segment of the industry to the next. For example, the relatively small number of state based research firms are less affected by the ongoing competition in the industry than are the large numbers of academic diversified firms. Porter points out that for strategic groups of firms like the academic diversified PPRIs, "achieving stability will be extremely difficult...and outbreaks of aggressive warfare are likely to insure a competitive outcome for it."[193]

Once again, AEI is a useful illustration of this point. During the past ten years, AEI has been besieged by firms who are competing for the same market segment (conservative policy makers), but who employ different approaches to delivering their products to their customers. Heritage and AEI, for example, share the same conservative orientation but their methods for reaching policy makers and influencing policy debate are radically different. AEI's books and reports tend to be academic in their orientation while Heritage views itself and its products as an activist version of both Brookings and AEI. While there is considerable overlap in the markets for AEI's and Heritage's products, AEI has

---

[192]Landers, "Think Tanks: The New Partisans," p. 193.
[193]Porter, *Competitive Strategy*, p. 140.

primarily targeted mainstream conservatives while Heritage has focused on those conservatives who are right of center. Heritage's strategies for reaching policy makers have helped Heritage distinguish itself from the academic oriented PPRIs although they are still competing for some of the same customers.

Politics, the Prince and the Policy Entrepreneur

Without doubt, the leading policy enterprise in Washington these days is the Heritage Foundation, which has made a name for itself not only as a producer of policy proposals but as a major marketer of ideas to policy makers and their constituents throughout the U.S. In the "war of ideas," Heritage has gone to battle armed with new products, marketing techniques and sales forces that have been described as the intellectual shock troops of the conservative movement. Putting philosophy and politics aside, this new PPRI has had a dramatic impact on the policy process and competition for dollars, scholars and influence.

The Heritage Foundation, established in 1973 with a $ 250,000 gift from Joseph Coors, set out to make conservative voices heard in Washington and in doing so sent shock waves through political establishment and set the policy research community on its ear. In a short span of time, this brash new kid on the block has become one of the leading PPRIs in Washington. The innovative strategies Edwin J. Feulner, Jr. and Paul Weyrich designed for Heritage were consciously intended to challenge the status quo. According to Feulner, the mandate for change came to him during the congressional debate on supersonic transport in 1971 when an AEI study on the subject arrived at his office shortly after Congress voted to kill the project. This experience lead Feulner to conclude that "it doesn't matter how many books or studies you produce...You've got to got to market your product, get it off the bookshelf."[194] In recent years some of the greatest innovations in policy products have come from policy entrepreneurs like Heritage Foundation who have developed effective products to deliver their messages to policy makers.

Feulner explained to Linden the forces that helped shape the new strategies and structures he introduced:

> The Wharton School taught him marketing techniques; how to target an audience and fill its needs. The hands-on jobs with Congressmen taught him that the right people (policy-makers and especially their aides) weren't getting the right information (neo-conservative gospel) delivered to them at the right time (when issues are about to be decided). Feulner forged the missing link: a policy-paper manufacturing and delivery system. In his words, "We forced our way into a town that had decided it didn't need more paper, flooded it with paper and made ourselves an integral part of the decision process."[195]

---

[194]Carol Matlack, "Marketing Ideas," *National Journal*, June 22, 1991, p. 1553.
[195]Linden, "Powerhouses of Policy," p. 103.

Unsurprisingly, Feulner attributes much of Heritage's success to its marketing and product development strategies. Feulner's business and marketing background are complemented by the newspaper background of Burton Pines, Heritage's senior vice president. This powerful combination has lead the New Republic to conclude that:

> Heritage's innovation is to combine the structures of a research group, a public relations firm, a special interest lobby and an employment agency [and I would add, newspaper] into one organization. If Heritage isn't as powerful or as influential as it claims, it is certainly better at what it doses than anyone else.[196]

My visit to Heritage revealed that it is run much like a newspaper; weekly editorial meetings are held to set production schedules, identify hot issues and develop marketing strategies and policy angles. The dominant culture is clearly a corporate/journalistic one rather than the university/academic culture that is so prevalent at other research institutes in and around the Beltway.

Heritage puts a premium on marketing its product. Feulner is quoted as saying that "our concept is to make marketing of the product an integral part of it."[197] Heritage's innovative strategies and structures have enabled it to effectively target policy makers and opinion leaders in Washington and in communities throughout the United States. By 1986 Heritage had the names, areas of interest and profiles of 1,500 congressional aides, 700 executive branch staffers and 3,000 journalists in its computer so that they could target mailings to them. Shut out of the traditional media outlets in Washington, Heritage turned to the 1,600 dailies and weeklies around the country and found them to be a potent weapon in the war of ideas. According to Gregg Easterbrook, each study mailed by Heritage to local newspapers resulted in 200-500 stories and its press releases were often published verbatim.[198]

Heritage's commitment to marketing is backed up with big bucks; approximately 37% of its budget is allocated to directly to marketing, while 13% is spent on fundraising which is another form of marketing. This commitment is further underscored by the fact that Heritage pays its direct-mail consultant more than it pays its President. In 1989, for instance, Stephen Winchell received $354,000 for his consulting services while Feulner received approximately $254,000 as Heritage's full time president. Some observers contend that the success of Heritage's marketing and direct mail operations has been demonstrated by the fact its proposals are being seriously considered by policy makers and its scholars are increasingly quoted on the floor of Congress and cited by the President and the news media.

---

[196]James Rosenthal, "Heritage Hype," *New Republic*, September 2, 1985.
[197]Critchlow, "Think Tanks, Anti-Statism, and Democracy," p. 65.
[198]Gregg Easterbrook, "Ideas Move Nations," *Atlantic*, January 1986, p. 73.

Conclusions and Implications 131

The hallmark of Heritage's success however, has been a set of timely policy research products carefully designed to meet the needs of the busy policy maker. These new products are short, fact filled, action oriented policy briefs that are designed to grab the attention of policy makers. Leslie Lenkowsky, the current president of the Hudson Institute, once described Heritage as the Wal-Mart or K Mart of PPRIs because its "packages were much more accessible" to policy makers and the public than the policy research outputs produced by the academic oriented institutes in Washington. According to Feulner, if the study is thin enough to fit into a congressional representative's briefcase, half the battle is won. Heritage thus applies what has become known as 'the brief-case test,' to all its products: they should must be short and to the point so that they can be read by members of Congress in the time it takes to ride from Washington National airport to Capital Hill.

Timing and packaging are everything. No Heritage product exemplifies these principles better than Heritage's Mandate for Leadership series which contains a detailed series of policy recommendations for nearly every federal agency and has been delivered to each administration shortly after the November election since 1980. Mandate For Leadership I, a 1000 page policy blueprint for the Reagan Administration, first brought Heritage into national prominence.

> Probably no other documents have been as widely circulated in Washington during the past five years as Mandate I and Mandate II, and by any standard they have been impressive. Each reflects a detailed understanding of how the federal government actually works (as opposed to how it officially works) and addresses the questions that are short on media appeal but crucial in Washington: how to motivate the bureaucracy, how to get the bills through committee and so on.[199]

Many of the policy proposals contained in Mandate I were not new and many were actually a reformulation of the works of scholars at AEI and the Hoover Institution. However, the package, a single action oriented volume, was new and Heritage combined this with excellent timing, which made it an instant success.

Heritage's other product innovations include: Executive Memoranda (timely one-page issue analysis), the Backgrounder series (addresses long-range issues), Issues Bulletins (address specific legislation) and Critical Issues (short monographs) which have had a profound effect on the way PPRIs operate.

> Before Heritage, most research groups published books and monographs and distributed them to scholars and executive branch contacts. Heritage, by contrast, prepared snappy issue briefs – easily digested in a few minutes' reading – and dropped them into in-boxes on the eve of important decisions.[200]

---

[199]Ibid., p. 72.
[200]Matlack, "Marketing Ideas," p. 1553.

Clearly, Heritage's strategy was to distinguish itself from the academic diversified and academic specialized firms that produced research studies in a book form that was often more marketable to academics than policy makers. Heritage also saturated the market (specifically, Congress and the national and local media) with its products, most of which were hand delivered just before a critical vote or debate on an issue. In any given year Heritage is likely to produce two to three hundred publications, as well as scores of op-ed pieces and policy briefs which are produced at a rapid fire pace.

The final weapon in Heritage's arsenal is a dedicated young sales force, most of whom are under forty and have been recruited from its national network of neo-conservative scholars at colleges and universities throughout the US. These new M.A.s and Ph.D.s are expected to know the issues, to work on tight deadlines and to turn their ideas into action. In addition, they are encouraged to cultivate contacts among the staffers on the Hill and key staff in the bureaucracy. According to Easterbrook, Heritage helps recruit young converts to the conservative cause by hosting daily events "at which food is served – cold cuts and beer being the reliable bait for young staff."[201] After a year or two at Heritage, staff are encouraged to get government experience by taking positions in the executive and legislative branches of government. To facilitate the placement of its staff, Heritage maintains a job bank of key government posts in hopes that its former staffers will continue to sell Heritage's neo-conservative agenda after they are on the inside.

Heritage benefited tremendously from the conservative intellectual foundation laid by AEI and consciously copied many of its media and public relations strategies. But this is where the similarities end – Heritage is a lean, mean, policy machine that eschews expensive scholars and labor and cost intensive book length publications. Its strategy of emphasizing policy briefs over scholarly books and hiring young policy analysts over established scholars has paid off, for it is now considered one of the most important PPRIs in the nation's capital. Heritage's impact on other PPRIs has been tremendous; prior to 1980 most of these organizations did not produce policy briefs or newsletters, and outreach to the media and policy makers was viewed as inconsistent with scholarly pursuits and non-profit status. Heritage changed all that. And while much of the Washington establishment continues to be uncomfortable with its political orientation or its approach to policy analysis, most agree that it has developed a highly effective medium for conveying its message. Heritage's longevity and growing influence and budget continue to defy its critics and make its competitors nervous.

The Number of Strategic Groups and Their Relative Sizes
The third major factor that influences the level and intensity of competition in an industry is the number of strategic groups and their relative

---

[201] Easterbrook, "Ideas Move Nations," p. 72.

sizes. It is only logical to assume that as the number and size of PPRIs increases, the competition will intensify.

In my structural analysis of the industry, I identified seven major strategic groups: 1) academic diversified; 2) academic specialized; 3) contract/consulting; 4) advocacy; 5) policy enterprise; 6) literary agent/publishing house, and 7) state based. According to Porter, the number of strategic groups and the share of the market each group controls will determine the nature of the competition in an industry.

> The more numerous and more equal in size (market share) the strategic groups, the more their strategic asymmetry generally increases competitive rivalry, other things being equal. Numerous groups imply great diversity and a high probability that one group will trigger an outbreak of warfare attacking the position of the other groups through price cutting or other tactics. Conversely, if groups are greatly unequal in size – for example, one strategic group constitutes a small share of an industry and another is a very large share – their strategic differences are likely to have little impact on they compete with each other, since the power of the small group to affect the large groups through competitive tactics is probably low.[202]

By Porter's standards, the number of strategic groups in the public policy research industry is quite large, which would tend to increase competition. The large number of strategic groups in the industry is offset, however, by the considerable variation in the groups' size. In the public policy research industry, the market share of the various strategic groups is not at all symmetrical. There are, however, a number of groups within the industry that approach parity. The net result of this type of configuration in an industry is that competition tends to affect some groups more than others.

The asymmetry in the industry is best illustrated by the literary agent/publishing house, diversified and specialized, and academic-oriented research organizations. The difference in the size of the market share held by the diversified and specialized groups is so great that the competition between them and the literary agent/publishing house is almost nonexistent. The diversified and specialized firms control such a large share of the market when it comes to publishing book length studies that the threat of competition from the much smaller literary agent/publishing house strategic group is almost non-existent. The rivalry between and among the academic diversified and academic specialized groups is quite intense because their strategies, structures and market shares are very similar.

The Manhattan Institute poses no real threat to the Brookings Institution because its publishing operation and share of the market are relatively small. In contrast, the National Bureau of Economic Research and the Institute for

---

[202]Porter, *Competitive Strategy*, p. 139.

International Economics are in almost constant competition with Brookings for scholars, dollars and influence because they are all fighting over the same market segment: centrist academics and policy makers who are concerned about economic issues. Clear evidence of this can be seen in Brookings' decision to significantly reduce its research in the area of international economics because it can no longer compete with firms like the Institute for International Economics which specializes in this area.

The Institute for International Economics, a specialized, academic oriented organization that conducts research in the area of international economics for academics and policy makers, is a good example of this new wave of specialization. Its books and policy briefs are geared to a highly specialized customer target – international economists and policy makers.[203] This move toward specialization has had major and direct effects on academic diversified think tanks like AEI and Brookings. Specialty tanks have forced both of these institutions to eliminate or drastically reduce programs in areas where they can no longer compete with the smaller specialized firms.

Metamorphosis, Meaning and the Middle: The Brookings Institution
Focusing on the case of Brookings will illustrate how competitive pressures influenced its decision to develop new marketing and product strategies. I will examine a series of strategic decisions made by Brookings' board and staff that influenced its structure during the ten year period from 1977 to 1987. The material for the case was drawn from a series of interviews with key staff, annual reports, the institution's charter, and popular and scholarly books and articles written on the institution.

Brookings is the oldest and one of the largest non-profit PPRIs. It has a long-standing reputation for producing empirical, scholarly, policy oriented research in economics, social policy, and security and international affairs. Since its inception, Brookings has prided itself on its ability to help shape public policy in the United States In the 1920s, Brookings helped establish the federal budgeting process. During World War II, it guided the war mobilization effort, and in the post war years it designed the Marshall Plan. It provided the inspiration for many of Johnson's Great Society programs of the 1960s. Throughout most of its history, Brookings has effectively asserted its influence without becoming overly affiliated with one political party or administration.

The Brookings Institution has a long standing reputation for producing empirical, scholarly, policy oriented research in economics, social policy, and security and international affairs. Its annual budget is over $ 15 million which enables it to maintain a large staff, publish a variety of studies, and conduct a range of public education activities for politicians, policy makers, and journalists. Brookings currently employs fifty senior researchers and a total staff of about

---

[203]For further information on the Institute for International Economics and its president Fred Bergsten see Mike McNamee, "Fred Bergsten Sure Knows How To Sell An Idea," *Business Week*, August 29, 1988, pp. 48-50.

250. While Brookings' history reflects its strong non-partisan and centrist tendencies it has been characterized as the "Democrats' Think Tank" or as described by Fortune Magazine a years ago as a "citadel of liberalism." It is precisely this image and Brookings' attempts to alter it that will be the focus of this case.

Throughout most of its history Brookings has effectively asserted its influence without becoming overly affiliated with one political party or administration. Brookings "has been called everything from flaming pinko to rightist, stodgy, bland and mugwump – wisecrackers in the Eisenhower years referred to the center as CBI, the Conservative Businessmen's Institution."[204]

Yet, it was one of the most ardent opponents of Roosevelt's New Deal and Truman's Fair Deal. Brookings' attacks of Roosevelt's programs led one of his key aides, to charge that Brookings was "a kind of research organ for the conservatives."[205] The view of Brookings as a centrist or conservative institution changed quite dramatically during the sixties and seventies.

Brookings acquired its reputation as a liberal institution after Kermit Gordon, a member of the Council of Economic Advisors in the Kennedy administration and director of the Bureau of the Budget during the Johnson administration, became its president in 1967. During this period Gordon recruited an unprecedented number of ex-Johnson and Kennedy administration officials including Arthur Okun, who had been chairman of the Council of Economic Advisors and Charles Schultze who had succeeded Gordon as budget director. These and other appointments helped establish Brookings' reputation as liberal partisan institution.

> Brookings' reputation as a liberal, democratic think tank became further entrenched – when Johnson made an unexpected appearance at Brookings' fiftieth anniversary meeting in 1966 in order to declare, 'you are a national institution, so important too, at least to the executive branch – and I think to Congress and the country – that if you did not exist we would have to ask someone to create you.'[206]

With this pronouncement Brookings' liberal image was fixed. While these affiliations served it well during the Kennedy, Johnson and Carter years, they began to present problems when the political winds started to blow to the right.

These image problems, as they are now called, were compounded by the fact that Gordon developed a research agenda and publication program that Critchlow describes as being of "more interest to academics than policy

---

[204]Linden, "Powerhouses of Policy," p. 101.
[205]Rexford G. Tugwell, quoted in Saunders, The *Brookings Institution: A Fifty Year History*, p. 57.
[206]Critchlow, "Think Tanks, Anti-Statism and Democracy," p. 33.

makers."[207] Moreover, Brookings had effectively alienated itself from the business community by its quite visible and vocal support for Johnson's Great Society programs and its opposition to the Vietnam War. The business community's disillusionment with Brookings prompted a number of prominent businessmen to support think tanks such as Heritage, the American Enterprise Institute and the Center for Strategic and International Studies, that they felt would be more sensitive to their interests. Soon after their emergence, these institutions began to challenge Brookings' position.

According to Critchlow and others, Brookings' close affiliation with the Democrats, its lack of policy relevance, its alienation from the business community, and the increased competition from the new conservative think tanks, began to affect its public image and financial position in the mid-seventies. Facing isolation from the corporate sector and the Nixon and Ford White Houses, Brookings found that it had to draw on its endowment at a higher than usual rate in order to meet its 1976 annual budget.[208] After Gordon's death in June 1976, Brookings' board went through a major reassessment process that resulted in a number of strategic decisions that altered the structure and course of the institution.

It is clear from the interview I conducted with Bruce MacLaury, the president of the Brookings Institution (see appendix) and popular and scholarly articles written on this subject, that Brookings set out to develop "an integrated functional plan in response to a problem...thrust upon the company by the environment."[209] It attempted to respond to the competition from the right while simultaneously trying to increase its impact on the policy community. This strategy manifested itself in 1977 when Brookings selected Bruce MacLaury to succeed Kermit Gordon as president. MacLaury, a conservative, midwestern Republican economist who was Nixon's deputy undersecretary of the treasury for monetary policy, represented a radical shift for Brookings. MacLaury is also a non-academic with solid credentials and strong ties to the business community. It is clear that, as the antithesis of Gordon, his selection fit into a larger strategy to move Brookings back to the center of American politics. Critchlow confirms this when he writes "In choosing Bruce MacLaury to succeed Gordon, the trustees deliberately sought a man who would be acceptable to business and a man in touch with the times.... MacLaury seemed to be an ideal choice."[210] Linden characterized the decision this way: "And now, the Institution is on a new track led by Bruce K. MacLaury, Brookings' president since 1977, the tank is steering its image back to the center."[211] MacLaury's mission was to develop a more

---

[207]Ibid., p. 32.
[208]Ibid., p. 29.
[209]William F. Glueck, *Business Policy: Strategy Formation and Management Action*, (New York: McGraw-Hill Inc., 1972).
[210]Critchlow, "Think Tanks, Anti-Statism, and Democracy," p. 33.
[211]Linden, "Powerhouses of Policy," p. 101.

moderate reputation for the institution. MacLaury has himself said, "I must eliminate the public perception that Brookings is a Democratic proxy."[212]

During the first five years of his tenure as president, MacLaury developed a strategy designed to address the board's concerns about the financial status of the institution and the organization's isolation from much of the business community. In 1986, Brookings' endowment covered only twenty-one percent of the institution's annual expenses, a sharp decline from 1980, when the endowment had met twenty-eight percent of the budget. MacLaury saw that "the obvious course was to broaden the institution's corporate and government support. Under MacLaury, all limits would be lifted on government contract work. At the same time, the Brookings board was to be transformed to ensure corporate support."[213]

MacLaury also encouraged his staff to develop more policy oriented papers and publications that would be of use to businessmen and policy makers. He hired new staff who were more receptive to the new policy orientation, and took advantage of retirements and resignations to re-energize the institution. The new staff included:

> In Economic Studies, Alice Rivlin [who had] returned from her work at the Congressional Budget Office to head the program. Robert B. Crandall, Daniel J. B. Mitchell, Ralph C. Bryant, Anthony Downs, and Robert Solomon also were brought into the program. In Government Studies, Paul Peterson, a political scientist from the University of Chicago, was hired after an arduous search to head the program. He was joined by John E. Chubb, Samuel H. Kernell, and Terry M. Moe. In Foreign Policy Studies, former director Henry Owens was replaced by John D. Steinbruner.[214]

These changes in staff prompted the media to observe that Brookings had "been trying to alter its political image by hiring more Republicans."[215] MacLaury contended that this charge is not entirely accurate, asserting "I've attempted to recruit staff that are non-partisan, in order to achieve some balance."[216] This point is echoed by Herbert Stein, a former Brookings scholar now at AEI who stated "I think Brookings wanted to have some Republicans around because it's not good for their image to be just a little nest of Democrats. It's not good for fundraising and it's not good for general credibility."[217]

MacLaury's selection of Roger Semerad, a Republican businessman and political consultant, who helped draft the 1980 Republican platform, as executive

---

[212] Ibid.
[213] Critchlow, "Think Tanks, Anti-Statism and Democracy," p. 34.
[214] Ibid., p. 36.
[215] John Powers, "Double Think Tank," *Regardie's*, May/June 1983, p. 59.
[216] Author's interview with Bruce MacLaury, October 18, 1988.
[217] Herbert Stein, quoted in Powers, "Double Think Tank," p. 50.

vice president for external affairs in 1981 was a further manifestation of Brookings' new strategy. The establishment of an external affairs office and the appointment of Semerad as its head represented a dramatic restructuring. Semerad's role was to "raise corporate contributors, and make the institution more visible in business, media, and government circles."[218] By all accounts, he developed an effective strategy aimed at marketing Brookings through a sophisticated public relations campaign.

The institutional commitment to implementing this strategy is reflected in Semerad's free rein to develop new programs and launch bold initiatives.

> He saw Brookings establish a public affairs office, set up a system to produce press releases and place Op-Ed articles and created a directory to service the press. He launched a series of briefings and breakfasts, encouraged media interviews with Brookings analysts and founded the quarterly Brookings Review. He energized the tank's fabled board of eminent directors and invented the Brookings Council, a body composed of the cream of America's corporate and financial heavy hitters whom he prodded for large gifts and rewarded by making them Brookings ambassadors. He launched a campaign for endowment giving; turned the Institution's 25 year old revenue-producing Advanced Study Program for executives into the Center for Public Policy Education; and added seminars for American executives in Korea and Tokyo.[219]

This aggressive approach involved a conscious strategy that addressed many of the concerns expressed by Brookings' trustees, policy makers, and the media. The external affairs office was the new administrative structure developed to coordinate the marketing and fundraising Brookings so desperately needed. The op-ed pieces, briefings, and media interviews were designed to give Brookings more visibility and to promote its new image. The direct work with the trustees and corporate leaders helped re-establish much-needed connections with the business community. In addition, the corporate seminars and the Center for Public Policy Education were consciously designed to help Brookings secure corporate contributions. These actions, when taken in conjunction with the other changes that were being implemented at the board and staff level, constituted an integrated functional plan that was designed to address the challenges presented to Brookings by its environment.

All of these activities were designed to shed Brookings' liberal image and to present a new one to Congress and the press. This strategy also proved successful with corporations, who increased their contributions from a low in 1978 of $ 95,450 to $ 1.6 million in 1984. Structural changes also occurred at the board level where MacLaury changed its "composition, size, and

---

[218] Critchlow, "Think Tanks, Anti-Statism, and Democracy," p. 35.
[219] Linden, "Powerhouses of Policy," p. 101.

responsibilities."[220] While Brookings has not fully erased its liberal image, because "big ships turn slowly"[221] it appears that Brookings has developed a successful strategy that will further alter its image over time.

Howard Wiarda, a conservative who is currently writing a book on the role of PPRIs in shaping foreign policy, agrees that Brookings has moved to the center, observing that:

> Over the years Brookings has moved steadily toward the center. That is where the money is and that is where the bulk of public opinion lies. Brookings has a Republican president and a Republican vice president, is recruiting more centrist scholars, and raises the bulk of its money from the same corporate sources as do the more conservative Think Tanks. Brookings has moved away from a strong ideological posture, and its foreign policy activities and publications are also serious, scholarly, and middle-of-the road. Most observers, in fact, do not see any ideological difference at this stage between Brookings' foreign policy positions and those of CSIS or AEI. But as Brookings has moved to the center, that has left a hole on the liberal left which no major Think Tank at present occupies.

The Brookings case effectively demonstrates the relationship between the competition in the industry and strategy and structure of firms operating in the industry. In an effort to re-establish its position as the leading PPRI in Washington and to regain its corporate supporters, Brookings has fought back by aggressively marketing itself as a centrist organization, by hiring scholars and administrators who are Republicans or non-partisan and by attempting to increase corporate contributions through a series of public relations and outreach efforts designed to engage corporate leaders. The changes in staff and Board composition and the administrative structure clearly demonstrate the impact of this strategy on the overall structure of the organization. Despite its success, the labels endure.[222]

Divergent Strategies and Strategic Distance

Porter contends that "if divergent strategies lead to distinct and differing brand preferences by customers, then rivalry among the groups will tend to be less than if the products are seen as interchangeable."[223] Before the mid-seventies, the customers of the leading PPRIs were relatively undifferentiated. Until then, most of the research organizations were non-partisan and produced book length studies that were more academic than policy oriented. Rand, which produced reports under contract with the government, was the obvious exception. All of this

---

[220]Critchlow, "Think tanks, Anti-Statism, and Democracy," p. 34.
[221]Linden, "Powerhouses of Policy," p. 101.
[222]John Powers, "Double Think Tank," *Regardie's*, May/June 1983, p. 59 (an irreverent take on these efforts).
[223]Porter, *Competitive Strategy*, p. 139.

changed in the 1970s and early 1980s when the public policy research industry entered into a period that Daft and others would describe as the variation stage of development.[224] The number of firms grew rapidly and the firms that entered the industry during this period took on a variety of organizational forms and introduced a series of strategies that created new brands of public policy research.

According to Porter, strategic distance "refers to the degree to which strategies in different groups diverge in terms of key variables, such as brand identification, cost position and technological leadership."[225] The analysis of the strategic dimensions presented in chapter six demonstrates the degree of strategic divergence in the public policy research industry. These differences in the strategy and structure of the major groups have made competition in the industry more vigorous because these firms "tend to have quite different ideas about how to compete and a difficult time understanding each other's behavior and avoiding mistaken reactions and outbreaks of warfare." The institution that has achieved the greatest strategic distance from its competitors has been the Rand Corporation.

Rand: Where Strategic Defense and Strategic Distance Meet
If there is an institution that defines strategic distance, it is the Rand Corporation. Founded in 1946 as Project Rand with the help of the Air Force and Douglas aircraft, it has become the largest and most distinctive PPRI. To avoid an obvious conflict of interest, Rand became an independent research center in 1948 with the help of the Ford Foundation. The name Rand itself is an acronym for research and development.

Over the years, Rand has achieved strategic distance from its competitors on the east coast through its policy orientation, close working relationship with various government agencies, role as program/ policy consultant, and reliance on government contracts. Rand's position as the leading contract research organization in the U.S. has provided it with significant brand recognition. It has achieved this status primarily through its application of systems analysis, which has become a trademark of sorts for the organization.

Rand successfully demonstrated the utility of systems analysis to the military in the early 50s. "Rand advised the Air Force to base its bombers in the U.S. rather than Europe. Paul Hill, director of Rand's 90-person Washington office, says, 'That one study saved the Air Force billions of dollars over the years, and Rand paid for itself in perpetuity with the Air Force.'"[226]

Rand capitalized on the early successes of its unique brand of policy analysis and has marketed it to customers ever since. Rand's success with this methodology for the analysis of military questions has enabled it to expand into

---

[224]Daft, *Organizational Theory and Design*, pp. 78-79.
[225]Porter, *Competitive Strategy*, p. 139.
[226]Linden, "Powerhouses of Policy," p. 105.

CONCLUSIONS AND IMPLICATIONS   141

other areas. While Rand continues to expand into non-defense-related areas, its success in these areas is limited and so is its brand recognition.

As a federally funded contract center, it has been required to produce reports and memos rather than book-length studies. Research is often conducted according to the specifications of the agency or department that is paying for the study, and therefore, researchers do not have the same degree of independence as researchers in the other strategic groups. It also tends to conduct a higher level of interdisciplinary research because the issues and the contracting agency require that a number of disciplines be involved in the research.

Thus, Rand's strategy and structure differs markedly from the academic-oriented public policy research institutions in that the reward system, production schedule, degree of independence and final product are all determined, in a large measure, by the contracting agency. At academic oriented institutions like Brookings, the production schedule is set by the scholar; at Rand, it is largely determined by the needs of the client. A contract researcher is more likely to be promoted for his/her agency contacts and ability to produce reports on schedule than on the number of books published or his/ her standing in the academic community. All of these factors serve to limit the degree of freedom that researchers have at Rand.

Rand further distinguishes itself from it competitors by its size. In 1989 Rand employed 1,132 people of whom 522 were full time researchers. Brookings pales in comparison, having only seventy full time researchers. Rand's 1989 annual budget was more than $ 84 million, approximately four times the size of Brookings' annual budget. These factors create significant barriers to entry into this group for other PPRIs that simply do not have the resources or workforce to compete for certain government contracts. Consequently, Rand's real competitors tend to be for-profit research and development centers. This may explain why Rand is frequently not included in directories of public policy research institutes.[227] Despite the down turn in the defense industry Rand continues to be a dominant force in the field of public policy research. No institution has successfully challenged its position as the leading contract PPRI in the nation.

These cases have clearly illustrated how the nature and makeup of the strategic groups have a dramatic impact on the competition that takes place within an industry. The specific dimensions of the competition in the industry are presented in the map of the strategic groups in the public policy research industry.[228] The horizontal axis is the target customer segment of the strategic group that illustrates the degree of market interdependence among the groups. The vertical axis represents a composite of the strategic dimensions of the seven groups. The numbered figures correspond to the seven strategic groups within the

---

[227]Public Interest Profiles, published by *Congressional Quarterly*, is the oldest and most comprehensive listing of think tanks in the nation but does not include Rand.
[228]This map is based on the strategic group mapping techniques developed by Porter.

industry. The shape of the figure represents the relative differences among the groups, and the size of the figure is roughly proportional to its market share.

Drawing on the analysis presented in the previous two chapters, it is clear that Groups 1, 2, 4 and 5 are all competing for the same basic customer segment, but use different marketing and production strategies. Because of the overlap in their customer segment and the relative parity in their share of the market, the competition among them is intense and ongoing. Group 7, on the other hand, is insulated from the competition among the major groups because its segment of the market does not overlap with that of the major groups. Group 7 is structured as a policy enterprise (rectangle) because its example of Commonwealth is modeled after Heritage (Group 5). State-based PPRIs, however, can model themselves on any type of PPRI. Group 3 has been able to largely insulate itself from the competition by developing a highly specialized product line, while Group 6 is shielded by its size; it is simply too small to draw much competition from the other groups.

Figure 8.1

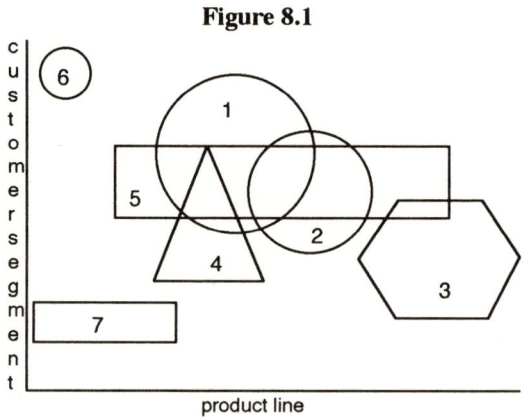

1. Academic Diversified
2. Academic Specialized
3. Contract/Consulting
4. Advocacy
5. Policy Enterprise
6. Literary Agent/Publishing House
7. State-Based

Throughout this study, I have identified a number of trends that have influenced the nature of the competition in the industry and the strategy and structure of the firms that operate within it. Four trends, however, are key to understanding the competition that exist in the industry today:

1. Proliferation of PPRIs

The dramatic increase in the number and type of PPRIs has increased the competition for limited resources. The number of PPRIs has increased tenfold in the last seventy-five years and doubled since 1965. Over two-thirds of the firms that have come into being in the last twenty years have been specialized research organizations.

2. Capital Flight

In the last fifteen years there have been major shifts in the funding patterns of some of the leading private and public sector supporters of public policy research. Federal grants and contracts for public policy research decreased dramatically during the Reagan years. Private foundation grants have shifted from unrestricted grants for programs and operations to restricted project grants. In addition, the recent tendency of some traditional supporters of policy research to grant funds for programs outside the United States (what I describe as the flight of philanthropic capital) has served to intensify the competition for resources. These new realities have made it necessary for institutions to develop new and innovative ways to generate revenues. For example, Brookings established a successful executive training program and Heritage has tapped the vast pool of individual donors to help offset declining revenues in other areas.

3. High Operating Costs

The increasing costs associated with operating PPRIs have forced many institutions to cut programs or rethink their staffing methods and organization. The academic diversified firms have been the hardest hit because of the significant overhead and salary costs associated with their reliance on a highly trained staff.

4. Changes in Consumer Preferences and Demand

Changes in consumer preferences and demand have served to intensify competition in every segment of the industry. The disintegration of the post-World War II policy consensus, changes in party politics and the rise of special interests have created a greater demand for policy research and fostered the growth of the specialized PPRI. These changes have created a marketplace of ideas where politicians, bureaucrats and the public go shopping for research and analysis that meets their needs and provides answers, not just advice.

The intense competition within the public policy industry has had both positive and negative implications for the firms in the industry and the customers they serve. The new entrants to the industry have introduced new products and services, which have forced the more established firms to improve the quality of their products. In addition, the specialized firms are reaching segments of the market that the diversified firms are incapable of reaching. On the negative side, the competition has a tendency to obscure the issues and reduce policy debate to the survival of the fittest, which does not always result in the best policies.

CHAPTER NINE
STUDY HIGHLIGHTS AND SUGGESTIONS FOR FUTURE RESEARCH

When I began my study of PPRIs, I knew something big was in front of me but I did not how to describe it. In some respects the task was made easier by the fact that no one had done a comparative or industry-wide study of PPRIs. I was therefore not bound by other scholars' conceptions of these institutions and was free to create the analytical framework for the study. Although liberating, it was not without cost or struggle; the lack of scholarly work in this area made it necessary for me to find my own way in an unfamiliar area. Developing a conceptual framework and gathering empirical data on each institution took far longer than would have liked. Now that it is behind me, I can say it was worth it. My only hope now is that each person who reaches this point in the study will feel the same way.

The descriptions and analysis contained in this study are not meant to be the definitive word on PPRIs but rather the beginnings of a discourse on the nature and role of these institutions in the policy planning and formulation process in the United States. Before I discuss some of the areas where additional research is needed, I will highlight some of the major findings of the study.

This effort provides a profile of PPRIs and differentiates them from other organizations that conduct research and analysis. The generic term 'think tank' does not begin to describe the diversity represented in this class of institutions discussed in this study. The terms of reference and the concept of the seven strategic groups will hopefully enable others to understand the diversity and range of strategies and structures that exist in the industry.

In addition to providing a general framework for analyzing PPRIs, the study presents a means for examining the vast differences that exist in the funding patterns, constituency base, research orientation, staffing patterns and organizational culture of the more than one hundred firms in the industry. The objective here was to extend the existing research, which focuses almost exclusively on individual case histories, to a more general assessment of the industry. The descriptions and analysis presented in Section II are intended to provide scholars and others interested in PPRIs with the tools for assessing the current and future state of the industry.

Another important objective of the study was to introduce some much needed empirical data on these organizations. Although I have only begun to scratch the surface in this regard, the survey and the data collected represent an important step in the right direction. Finally, it is my hope that the data presented clearly demonstrate that market and other forces in the environment have influenced and will continue to influence the strategy and structure of the firms in this industry.

Since so little research has been done in this area, it cries out for more scholarly and empirically based studies. Future studies might fall into three categories: industry-wide studies, strategic groups studies and individual firm studies. Clearly, further data needs to be collected and analysis needs to be done in each one of these areas. In addition, the analytical frame needs to be expanded in order to determine how other research organizations have affected the public policy research industry. Still other studies might focus on the people and institutions (primarily academics and policy makers) who use the products of these institutions. This field of study is ripe for the picking.

APPENDICES

MacLaury Interview Questions

1.   How would you characterize the strategy and structure of Brookings prior to your arrival in 1977?

2.   In your estimation what were the major flaws/problems with the strategies employed by your predecessor?

3.   What were the internal and external forces that influenced the decision to hire you in 1977?

4.   Was your selection by the Board a conscious effort to alter the course of the institution?

5.   Did you have a blueprint for altering the strategy and structure of the organization when you came on board? Did the Board?

6.   How did your strategy manifest itself? Can you cite specific examples such as changes in staffing patterns, the research agenda, outreach activities, fund raising, etc.?

7.   Whose decision was it to hire Roger Semerad, yours or the Board's?

8.   What are some of the things that you can point to that demonstrate the success of the strategies that you have employed since becoming president?

9.   What are some of the financial, environmental constraints/opportunities that are on the horizon that may influence the strategy and structure of Brookings in the future?

INSTITUTIONAL PROFILE

(Please return questionnaire by 1/5/91)

Section I: Background
1.   Institution: _____
2.   Address: _____
     _____
3.   Telephone Number: _____
4.   Chief Executive Officer: _____
5.   Name of Person Completing Profile: _____
     Telephone Number _____

Section I: Origins and Purposes
6.   Date Founded: _____
7.   Mission Statement: _____
     _____
     _____

8.   Brief History _____
     _____
     _____

8.   Founder(s)' Name(s):

Section II: Program
9.   Primary activity of your organization (choose one):
     a.   Scholarly research   _____
     b.   Policy-oriented research   _____
     c.   Contract research   _____
     d.   Public policy advocacy   _____

APPENDICES 149

    e.   Training and technical assistance   _____

    f.   Public education   _____

    g.   Other (please specify)   _____

10.   Please list the major programs and research priorities of your organization:

_____

_____

11.   What are the products of your organization? For each of the following items, estimate the number produced during the period specified below:

	1970	1980	1988	1989
a. Books				
b. Monographs				
c. Journals				
d. Issue/ Policy Briefs				
e. Newsletters				
f. Magazines				
g. Seminars				
h. Major Conferences				
i. Films				
j. Other (specify)				

12.   Who are the major users of these products and services?

_____

13.   How do you differentiate your products from your competitors'?

_____

_____

14.   Your organization is best known for its research in (choose one):

    a.   Domestic economics   _____

    b.   International economics   _____

    c.   Political science   _____

    d.   Security studies   _____

    e.   Regional studies (specify)   _____

    f.   Social policy   _____

150   THE COMPETITION FOR DOLLARS, SCHOLARS AND INFLUENCE

    g.   Education policy   _____

    h.   International relations   _____

    i.   Other (specify)   _____

15. Please attach a list of the publications and programs produced by your organization during the last year.

16. Please identify what you consider to be the most influential publications and programs produced by your organization in the last five years in rank order.

	Publications	Programs
a.		
b.		
c.		
d.		
e.		

17. Who has primary responsibility for establishing the research agenda for your institution? (choose one)

    a.   Board of directors   _____

    b.   Chief executive officer   _____

    c.   Department heads   _____

    d.   Individual scholars   _____

    e.   Other (specify)   _____

18. What mechanisms does your organization employ to assure the quality and timeliness of your products?

_____

_____

Section III: Finances

Answer each of the following questions for 1970, 1980, 1988 and 1989 for the fiscal or calendar years closest to those dates for which data are available.

19. What was your organization's total income in:

                                                          1970? _____

                                                          1980? _____

1988? _____
1989? _____

20. What proportion of your organization's total income came from each of the following sources?

		1970	1980	1988	1989
a.	Endowment				
b.	University subsidy				
c.	Private foundations				
d.	Corporate foundations				
e.	Individual contributions				
f.	Corporate contributions				
g.	Government grants				
h.	Government contracts				
i.	Private contracts				
j.	Membership subscriptions				
k.	Sales of publications, etc.				
l.	Other (specify)				

21. What were your total operating expenditures in:

    1970? _____
    1980? _____
    1988? _____
    1989? _____

22. What was your total operating surplus or deficit in:

    1970? _____
    1980? _____
    1988? _____
    1989? _____

23. What was the total value of your endowment in:

    1970? _____
    1980? _____
    1988? _____
    1989? _____

152   THE COMPETITION FOR DOLLARS, SCHOLARS AND INFLUENCE

24. What percentage of your income was contributed to your endowment in:

                                                        1970? _____

                                                        1980? _____

                                                        1988? _____

                                                        1989? _____

25. At what rate do you expect your operating budget to expand over the next three years?

                                                        1990? _____

                                                        1991? _____

                                                        1992? _____

26. What percentage of your organization's expenditures were allocated for the following purposes?

		1970	1980	1988	1989
a.	Research				
b.	Printing & publications				
c.	Salaries & related				
d.	Conferences & seminars				
e.	Fund raising				
f.	Outreach activities				
g.	Overhead				
h.	Other (specify)				

27. List your organization's ten largest sources of private support (corporations, foundations and individuals) in each of the following three years, along with percentage of total income for which each accounted:

		1970	1980	1989
a.	source/%			
b.	source/%			
c.	source/%			
d.	source/%			
e.	source/%			
f.	source/%			
g.	source/%			
h.	source/%			
i.	source/%			
j.	source/%			

28. Do you own _____ or rent _____ the space that houses your organization?

Section IV: Staffing and Structure

29. Board of directors (list of current members)

30. What are the major disciplines/ professions represented on your staff?

_____
_____

31. What are the functional areas in which your staff works?

_____
_____

32. What institutions would you consider your peers?
a. _____
b. _____
c. _____
d. _____
e. _____

33. What organizational structure comes to mind when describing the structure of your organization?

      a.   Academic institution   _____
      b.   Consulting firm   _____
      c.   Literary agent/ publishing company   _____
      d.   For-profit corporation   _____
      e.   Newspaper/ magazine   _____
      f.   Advocacy organization   _____

34. Indicate where you feel your organization belongs on the philosophical scale provided below:
Ultraliberal____ Liberal____ Centrist____ Conservative____ Ultraconservative____

35. Do you feel that it is important for your organization to be nonpartisan? Yes____. No____.

36. What have been the most enduring programs or areas of research conducted by your organization?

37. Please list the number of staff members employed by your organization for the periods listed below:

1970 Administration____   Program____   Support____
1980 Administration____   Program____   Support____
1988 Administration____   Program____   Support____
1989 Administration____   Program____   Support____

38. What is the total number of researchers on your staff?_____

39. How many of these researchers are:
    a.   part time?   _____
         full time?   _____
    b.   resident?   _____
         non-resident?   _____

40. What percentage of the total staff have Ph.D.s?   ____%

41. Where are you most likely to draw your staff from?
    a.   business   _____
    b.   government   _____
    c.   academic   _____
    d.   other (specify)   _____

42. Is your organization organized along traditional academic departments and discipline or according to functional problems and issues:
    a.   Academic departments   _____
    b.   Issue/ problems departments   _____
    c.   Other (specify)   _____

43. What portion of the research conducted by your organization is conducted by:
    a.   Individual specialists   _____
    b.   Interdisciplinary teams   _____
    c.   Others (specify)   _____

44. How many of your staff are engaged in fundraising and outreach?
    Fundraising_____   Outreach_____

45. Does your research staff sign a contract with your organization?
    Yes___   No_____

46. What restrictions does your organization place on your research staff engaging in outside teaching, consulting and publishing?

---

47. Do you see your organization primarily as:
    a.   Source of policy ideas   _____
    b.   Evaluator of policy proposals   _____
    c.   Evaluator of government proposals   _____
    d.   An advocate of a particular philosophy or cause _____

48. Rate the following according to their importance in your selection of new staff (1 being the least important and 10 being the most important):
    a.   Academic credentials   _____
    b.   Ideological orientation   _____
    c.   Methodological orientation _____
    d.   Government experience   _____
    e.   Publication record   _____
    f.   Political affiliation   _____
    g.   Substantive experience   _____
    h.   Other (specify)   _____

49. Does the research conducted by your organization focus on:
    a.   Systems approach (whole)   _____
    b.   Issue approach (parts)   _____

In answering questions 50-53, you should describe how the factors outlined below have affected the strategy and structure of your organization. For example, how have they affected the output, research priorities and staffing patterns of your organization ?

50. How has the single-issue orientation of Congress and the executive branch affected your mode of operation?

51. How have advances in computers and telecommunications affected your mode of operation?

52. How have changes in funding patterns affected your mode of operation?

53. How has (specify)_____ affected your mode of operation?

Section V: Outreach

54. Rate the following according to their importance to your organization (1 being the least important and 10 being the most important).

Congress _____
Executive branch _____
Corporate community _____
Academic/ scholarly community _____
Media _____
General public _____
Others (specify) _____

55. Please provide an estimate of the number of media-related outreach activities conducted for the periods listed below:
    a.   Press briefings   1988-89_____
    b.   Television/ radio interviews   1988-89_____
    c.   Newspaper editorials   1988-89_____

56. On a scale from one to ten, how would you rate the strength of your networks in the following communities?

          Weak   Strong
   1   2   3   4   5   6   7   8   9   10

Academic

Policy maker

Corporate

Foundation

Media

Other (specify)

57. How do you disseminate your products?
_____
_____

58. Please list the outreach activities you conduct for your primary constituencies.
_____
_____

59. What is your primary means of marketing your organization to private donors?
_____
_____

60. If additional private funds were made available to you (above and beyond what you anticipate in the coming year) what amount, over what period of time, for what purpose, would you use?

Amount $_____

Time period   _____

Purpose _____
_____

61. Please provide the annual report for your organization for the following years:
 1970_____   1980_____   1988_____   1989_____

Please return questionnaire to:
James G. McGann
[address]
[telephone number]

Institutions Surveyed[+]

1. Accuracy In Media
2. American Enterprise Institute for Public Policy Research
3. The Atlantic Council of the United States
4. The Brookings Institution
5. Carnegie Endowment for International Peace*
6. Cato Institute*
7. Center on Budget and Policy Priorities
8. Center for International Business*
9. Center for National Policy*
10. Center for Strategic and International Studies
11. Center of International Studies (Princeton University)
12. Citizens Network for Foreign Affairs
13. Committee for Economic Development
14. Commonwealth Foundation
15. Council on Foreign Relations, Inc.
16. Economic Policy Institute
17. Economic Strategy Institute*
18. Environmental Policy Institute*
19. Ethics and Public Policy Center
20. Foreign Policy Research Institute
21. Heritage Foundation
22. Hoover Institution on War Revolution and Peace (Stanford University)
23. Hudson Institute
24. Independent Institute
25. Institute for Contemporary Studies
26. Institute for International Economics
27. Institute for Policy Studies
28. Institute for Research on Poverty (University of Wisconsin)
29. Joint Center for Political and Economic Studies*
30. Manhattan Institute
31. Media Institute*
32. National Bureau of Economic Research
33. National Center for Policy Analysis
34. National Strategy Information Center*
35. Overseas Development Council
36. Pacific Research Institute for Public Policy
37. Public Policy Institute (AARP)*
38. The Rand Corporation
39. Reason Foundation
40. Resources for the Future
41. Scientists Institute for Public Information*
42. SRI International
43. Urban Institute

44. Woodrow Wilson International Center (Smithsonian)*
45. World Resources Institute
46. World Watch Institute*

+ A twelve page survey was sent to each of the institutions listed above. Thirty-four institutions agreed to participate in the study.
* Did not agree to participate in the study.

BIBLIOGRAPHY

The bibliography has been divided into two sections to make it easier to use. Section I contains the literature on PPRIs and the public policy formulation process. Section II contains the relevant literature on organizational theory, business management and knowledge utilization and public policy.

SECTION I: PUBLIC POLICY RESEARCH INSTITUTES

Books

Aaron, Henry. *Politics and the Professors: The Great Society in Perspective.* Washington, DC: Brookings Institution, 1978.

Advisory Committee for the Assessment of University Based Institutes for Research on Poverty, *Policy and Program Research in a University Setting: A Case Study*, Washington, DC: Division of Behavioral Sciences, National Research Council-National Academy of Sciences, 1971.

Alchon, Guy. *The Invisible Hand of Planning Capitalism, Social Science and the State in the 1920s.* Princeton, NJ: Princeton University Press, 1985.

Anderson, Annelise & Bark, Dennis L., eds. *Thinking About America: The United States in the 1990s.* Stanford, CA: Hoover Institution Press, 1988.

Anderson, Martin. *Revolution.* San Diego, New York, London: Harcourt Brace Jovanovich, 1988.

Andrews, F. Emerson, Brandt, Lillian & Glenn, John M. *Russell Sage Foundation, 1907-1946.* New York: Russell Sage Foundation, 1947.

Banfield, Edward. "Policy Science as Metaphysical Madness," in Bureaucrats, Policy Analysts, Statesmen: Who Leads? Goldwin, Robert A., ed. Washington, DC: American Enterprise Institute, 1980.

Bassett, Grace. *The Urban Institute: A History of Its Organization.* Washington, DC: Urban Institute, July 1969. (Unpublished)

Bell, Daniel. *The End of Ideology.* Glencoe, IL: Free Press, 1960.

Berle, Adolf A. *Leaning Against the Dawn, 1919-69.* New York: Twentieth Century Fund, 1969.

Blumenthal, Sidney. *The Rise of the Counter-Establishment: From Conservative Ideology to Political Power.* New York: Times Books, 1986.

Boaz, David & Crane, Edward H., eds. *Beyond the Status Quo: Policy Proposals for America.* Washington, DC: Cato Institute, 1985.

Brewer, G.D. *Politicians, Bureaucrats, and the Consultant: A Critique of Urban Problem Solving.* New York: Basic Books, 1973.

Cannon, Lou. *Reagan.* New York, 1983.

Cater, Douglass. *Power in Washington*. New York: Random House, 1964.

Chipman, John. *Survey of International Relations Institutes in the Developing World*. London: Institute for Strategic Studies, 1987.

Chipman, John & van der Woerd, N. *World Survey of Strategic Studies Centres*. London: International Institute for Strategic Studies, 1988.

Coleman, J. S. *Policy Research in the Social Sciences*. Morristown, NJ: General Learning Systems, 1972.

Crawford, Alan. *Thunder on the Right: The 'New Right' and the Politics of Resentment*. New York: Pantheon, 1980

Critchlow, Donald T. *The Brookings Institution, 1916-1952: Expertise and the Public Interest in a Democratic Society*. DeKalb, IL: Northern Illinois University Press, 1985.

DeLeon, Peter. *Advice and Consent: The Development of the Policy Sciences*. New York: Russell Sage Foundation, 1988.

Destler, I.M., Gelb, Leslie H. and Lake, Anthony. *Our Own Worst Enemy*. New York: Simon & Schuster, 1984.

Dickson, Paul. *Think Tanks*. New York: Atheneum, 1972.

Doern, G.B. and Aucoin, P., eds. *The Structure of Policy-Making in Canada*. Toronto: Macmillan of Canada, 1971.

Doern, G.B. and Phidd, R.W. *Canadian Public Policy: Ideas, Structure, Process*. Toronto: Methuen, 1983.

Domhoff, William G. *The Higher Circles: The Governing Class in America*. New York, 1970.

Domhoff, William G. *The Powers That Be: Processes of Ruling Class Domination in America*. New York: Vintage, 1979.

Domhoff, William G. *Who Rules America Now? A View for the 80's*. New Jersey: Prentice Hall, 1983.

Danhof, Clarence H. *The Expanding Roles of Non-Profit Organizations as Contractors with Government: Some Research Needs, Program of Policy Studies in Science and Technology*. Washington, DC: George Washington University Press, 1968.

Danhof, Clarence H. *Government Contracting and Technological Change*. Washington, DC: Brookings Institution, 1968.

Douglas, George W. & Miller, James C., III. *Economic Regulation of Domestic Air Transportation: Theory and Policy*. 1974.

Draper, Theodore. *Present History: Nuclear War, Detente and Other Controversies*. New York: Random House, 1984.

Dror, Yehezkel. *Design for Policy Science*. New York: Elsevier, North Holland, 1971.

Dror, Yehezkel. "Think Tanks: A New Invention in Government" in Weiss, Carol H. & Barton, Allen H., *Making Bureaucracies Work*. Beverly Hills & London: Sage, 1980.

Duignan, Peter, ed. *The Library of the Hoover Institution on War, Revolution and Peace*. Stanford, CA: Hoover Institution Press, 1985.

Duignan, Peter, *The Hoover Institution on War, Revolution and Peace: Seventy-five Years of Its History*. Stanford, CA: Hoover Institution Press, 1989.

Dye, Thomas R. *Who's Running America? Institutional Leadership in the U.S.* Englewood Cliffs, NJ: Prentice Hall, 1976.

Dye, Thomas R. *Who's Running America. The Bush Era*. Englewood Cliffs, NJ: Prentice Hall, 1990.

Eakins, David W. *The Development of Corporate Liberal Policy Research in the United States*. Ph.D. dissertation, University of Wisconsin, 1966.

Enthoven, Alain & Smith, Wayne C. *How Much is Enough?* New York: Harper Row, 1971.

Fenno, Richard. *Homestyle and Washington Work*. Ann Arbor, MI: University of Michigan Press, 1989.

Formaini, Robert. *The Myth of Scientific Public Policy*. New Brunswick, NJ: Transaction Publishers, 1990.

Fox, Harrison W. & Webb Hammond, Susan. *Congressional Staffs: The Invisible Force in American Lawmaking*. New York: Free Press, 1977.

Freeman, J. Leiper. *The Political Process: Executive Bureau Legislative Committee Relations*. Garden City, NY: Doubleday, 1955.

Friedman, John S. *First Harvest: The Institute for Policy Studies, 1963-83*. New York: Grove Press, 1983.

Fugwell, R.G. *The Brains Trust.* New York: Viking, 1968.

Gilder, George. *Wealth and Poverty.*

Glenn, John M., Brandt, Lillian & Andrews, F. Emerson. *Russell Sage Foundation, 1907-46*, 2 vols. New York: Russell Sage Foundation, 1947.

Gottfried, Paul & Fleming, Thomas. *The Conservative Movement.* Boston: Twayne Publishers, 1988.

Greenberg, D.S. *The Politics of Pure Science.* New York: New American Library, 1967.

Grossman, David M. *Professors and Public Service 1885-1965.* Ph.D. dissertation, Washington University of St. Louis, 1973.

Hagedorn, Herman. *Brookings: A Biography.* New York: Macmillan Co., 1936.

Harned, Joseph W. & Pagliano, Gary J. *The Role of Non-Governmental Organizations in the Formulation of U.S. Foreign Policy.* Washington, DC: The Atlantic Council of the United States.

Hayes, Frederick O'R., Japha, Anthony F., & Kaysen, Carl. *The Urban Institute, 1968-78: An Evaluation of Its Performance, Prospects and Financial Problems.* New York: Ford Foundation, 1978.

Heatherly, Charles L. *Mandate for Leadership: Policy Management in a Conservative Administration.* Washington, DC: Heritage Foundation, 1980. (Also see *Mandate for Leadership II* (1984) and *Mandate for Leadership III* (1989).

Heclo, Hugh. "The In and Outer System: A Critical Assessment," in MacKenzie. G. Calvin, *The In-and-Outers: Presidential Appointees and Transient Government.* Washington, Baltimore, London: *Johns Hopkins University Press*, 1987.

Heclo, Hugh. "Issue Networks and the Executive Establishment," in King, A., ed., *The New American Political System.* Washington, DC: American Enterprise Institute, 1978.

Heclo, Hugh. *The Private Government of Public Money.* Berkeley: University of California Press, 1974.

Heclo, Hugh. *The Government of Strangers.* Washington, DC: Brookings Books, 1972.

Himmelstein, Jerome L. *To the Right: The Transformation of American Conservatism*. Berkeley: University of California Press, 1990.

Hitch, Charles J. & McKean, Roland N. *The Economics of Defense in the Nuclear Age*. Cambridge, MA: Harvard University Press, 1960.

Hoos, Ida. *Systems Analysis in Public Policy: A Critique*. Berkeley: University of California Press, 1972.

Huberty, R. & Hobbach, Barbara D., eds. *The Annual Guide to Public Policy Experts, 1990*. Washington, DC: Heritage Foundation, 1990.

Kahn, Herman. *An Escalation: Metaphors and Scenarios: Hudson Institute Series on National Security and International Order*. New York: Praeger Press, 1965.

Kamura, Hiroshi Peter. *International Relations Research: Emerging Trends outside the United States, 1981-1982*. New York: Rockefeller Foundation, 1982.

Kaplan, Fred. *The Wizards of Armageddon*. New York: Simon & Schuster, 1983.

King, Anthony. *The New American Political System*. Washington, DC: 1979.

Kingdon, John W. *Agendas, Alternatives and Public Policy*. New York: Little, Brown & Co., 1984.

Kiger, Joseph C. *Research Institutions and Learned Societies*. Greenwood Press, 1982.

Kolko, Gabriel. *The Triumph of Conservatism*. New York, 1963.

Lagemann, Ellen Condliffe. *The Politics of Knowledge: The Carnegie Corporation, Philanthropy and Public Policy*. Middletown, CT: Wesleyan University Press, 1989.

Lesher, Richard L. *Independent Research Institutes and Industrial Application of Aerospace Research*, Ph.D. dissertation, Graduate School of Business, Indiana University, 1963.

Lindbloom, Charles E. *The Policy Making Process*. Englewood Cliffs, NJ: Prentice Hall, 1980.

Lindquist, Evert A. *Behind the Myth of Think Tanks: The Organization and Relevance of Canadian Policy Institutes*. Ph.D. dissertation, University of California at Berkeley, 1989.

Lustig, R. Jeffrey. *Corporate Liberalism: The Origins of Modern Political Theory, 1890-1920.* Berkeley: University of California Press, 1982.

Lynd, Robert. *Knowledge for What? The Place of Social Science in American Culture.* Princeton, NJ: Princeton University Press, 1939.

Lynn, Laurence E., ed. *Knowledge and Policy: The Uncertain Connection.* Washington, DC: National Academy of Sciences, 1978.

Lyons, Gene M. *The Uneasy Partnership: Social Science and the Federal Government in the Twentieth Century.* New York: Russell Sage Foundation, 1969.

MacRae, D., Jr., & Wilde, J.A. *Policy Analysis for Public Decisions.* Belmont, CA: Duxbury Press, 1979.

Malbin, Michael. *Unelected Representatives.* New York: Basic Books, 1980.

Marver, J. *Consultants Can Help.* Lexington, MA: Lexington Press, 1979.

McQuaid, Kim. *Big Business and Presidential Power: From FDR to Reagan.* New York: William Morrow & Co., 1982.

Meltsner, A. J. *Policy Analysts in the Bureaucracy.* Berkeley: University of California Press, 1976.

Merton, Robert K. "Role of The Intellectual in Public Bureaucracy," in *Social Theory and Social Structure*, revised. New York: Free Press, 1957.

Milliken, John Gordon: *An Analysis of Selected Management Problems of Federal-Auxiliary Contract Research and Development Centers.* Ph.D. dissertation, University of Colorado, 1969.

Mosher, Frederic, C. *A Tale of Two Agencies: A Comparative Analysis of the General Accounting Office and the Office of Management and Budget.* Baton Rouge, LA: Louisiana State University Press, 1984.

Moynihan, Daniel Patrick. *Maximum Feasible Misunderstanding: Community Action in the War on Poverty.* New York: Free Press, 1969.

Moynihan, Daniel Patrick. *On Understanding Poverty.* New York: Basic Books, 1969.

Moynihan, Daniel Patrick. *Toward a National Urban Policy.* New York: Basic Books: New York, 1970.

Moynihan, Daniel Patrick. *Coping: Essays on the Practice of Government.* New York: Random House, 1973.

Nash, George H. *The Conservative Intellectual Movement in America Since 1945.* New York: Basic Books, 1976.

Nathan, Richard P. *Social Science in Government: Uses and Misuses.* New York: Basic Books, 1988.

Nelson, Sidney G. *The Creation, Evaluation, and Selection of Research Projects in Not-for-Profit Contractors.* Ph.D. dissertation, Ohio State University, 1968.

Orlans, Harold. *Non-Profit Organizations: A Government Tool.* New York: McGraw-Hill, 1972.

Orlans, Harold. *The Non-Profit Research Institute: Its Orgins, Operation, Problems and Prospects.* New York: McGraw-Hill, 1972.

Peschek, Joseph G. *Policy-Planning Organizations, Elite Agendas and America's Rightward Turn.* Philadelphia: Temple University Press, 1987.

Pines, Burton Yale. *Back to Basics: The Traditionalist Movement That Is Sweeping Grass-Roots America.* New York: William Morrow & Co., 1982.

Polsby, Nelson. *Policy Innovations in America: The Politics of Policy Initiation.* New Haven, CT: Yale University Press, 1986.

Powell, S. Steven. *Covert Cadre: Inside the Institute for Policy Studies.* Ottawa, IL: Green Hill Press, 1988.

Presthus, Robert. *Elites in the Policy Process.* Cambridge, England: Cambridge University Press, 1974.

Prewitt, K. and Stone, A. *The Ruling Elites: Elite Theory, Power, and American Democracy.* New York: Harper and Row, 1973.

Raskin, Marcus. *Being and Doing.* Boston: Beacon Press, 1973.

Reeves, Richard. *The Reagan Detour.* New York: Simon & Schuster, 1986.

Rosen, Elliot A. *Hoover, Roosevelt and the Brain Trust: From Depression to New Deal.* New York: Columbia University Press, 1977.

Saloma, John S., III. *Ominous Politics: The New Conservative Labyrinth.* New York: Hill & Wang, 1984.

Saunders, Charles B., Jr. *The Brookings Institute, A Fifty-Year History.* Washington, DC: Brookings Books, 1966.

Schriftgiesser, Karl. *Business Comes of Age: The Impact of the Committee for Economic Development, 1942-60.* New York: Harper Brothers, 1960.

Schriftgiesser, Karl. *Business and Public Policy: The Role of the Committee for Economic Development: 1942-67.* Englewood Cliffs, NJ: Prentice Hall, 1967.

Schultzinger, R.D. *The Wise Men of Foreign Affairs: The History of the Council on Foreign Relations.* New York: Columbia University Press, 1984.

Sclee, Smith P.I. *Think Tanks and Problem Solving.* London: Business Books, 1971.

Silk, L. & Silk, M. *The American Establishment.* New York: Avon, 1981.

Singer, Max. *The Work of the Hudson Institute: A Background Statement.* Croton-on-Hudson, NY: The Hudson Institute, 1969.

Smith, Bruce L. *The Rand Corporation, Its Origins, Evolutions and Plans for the Future.* Santa Monica, CA: Rand Corporation, 1987.

Smith, Bruce L. & Hague, D.C., eds., *The Dilemma of Accountability in Modern Government: Independence Versus Control.* New York: St. Martin's Press, 1971.

Smith, Bruce L. *The Rand Corporation: Case Study of a Nonprofit Corporation.* Cambridge, MA: Harvard University Press, 1966.

Smith, Bruce L. *The Rand Corporation: The First Fifteen Years.* Santa Monica, CA: Rand Corporation, 1965.

Smith, James A. *Brookings at Seventy-Five.* Washington, DC: Brookings Books, 1991.

Smith, James A. *The Idea Brokers: Think Tanks and the Rise of the New Policy Elite.* New York: The Free Press, 1991.

Smith, James A. "Think Tanks and the Politics of Ideas," in Colander, David & Coats, A.W., *The Spread of Economic Ideas.* Cambridge, England: Cambridge University Press, 1989.

Soley, Lawrence C. *The News Shapers.* St. Paul: University of Minnesota, 1989.

Sowell, S. Steven. *Covert Cadre: Inside the Institute for Policy Studies*, Introduction by David Horowitz. Ottawa, IL: Green Hill Press, 1987.

Stokey, E. & Zeckhauser, R. *A Primer for Policy Analysis*. New York: Norton, 1978.

Swatez, Gerald. *Social Organization of a University of California*. Berkeley: University of California, 1966.

The 1989 Roe Foundation Report on Twelve State Policy Institutes. Greenville, SC: The Roe Foundation, 1990.

Thomson, Charles. *The Institute for Government Research*. Washington, DC, 1959.

de Tocqueville, Alexis. *Democracy in America*, vol. 1, Henry Reeve text as revised by Francis Bowen, edited by Phillips Bradley. New York: Alfred A. Knopf, 1963.

Walker, Jack. "The Diffusion of Knowledge, Policy Communities, and Agenda Settings: The Relationship of Knowledge and Power," in Tropman, John, Dlahey, Milar & Lind, Roger eds., *Strategic Perspectives of Social Policy*. New York: 1973.

Weaver, Richard. *Ideas Have Consequences*. Chicago: University of Chicago Press, 1948.

Weinstein, James. *The Corporate Ideal in the Liberal State*. Boston: 1968.

Weiss, Carol, ed. *Organizations for Policy Analysis: Helping Governments Think*. Newbury Park, CA: Sage Publications, Inc., 1992.

White, Theodore H. *America in Search of Itself*. Warner Books, 1982.

Wiarda, Howard J. *Foreign Policy Without Illusion: How Foreign Policy Works and Fails to Work in the United States*. Glenview, IL: Scott, Foresman & Co., 1990.

Wildavsky, Aaron. *Speaking Truth to Power: The Art and Craft of Policy Analysis*. Boston: Little, Brown & Co., 1979.

Willner, Barry. *The Shadow Government*. New York: 1976.

Winch, Donald. *Economics and Policy: A Historical Study*. New York: Simon & Schuster, 1984.

Wolfe, Gregory. *Right Minds: A Source Book of American Conservative Thought*. Chicago: Regnery Books, 1987.

Journals, Periodicals & Reports

Adams, Bruce. "The Limitations of Muddling Through: Does Anyone in Washington Really Think Anymore?" *Public Administration Review*, November-December 1979, pp. 545-52.

U.S. Air Force. "Air Force Relations with the Not-for-Profit Corporations: Report of Air Force Systems Command Board of Visitors' Ad Hoc Group." 1966.

Alpert, I. & Markusen, A. "The Professional Production of Policy, Ideology and Plans: Brookings and Resources for the Future." *Insurgent Sociologist*, vol. 9, 1980, pp. 94-106.

Anderson, Jack. "Heritage Foundation Throws a Right." *Washington Post*, December 7, 1984.

Anderson, Charles. "Research: A Retreat from the Universities." *Scientific Research*, November 24, 1969.

Averch, Harvey A. "Applied Social Science, Policy Science, and the Federal Government." *Knowledge: Creation, Diffusion, Utilization*, vol. 8, no. 3, March 1987.

Bachrach, P. & Baratz, S.M. "Two Faces of Power." *American Political Science Review*, vol. 56, 1962, pp. 947-52.

Baer, Walter S. "Interdisciplinary Policy Research in Independent Research Centers." *The Rand Paper Series*, January 1975, p. 5347.

Balz, Daniel J. "Moderate, Conservative Democrats Buck 'Constraints,' Form Think Tank." *Washington Post*, June 30, 1989, p. A21.

Balz, Daniel J. "Washington Pressures: AEI/Hoover Institution Voices Grow In Policy Debates During Nixon Years." *National Journal*, December 22, 1973, pp. 1893-1901.

Balzano, Michael P., Jr. "The Sacking of a Centrist." *Washington Post*, July 6, 1986.

Barnes, Fred. "The New Parasite Culture of Washington." *The New Republic*, July 28, 1986.

"Baroody Looks at the Presidency." *Government Executive*, February 1982, pp. 13-16.

Baroody, William J., Sr. "Remembered by Paul McCracken, Robert H. Bork, Irving Kristol and Michael Novak." *American Enterprise Publication*, 1981.

Baroody, William J., Jr. "Think Tanks." *1986 Public Interest Profiles: Foundation for Public Affairs*, 1986, pp. 71-76.

Bast, Joseph L. "Two Strategies for State-Based Think Tanks." *The Madison Report*, September/October 1990, pp. 1-3.

Beloff, Max. "The Think Tank and Foreign Policy." *Public Administration*, vol. 55, 1977, pp. 435-44.

Bencivenga, Jim. "A Voice with Clout." *Christian Science Monitor*, September 28, 1984.

Bencivenga, Jim. "Young, Brash and Conservative." *Christian Science Monitor*, October 5, 1984.

Bernstein, P.W. "Brookings Tilts Right." *Fortune*, July 1984, p. 96.

Bethell, Tom. "Liberalism, Stanford Style." *Commentary 77*, January 1984, pp. 42-47.

Bethell, Tom. "The New Conservative Idea Men." *Dun's Review*, April 1976, pp. 39-41, 81.

Bethell, Tom. "The Rewards of Enterprise." *New Republic*, July 16, 1977, pp. 17-19.

Bjerre-Poulsen, Neils. "Heritage, A Second Generation Think Tank." *Policy*, vol. 3, no. 2, 1991, pp. 152-72.

Blodgett, Nancy. "The Ralph Naders of the Right." *American Bar Association Journal*, May 1984.

Bloom, Benjamin S. "Research and Development Centers: Promise and Fulfillment." *Journal of Research and Development in Education*, vol. 1, no. 4, 1968. pp. 181-189.

Blumenthal, Sidney. "A Well-Connected Conservative." *Washington Post*, June 22, 1986.

Blumenthal, Sidney. "Hard Times at the Think Tank." *Washington Post*, June 26, 1986, p. D1.

Blumenthal, Sidney. "The Ideology Makers." *Boston Globe Magazine*, August 8, 1982.

Blumenthal, Sidney. "The Left Stuff: IPS and the Long Road Back." *Washington Post*, July 30, 1986, pp. D1-3.

Blumenthal, Sidney. "Think Tank Adrift in the Center." *Washington Post*, June 26, 1986.

Boffey, Philip M. "Heritage Foundation: Success in Obscurity." *New York Times*, November 17, 1985.

Bonafede, Dom. "Issue-Oriented Heritage Foundation Hitches its Wagon to Reagan's Star." *National Journal*, March 20, 1982, p. 504.

Boorstin, David. "Directions of Policy Research." *Congressional Quarterly Editorial Research Reports*, vol. II, no. 13, October 10, 1975, pp. 725-44.

Bovbjerg, Randall & Shellow, Jill. "A Brief History of the Urban Institute." Washington, DC: September 1983 (unpublished).

Brim, Orville G., Jr. "Diversity in Social Research Organizations." *Russell Sage Foundation*, September 1, 1967.

Butler, Stuart M. "A Firm Foundation Amid the D.C. Mire." *Wall Street Journal*, February 21, 1985.

Calkins, Robert D. "Remarks." *Government and Critical Intelligence, An Address by President Lyndon B. Johnson Marking the Fiftieth Anniversary of the Brookings Institution*, September 29, 1966.

Campbell, Colin. "A Futurologist's Institute Looks to Middle West for Its Future." *New York Times*, June 18, 1984.

"The Capital Source." *National Journal,* Fall/ Spring 1990.

Caplan, Nathan. "The Use of Social Science Knowledge in Policy Decisions at the National Level." *Institute for Social Research*, 1975.

Cato Institute. *Annual Reports,* 1980-1987.

Clapp, Stephen. "The Intellectual Bombthrowers." *Washingtonian*, December 1969.

"Communophilism and the Institute for Policy Studies." *World Affairs*, Winter 1984-1985.

"The Conservative Brookings Institution." *Dun's Review*, April 1976, pg. 43.

"Conservative Think Tank: AEI Gains a Reputation, Even Among Liberals, for Scholarly, Balanced Work." *Business Week*, May 2, 1987, pp. 80-81.

Critchlow, Donald T. "Think Tanks, Anti-Statism and Democracy: The Career of the Nonpartisan Ideal in the American Political Order." Produced for the Program on American Society and Politics, Woodrow Wilson International Center for Scholars, Smithsonian Institution, Washington, DC, 1985.

DeLeon, Peter. "The Influence of Systems Analysis on U.S. Defense Policy." *Rand Paper* 7136, August 1985.

Devine, F. "Think Tanks Overflowing." *Australian*, July 12, 1990, p. 15.

Dionne, E. J., Jr. "A Conservative Call for Compassion." *New York Times*, November 30, 1987.

Dolan, Carrie. "Private Citizen Jerry Brown Divides His Time Between Law Practice, Non-Profit Think Tanks." *Wall Street Journal*, February 19, 1985.

Draper, Theodore. "Intellectuals in Politics." *Encounter*, 1977.

Dror, Yehezkel. "Required Breakthroughs in Think Tanks." *Policy Sciences* vol. 16, 1984, pp. 199-225.

Dror, Yehezkel. "Think Tanks: A New Invention in Government." In *Making Bureaucracies Work*, Weiss, C.H. & Barton, A.H., Beverly Hills, CA: Sage, 1980.

Durst, Samantha L. & Thurber, James A. "Studying Washington Think Tanks: In Search of Definitions and Data." Prepared for delivery at the 1989 Annual Meeting of the American Political Science Association, August 31 - September 3, 1989.

Dye, Thomas R. "Oligarchic Tendencies in National Policy- Making: The Role of Private Policy-Planning Organizations." *Journal of Politics*, vol. 40, May 1978, pp. 309-31.

Easterbrook, Gregg. "Ideas Move Nations." *Atlantic*, January 1986, pp. 66-80.

Ecenbarger, William. "He's Spending Millions to Help You Think Right." *Philadelphia Inquirer*, January 24, 1982.

Emery, Glenn. "New Troubles for an Old Think Tank." *Nation*.

Fabricant, Solomon. "Toward a Firmer Basis of Economic Policy: The Founding of the Bureau of Economic Research." *National Bureau of Economic Research*, 1984.

Farnsworth, Clyde H. "Washington Think Tanks Compete with Ideas." *New York Times*.

Fauriol, George A. "Think Tanks and U. S. Foreign Policy." A paper at the fourth Tamkang American Studies Conference, Tamkang University, Taipei, Taiwan, November 25-28, 1984. *Georgetown University, Center for Strategic and International Studies*.

Feder, Barnaby. "What's New at the Research Institutes." *New York Times*, April 6, 1986, p. F23.

"Federal Contract Research Centers, A Brief Historical Analysis Memorandum." *Office for Laboratory Management, Office of the Director of Defense and Engineering*, August 21, 1967.

Feulner, Edwin J. "Conservatives Aid Transition Plans Behind the Scenes." *New York Times*, December 5, 1990.

Feulner, Edwin J. "Ideas, Think Tanks and Governments." *Heritage Foundation*, 1985.

"Final Agreement Is Announced on Separation of University." *Stanford Report*, Stanford University, January 14, 1970.

Fly, Richard. "What's in for the Presidential Hopefuls: Think Tanks." *Business Week*, May 12, 1986, pp. 60-62.

Freeberg, Ellen M. & Miller, Ellen S., et. al. "Public Policy and Foundations: The Role of Politicians in Public Charities." *Center for Responsive Politics*, Washington, DC, 1987.

Gailey, Phil. "A New Hybrid, Political Foundations." *New York Times*, April 10, 1985.

Gellner, Winard. "Political Think Tanks: Functions and Perspectives of a Strategic Elite." Prepared for the 1990 Annual Meeting of the *American Political Science Association*.

Glass, E.M. "Evaluation of R&D Organizations." Management Analysis Memorandum, *Office for Laboratory Management, Office of the Director of Defense Research and Engineering*, July 31, 1969.

Gleckman, Howard. "A Washington Wallflower Starts to Bloom." *Business Week*, March 9, 1987, pp. 112-116.

Gordon, Suzanne. "Public Policy Publishing: Lobbying in Print." *Book World*, July 28, 1985.

"The Gordon Years." *The Brookings Bulletin..*

Gottlieb, Martin. "Conservative Policy Unit Takes Aim at New York." *New York Times*, May 5, 1986, p. B4.

Gray, C.S. "Think Tanks and Public Policy." *International Journal*, vol. 33, 1978, pp. 177-94.

Grayson, Cary T., ed. "Science and Policy Research." *A Comprehensive Directory of the Nation's Capital . . . Its People and Institutions.* Multiple volumes, Washington, DC, 1975-1988.

Green, Philip. "Science, Government and the Case of Rand." *World Politics*, vol. 20, no. 2, January 31, 1964, pp. 301-26.

Hagedorn, Herman. "Brookings: A Biography." New York, 1937.

Hay, J.R. "The Institute of Public Affairs and Social Policy in World War Two." *Historical Studies*, vol. 20, 1982, pp. 198-216.

Hayes, Frederick., et al. "The Urban Institute, 1968-1978: An Evaluation of its Performance, Prospects and Financial Problems." *Ford Foundation Evaluation Report*, New York: Ford Foundation, 1978.

Hallow, Ralph Z. "Donations Fuel Think Tank Battle to Control Field of Policy Ideas." *Washington Times*, November 25, 1985.

Henderson, Keith. "A 3,000-Mile Corridor of Power." *Christian Science Monitor*, October 9, 1984.

Herbers, John. "The Urban Institute, Then and Now." *New York Times*, August 20, 1986, p. B6.

"Heritage." *Washington Post*, October 3, 1983.

"The Heritage Report: Getting the Government Right with Reagan." *Washington Post*, November 16, 1987.

Hershey, Robert D., Jr. "Shifts at Enterprise Institute." *New York Times*, June 26.

Hicks, Sallie M., et al. "Influencing the Prince: A Role for Academicians?" *Policy*, vol. 15, Summer 1982, pp. 279-93.

Higgot, Richard & Stone, Diane. "The Limits of Influence: Foreign Policy Think Tanks in Britain and the USA." *Review of International Studies*, 20, 15, 34, 1994, pp. 15-34.

Hollander, Paul. "IPS Testimony Certain to be Anti U.S." February 12, 1985.

Holwill, Richard N. "The First Year." Washington, DC: 1981.

Hyer, Marjorie. "Bleeding Hearts In Unlikely Setting." *Washington Post*, July 29, 1989, p. C11.

"Industrial R&D: Competition from Universities, Non-Profits, Alarms Independent Laboratories." *Science*, vol. 144, no. 3616, April 17, 1964.

"Institute Quizzed on Political Tie." *Washington Post*, April 15, 1965.

"Institution Analysis." *Heritage Foundation*, May 1977.

"IPS (Institute for Policy Studies) Faces Life." *New Republic*, August 6, 1976.

Joseph, James A. "Private Philanthropy and the Making of Public Policy." *Council on Foundations*, 1985.

Karl, Barry D. "Foundations and Ruling Class Elites." *Daedalus*, Winter 1987.

Karl, Barry D. "Philanthropy, Policy Planning and the Bureaucratization of the Democratic Ideal." *Daedalus*, Fall 1976.

Kastor, Elizabeth. "Conservative and Loving It." *Washington Post*, October 4, 1981.

Kelley, Peter. "Think Tank Jobs Fall Between Pure Research and Lobbying." *Houston Chronicle*, March 9, 1988.

Kemble, Penn. "The Rise of the Counter-Establishment: From Conservative Ideology to Political Power." *The American Spectator*, September 1986.

Kidder, Rushworth M. "From Left to Center." *Christian Science Monitor*, October 2, 1984.

Kidder, Rushworth M., et al. "Public Policy Think Tanks," (series). *Christian Science Monitor*, September 25, 28; October 2, 5, 9, 1984.

Kidder, Rushworth M. "Think Tanks Shape Contemporary U.S. Life." *Peninsula Times Tribune*, September 30, 1984.

Kilian, Michael & Sawislak, Arnold. "Who Runs Washington?" *St. Martin's Press*, 1982.

Kissinger, Henry A. "The Policymaker and The Intellectual." *The Reporter*, March 5, 1959, pp. 30-35.

Knickerbocker, Brad. "Heritage Foundation's Ideas Permeate Reagan Administration." *Christian Science Monitor*, December 7, 1984.

Kondracke, Morton. "The Heritage Model." *New Republic*, December 20, 1980.

Landers, Robert K. "Think Tanks: The New Partisans?" *Editorial Research Reports, Congressional Quarterly*, vol. I, no. 23, June 20, 1986, pp. 455-72.

Lane, Chuck. "The Manhattan Project." *New Republic*, March 25, 1985, pp. 14-15.

Lane, Robert E. "The Decline of Politics and Ideology in a Knowledgeable Society." *American Sociological Review*, 1966, pp. 649-62.

Lanouette, William J. "The 'Shadow Cabinets' Changing Themselves as They Try to Change Policy." *National Journal*, February 25, 1978, pp. 296-297.

Lardner, James. "Thick and Think Tank." *Washington Post*, September 21, 1982.

Leavitt, William. "ANSER: USAF's 'Short-Order' Think Tank." *Air Force Space Digest*, August 1967.

Lefever, Ernest W., English, Raymond & Schuettinger, Robert L. "Scholars, Dollars and Public Policy." *Ethics and Public Policy Center*, Washington, DC: 1983.

Levien, Roger E. "Independent Public Policy Analysis Organization: A Major Social Invention." *The Rand Papers Series*, 1965, p. 4231.

Levien, Roger E. "National Institute of Education: Preliminary Plan for the Proposed Institute." *The Rand Papers Series*, February 1971.

Linden, Patricia. "Powerhouses of Policy." *Town and Country*, January 1987, pp. 99-106; 170, 174-75, 178-79.

Lowry, Ira S. "Reforming Rent Control in New York City: The Role of Research in Policy Making." *Rand Corporation*, November 1970.

Malone, Julia. "Right's New Weapon - Think Tanks." *Christian Science Monitor*, February 10, 1981.

"Management Trends in Federal Contract Research Centers (FCRCs)." Management Analysis Memorandum, *Office for Laboratory Management, Office of the Director of Defense Research and Engineering,* August 1, 1968.

Manoff, Robert. "For Think Tanks, Lots to Rethink." *Los Angeles Times,* February 2, 1990.

Marsh, I. "Globalisation, Governance and Think Tanks." Presented at the Canadian Institute for Research on Public Policy's Third International Workshop on Governance in the Asia Pacific Region, Kuala Lumpur, 1990.

Masters, Brook A. "Peace Institute's Course: A Balanced Approach." *Washington Post,* July 12, 1989, p. A21.

Matlack, Carol. "Marketing Ideas." *Washington, Inc.,* June 22, 1991, pp. 1552-55.

McBride, Stewart. "Leaning to the Right." *Christian Science Monitor,* April 18, 1980.

McCombs, Phil. "Building a Heritage In the War of Ideas." *Washington Post,* October 3, 1983.

McGann, James G. "Academics to Ideologues: A Brief History of the Public Policy Research Industry." *Political Science & Politics,* vol. XXV, no. 4, pp. 733-40.

McNamee, Mike. "Fred Bergsten Sure Knows How To Sell an Idea." *Business Week,* August 29, 1988, pp. 48-50.

Mitchell, Wesley C. "The National Bureau's First Quarter-Century." *25th Annual Report.* National Bureau of Economic Research, 1945.

Mone, Lawrence. "Thinkers and Their Tanks Move on Washington." *Wall Street Journal,* March 15, 1988, p. 34.

Moore, John W. "Local Right Thinkers." *National Journal,* October 1, 1988, pp. 2455-59.

Morgan, Dan. "Conservatives: A Well-Financed Network." *Washington Post,* January 4, 1981.

Muravachik, Joshua. "The Think Tank of the Left." *New York Times Magazine,* April 26, 1981, p. 46.

Muravachik, Joshua. "U.S. Political Parties Broad." *Washington Quarterly*, Summer 1989, pp. 91-100.

Muscatine, Alison. "Georgetown's Media Professors." *Washington Post*, May 11, 1986.

"Need for Improved Guidelines in Contracting for Research with Government-Sponsored Nonprofit Contractors." Report to Congress by the Comptroller General of the United States, February 10, 1969.

Nisbet, Robert. "The Future of the University." *Commentary*, vol. 51, no. 2, February 1971.

Noble, Kenneth B. "Research Unit Focuses on Progress for Blacks." *New York Times*, September 11, 1986, p. B14.

Oberdorfer, Don. "Foggy Bottom Woos Its Critics." *Washington Post*, December 29, 1985.

O'Conner, Colleen & Cohn, Bob. "A Baby Boomer's Think Tank." *Newsweek*, September 1, 1986, p. 22.

Orlans, Harold. "Contracting for Atoms." *Brookings Institution*, Washington, DC, 1967.

Orlans, Harold. "The Effects of Federal Programs on Higher Education." *Brookings Institution*, Washington, DC, 1962.

Otten, Alan L. "On Stanford's Campus, A Partisan Think Tank Has Political Problems." *Wall Street Journal*, June 15, 1984.

Pipes, Daniel. "First Annual Advisory Meeting of the Foreign Policy Research Institute." *Foreign Policy Research Institute*, September 14, 1988.

Podesta, Jane. "At 40, A Think Tank Sets Out to Win Dollars and Scholars." *Washington Times*, December 8, 1983.

Polsby, Nelson W. "Tanks But No Tanks." *Public Opinion*, vol. 6, April/May 1983, pp. 14-16, 58-59.

Powers, John. "Double-Think Tank." *Regardies*, April/May 1983.

"Policy Analysis Explosion." *Transaction: Social Science and Modern Society*, September-October 1979.

"The Private Research Organization." *Challenge*, February 1964, pp. 18-21.

"Public Interest Profiles, 1988-1989, Foundation for Public Affairs." *Congressional Quarterly*, 1989.

Ranzal, Edward: "Garelik Calls Rand Study of City's Police a Failure." *New York Times*, October 7, 1970.

Rattner, Steven. "A Think Tank for Conservatives." *New York Times*, March 23, 1975.

Rauch, J. "Giving Wings to Ideas." *National Journal*, October 22, 1988, pp. 2655-59.

Remnick, Daniel. "The Lions of Libertarianism." *Washington Post*, July 30, 1985.

"Report of the Stanford-SRI Study Committee" (Campus Report Supplement). *Stanford University*, April 14, 1969.

"Research Centers Directory." published by *Gale Research Company*.

"Resources for the Future." *Annual Reports*, 1975-1989. Washington, DC: Resources for the Future.

Rich, Spencer. "Think Tank Survives Lean Times." *Washington Post*, May 16, 1988, p. A13.

Richburg, Keith B. "Washington Awash in Think Tanks." *Washington Post*, December 7, 1984.

Roback, Herbert. "The Not-for Profit Corporation in Defense Contracting: Problems and Perspectives." *Federal Bar Journal*, Spring 1965, pp. 195-206.

Robinson, William H. "Policy Analysis for Congress: Lengthening the Time Horizon." *Journal of Policy Analysis and Management*, vol. 8, no. 1, 1989, p. 6.

Romano, Lois. "The Heritage Hurrah." *Washington Post*, April 8, 1987.

Rosen, Gerald R. "The New Conservative Idea Men." *Dun's Review*, April 1976.

Rosenthal, James. "Heritage Hype." *The New Republic*, September 2, 1985.

Rothmyer, Karen. "The Mystery Angel of The New Right." *Washington Post*, July 12, 1981.

Rowe, Jonathan. "Taking Conservatives Seriously." *Washington Monthly*, December 1986.

Rusher, William A. "The Rise of the Right." *New York*, 1984, p. 157.

Rushworth, M. Kidder. "Public Policy Think Tanks." *Christian Science Monitor*, September 25, 1984, pp. 19-21.

Safire, William. "Tanks for the Memories." *New York Times*, September 1, 1986, p. 23.

Salholz, Eloise. "A Think Tank at the Brink." *Newsweek*, July 7, 1986.

Salzman, H. & Domhoff, W. "Corporations, Non-Profit Groups and Government: Do They Interlock." *Insurgent Sociologist*, vol. 9, pp. 121-35, 1980.

Sanoff, Alvin P. "Matters Over Mind." *Regardie's*, January 1987, pp. 51-60.

Sawyer, Kathy. "Heritage Foundation Gives Reagan Passing Grade." *Washington Post*, November 22, 1981.

Schneider, William. "The New Shape of American Politics." *Atlantic*, January 1987.

Schick, Allen. "The Supply and Demand for Analysis on Capitol Hill." *Policy Analysis*, Spring 1976, p. 217.

Seabrook, John. "Capital Gain." *Manhattan, Inc.*, March 1987, pp. 71-79.

Seamans, Andrew C., Sr. "Heritage Study Sets Firm Foundation for Reagan." *Human Events*, January 10, 1981, pp. 10, 16-17.

Shils, Edward. "The End of Ideology." *Encounter*, vol. 5, November 1955, pp. 52-58.

Sieber, Sam D., & Lazarsfeld, Paul F. "Reforming the University: The Role of the Research Center." *Bureau of Applied Social Research*, Columbia University, New York, 1971.

Smith, B. L. R. "The Non-Governmental Policy Analysis Organization." *Public Administration Review*, May/June 1977, pp. 253-58.

Smith, James A. "Private Players in the Game of Nations." *Washington Quarterly*, vol. 2, Summer 1988, pp. 17-25.

Specht, R. D. "RAND - A Personal View of Its History." *Journal of the Operations Research Society of America*, no. 8, November-December 1960, pp. 825-39.

Stern, Lawrence: "Institute Quizzed on Political Tie." *Washington Post*, April 15, 1965.

Stone, Nahum I. "The National Bureau's First Quarter Century." *Twenty-Fifth Annual Report*. National Bureau of Economic Research, 1945, p. 6.

Stone, Peter H. "Conservative Brain Trust." *New York Times*, May 10, 1981.

Sundquist, James L. "Research Brokerage: The Weak Line." Lynn, Laurence E., Jr., ed., *Knowledge and Policy: The Uncertain Connection*, the National Academy of Science, Washington, DC 1978, pp. 126-44.

Sussman, Edward. "Conservative Think Tank Comes Back from Brink of Financial Disaster, Leaning More to the Right." *Wall Street Journal*, September 3, 1987, 210:42.

Sussman, Edward. "Research Institutes Battle Image as U. Orphans." *Daily Pennsylvanian*, University of Pennsylvania, Philadelphia, November 14, 1984.

Taylor, Paul. "Analyzing Alternatives in Labor's Think Tank." *Washington Post*, February 19, 1987, p. A25.

Teltsch, Kathleen. "Fund Selects Head for Study of Public Policy." *New York Times*, September 26, 1985.

Thimmesch, Nick. "The Right Kind of Think Tank at the Right Time." *Human Events*, October 7, 1978, pp. 12-21.

"Think Tanks." *Capital Source*, Fall 1990 - Spring 1991.

"Think Tanks." *Free China Review*, vol. 40, no. 2, February 1990.

Thomas, B.D. "The Legacy of Science, the Story of Battelle Memorial Institute." *The Newcomer Society in North America*, Princeton, NJ, 1963.

Thomas, Patrick. "In Washington's Marketplace of Ideas, Think Tanks are the Strongest Sellers." *Los Angeles Times*, November 6, 1988, part IV, p. 3.

Thurber, James A. "The Battelle Memorial Institute's Human Affairs Research Centers." *Political Science & Politics*, vol. XIV, no. 3, Summer 1981, pgp. 584-89.

Traub, James. "Intellectual Stock Picking." *New Yorker*, February 7, 1994, pp. 36-42.

Turner, Wallace. "Research Institute Rises with Reagan." *New York Times*, January 26, 1981.

"Twenty Years in the Strategic Labyrinth." (Interview with David M. Abshire.) *Washington Quarterly*, Winter 1982, pp. 83-105.

Van Dyne, Larry. "Idea Power." *Washington Post*, April 1985, pgs. 102-165.

Victor, Kirk. "After the Victory." *National Journal*, September 24, 1988.

Waks, Norman. "Problems in the Management of Federal Contract Centers." *MITRE Corporation*, Bedford, MA, September 1970.

Walsh, John. "Behavioral Sciences: The View at the Center for Advanced Study." *Science*, vol. 169, no. 3946, August 14, 1970, pp. 654-658.

Weaver, R. Kent. "The Changing World of Think Tanks." Revised version of a paper presented at the Ortega Y Gasset Foundation, Madrid, Spain, June 14, 1988. Appeared in *Political Science & Politics 22*, September 1989.

Weaver, Warren, Jr. "CATO Institute Marks 10 Years." *New York Times*, May 18.

Weinberg, Alvin M. "Social Problems and National Socio-Technical Institutes" in *Applied Science and Astronautics*, a report to the U.S. House of Representatives by the National Academy of Sciences, 1967, pp. 415-434.

Weintraub, Bernard. "Institute Plays Key Role in Shaping Reagan Programs." *New York Times*, January 15, 1981.

Welles, John G., Coddington, Dean C., et al. "Contract Research and Development Adjuncts of Federal Agencies: An Exploratory Study of Forty Organizations." Denver Research Institute, University of Denver, March 1969.

White, Theodore H. "The Action Intellectuals." *Life*, June 9, 16 & 23, 1967.

Whiteman, David. "The Fate of Policy Analysis in Congressional Decision Making: Three Types of Use in Committee." *Western Political Quarterly*, June 1985, pp. 294-311.

Whiteman, David. "Reaffirming the Importance of Strategic Use: A Two-Dimensional Perspective on Policy Analysis in Congress." *Knowledge: Creation, Diffusion and Utilization*, March, 1985, pp. 203-224.

Wilentz, Amy. "On the Intellectual Ramparts." *Time*, September 1, 1986, pp. 22-23.

Wills, Garry. "The Thinking of Positive Power." *Esquire*, p. 100.

Wolfle, Dael. "Unnecessary Research Institutes." *Science*, vol. 139, no. 3555, February 15, 1963.

Yoffe, Emily. "The Domains of Eminence: Great Minds Do Not Always Think Alike." *Washington Journalism Review*, November 1980, pp. 30-31, 33.

SECTION II: KNOWLEDGE UTILIZATION, ORGANIZATIONAL THEORY AND MANAGEMENT

Books

Aaron, Henry. *Politics and the Professors: The Great Society in Perspective*, Washington, DC: Brookings Institution, 1978.

Abt, Clark, ed. *Problems in American Social Policy Research*, Cambridge, MA: Abt Books, 1988.

Adams, Robert & Smelser, Neil, J., eds. *Part I, Behavioral and Social Science Research, a National Resource*. Washington, DC: National Academy Press, 1982.

Aldrich, H.E. *Organizations and Environment*. New York: Prentice-Hall, 1979.

Aldrich, H.E. & Mueller, S. "The Evolution of Organizational Forms: Technology, Coordination, and Control," in Cummings, L.L. & Straw, B., eds., *Research in Organization Behavior*, vol. 4, Greenwich, CT: JAI Press, 1982.

Aldrich, H.E. and Pfeffer, J. "Environments of Organizations" in Inkeles A., ed., *Annual Review of Sociology*, vol. 4, Palo Alto, CA: Annual Review, Inc., 1976.

Allison, G. T. *Essence of Decision: Explaining the Cuban Missile Crisis*. New York: Little, Brown, & Co., 1971.

Barber, Bernard. *Effective Social Science: Eight Cases in Economics, Political Science and Sociology*. New York: Russell Sage Foundation, 1987.

Barney, J. B. & Ouchi, W. G. *Information Cost and Organizational Form*. Unpublished paper, University of California, Los Angeles, 1983.

Bauer, Raymond A. & Gergen, Kenneth J., eds. *The Study of Policy Formulation*. New York: Free Press, 1968.

Ben-David, Joseph. *Centers of Learning: Britain, France, Germany, United States*. Essay prepared for the Carnegie Commission on Higher Education. New York: McGraw-Hill Book Company, 1977.

Ben-David, Joseph. *American Higher Education: Directions Old and New*. New York: McGraw-Hill Book Company, 1972.

Ben-David, Joseph. *The Scientists' Role in Society: A Comparative Study.* Englewood Cliffs, NJ: Prentice-Hall, 1971.

Ben-David, Joseph. *Fundamental Research and the Universities: Some Comments on International Differences.* Paris: Organization for Economic Co-operation and Development, 1968.

Bernard, Luther Lee & Bernard, Jessie. *Origins of American Sociology: The Social Science Movement in the United States.* New York: Publisher unknown, 1943.

Blau, Peter M. *Exchange and Power in Social Life.* New York: Wiley, 1964.

Blau, Peter M. *The Organization of Academic Work.* New York: Wiley Interscience, 1973.

Bulmer, Martin, ed. *Social Science Research and Government: Comparative Essays on Britain and the United States.* Cambridge, England: Cambridge University Press, 1987.

Chandler, Alfred D., Jr. *Strategy and Structure: Chapters in the History of the American Industrial Enterprise.* Boston: MIT Press, 1962.

Chandler, Alfred D., Jr. *The Visible Hand: The Managerial Revolution in American Business.* Cambridge: Harvard University Press, 1977.

Curtis, J.E. & Petras, J.W. *The Sociology of Knowledge.* New York: Praeger.

Daft, R. L. *Organization Theory and Design.* New York: West Publishing Company, 1983.

Davis, S.M. & Lawrence, P.R. *Problems of Matrix Organizations.*

De Leon, Peter. *Advice and Consent: The Development of the Policy Sciences.* New York: Russell Sage Foundation, 1988.

Dluhy, Milan J., Lind, Roger M., & Tropman, John F., eds. *New Strategic Perspectives on Social Policy.* New York: Pergamon Press, 1981.

Dunn, William N. *Public Policy Analysis: An Introduction.* Englewood Cliffs, NJ: Prentice-Hall, 1981.

Etzioni, Amitai. *A Comparative Analysis of Complex Organizations.* New York: Free Press, 1961.

Freeman, J.H. "Organizational Life Cycles and Natural Selection Processes," in Staw, B. M. & Cummings, L. L. *Research in Organizational Behavior*, vol. 4., Greenwich, CT: JAI Press, 1982.

Galbraith, J.R. *Designing Complex Organizations*. Addison-Wesley, 1973.

Galbraith, J.R. *Organization Design*. Addison-Wesley, 1973.

Hannan, M.T., Freeman, J.H., & Johnson, N.J. "Toward an Empirically Derived Taxonomy of Organizations," in Bowers, R. V., ed., *Studies on Behavior in Organizations*. Athens, GA: University of Georgia Press, 1966.

Haskell, Thomas. *The Emergence of Professional Social Science: The American Social Science Association and the Nineteenth Century Crisis of Authority*. Urbana: University of Illinois Press, 1977.

Haskins, Caryl P., ed. *The Search For Understanding*. Washington, DC: Carnegie Institute, 1967.

Holzner, Burkart, & John, Mary. *Knowledge Application: The Knowledge System in Society*. Boston: Allyn & Bacon, 1979.

Huber, G.P. *The Nature and Design of Post-Industrial Organizations*.

Kast, Fremont E. & Rosenzweig, James E. *Organization and Management: A Systems and Contingency Approach*. New York: McGraw Hill, 1979.

Kingdon, John W. *Agendas, Alternatives, and Public Policies*. Boston: Little, Brown & Co., 1984.

Lindblom, C.E. & D.K. Cohn. *Usable Knowledge*. New Haven, CT: Yale University Press, 1972.

Lynn L.E. Jr., ed. *Knowledge and Policy: The Uncertain Connection. Study Project on Social Research and Development*, vol. 5. Washington, DC: National Academy of Sciences, 1978.

Machlup, Fritz. *Knowledge: Its Creation, Distribution and Economic Significance*, vol. I. Princeton, NJ: Princeton University Press, 1980.

Machlup, Fritz. *The Production and Distribution of Knowledge in the United States*. Princeton, NJ: Princeton University Press, 1962.

MacRae, Duncan, Jr. *The Social Function of Social Science*. New Haven: Yale University Press, 1976.

Mark, Meliun M. & Shoctland, R. Lance, eds. *Social Science and Social Policy*. Beverly Hills: Sage Press, 1985.

McKelvey, W.W. *Organizational Systematics: Taxonomy, Evolution, Classification*. Berkeley: University of California Press, 1982.

Meyer, J.W. & Rowan, B. *Institutionalized Organizations: Formal Structure as Myth and Ceremony.*

Mintzberg, H. *Organization Design: Fashion or Fit?*

Peschek, Joseph G. *Policy-Planning Organizations: Elite Agendas and America's Rightward Turn.* Philadelphia: Temple University Press, 1987.

Pfeffer, J. "The Micropolitics of Organizations," in M. W. Meyer and Associates, eds., *Environments and Organizations.* San Francisco: Jossey-Bass, 1978.

Pfeffer, J. *Organizations and Organization Theory.* Marshfield, MA: Pitman, 1982.

Pfeffer, J. *Power in Organizations.* Marshfield, MA: Pitman, 1981.

Pfeffer, J. & Salancik, G. *The External Control of Organizations.* New York: Harper & Row, 1978.

Randolph, W.A. *Technology and the Design of Organization Units.*

Rumelt, Richard P. *Strategy, Structure, and Economic Performance.* 1974.

Scott, W.R. *Conceptions of Environments.*

Selznik, P. *TVA and the Grass Roots.* Berkeley, CA: University of California Press, 1949.

Snow, C.P. *The Two Cultures and the Scientific Revolution.* Cambridge, England: Cambridge University Press, 1965.

Taylor, Frederick Winslow. *The Principles of Scientific Management.* New York: Harper & Bros., 1911.

Thompson, James. *Organizations In Action.* New York: McGraw-Hill, 1967.

Ulrich, D.O. *The Population Perspective: Taxonomy and Selection in Niches and Environments.* Working paper, University of Michigan, 1983.

Ulrich, D.O. *United States and Japanese Electronics Industries: Description, Taxonomy, and Selection.* Ph.D. dissertation, University of California, Los Angeles, 1982.

Weber, M. *Theory of Social and Economic Organizations.* New York: Free Press, 1947.

Weiss, Carol H. *Social Science Research and Decision Making.* New York: Columbia University Press, 1980.

Weiss, Carol H. *Using Social Research in Public Policy Making.* Lexington, MA: Lexington Books, 1977.

Williamson, O.E. *Markets and Hierarchies: Analysis and Antitrust Implications.*
"The Organizational Failures Framework," Chapter 2, (pp. 20-40);
"Intermediate Product Markets and Vertical Integration," Chapter 5, (pp. 82-105);
"Limits of Vertical Integration and Firm Size," Chapter 7, (pp. 117-131);
"The Multidivisional Structure" Chapter 8, (pp. 132-154).

Williamson, O.E. & Ouchi, W.G. "The Markets and Hierarchies and Visible Hand Perspectives: The Markets and Hierarchies Program of Research: Origins, Implication, Prospects," in van di Ven, A. & Joyce, J. *Perspectives on Organization Design and Behavior.* New York: Wiley, 1981.

Journals, Periodicals and Reports

Atal, Yogesh. "Using the Social Sciences for Policy Formulation." *International Social Science Journal*, vol. 35, 1983, pp. 367-377.

Bardach, Eugene. "The Dissemination of Policy Research to Policymakers." *Knowledge - Creation, Diffusion, and Utilization*, vol. 6, no. 2, December 1984.

Blau, Peter M. "Interdependence and Hierarchy in Organizations." *Social Science Research*, vol. 1.

Blau, Peter M. "The Formal Theory of Differentiation in Organizations." *American Sociological Review*, vol. 35, 1970. pp. 201-18.

Beal, George M. & Meehan, Peter. "Knowledge Production and Utilization." Conference Paper, 1978.

Blute, M. Sociocultural Evolutionism: An Untried Theory. *Behavioral Science*, 1979, 24, 46-59.

Boland, M., Boland, W. & Hawley, A. "Population Size and Administration Size in Institutions of Higher Education." *American Sociological Review*, vol. 30, 1965, pp. 252-55.

Caplan, Nathan. "The Two Communities: Theory and Knowledge Utilization." *American Behavioral Scientist*, vol. 22, no. 3., January-February 1979, pp. 459-70.

Caplan, Nathan. "What Do We Know About Knowledge Utilization?" *New Directions for Program Evaluation*, vol. 5, 1980, pp. 1-10.

Coase, R. J. "The Nature of the Firm." *Economics*, 1937, 4, 386-405.

Coats, A. W. "The First Two Decades of the American Economic Association." *American Economic Review*, vol. 50, September 1960, pp. 555-72.

Dahl, R.A. "The Concept of Power." *Behavioral Science*, 1957, 2, 201-215.

Dalton, D.R. & Tudor, W.D., et al. "Organization Structure and Performance: A Critical Review." *Academy of Management Review*, 1980, 4, 49-64.

Duncan, Robert B. "Characteristics of Organizational Environments and Perceived Environmental Uncertainty." *Administrative Science Quarterly*, pp. 313-327.

Dunn, William N. "Methodological Research on Knowledge Use and School Improvement." *Measuring Knowledge Use: A Procedural Inventory*, vol. III, National Institute for Education, 1982.

Dunn, R.B. "Characteristics of Organizational Environments and Perceived Environmental Uncertainty." *Administrative Science Quarterly*, vol. 17, 1972, pp. 313-27.

Galbraith, J.R. "Organization Design: An Informative Processing View." *Interfaces*, May 1974.

Granz, C. "Linkages Between Knowledge Creation, Diffusion, and Utilization." *Knowledge-Creation, Diffusion, and Utilization*, vol. 1, no. 4, 1980, pp. 592-612.

Hannan, Michael T. & Freeman, John H. *Niche Width and the Dynamics of Organizational Populations*. Technical Report #2, Organizational Studies Section, Institute for Mathematical Studies in the Social Sciences, Stanford University, 1981.

Hannan, Michael T. & Freeman, John H. "The Population Ecology of Organizations." *American Journal of Sociology*, vol. 82, no. 5, pp. 929-963.

Hastings, Margaret H. "Summing Up, Starting New: Knowledge Transfer, Public Policy, and a New Society." *Knowledge: Creation, Diffusion, and Utilization*, vol. 8, no. 2, December 1986.

Holzner, Burkart. "The Sociology of Knowledge." *Knowledge: Creation, Diffusion, and Utilization*, vol. 4, no. 1, September 1982.

Holzner, Burkart, & Salmon-Coy, Leslie. "Knowledge Systems and the Role of Knowledge Synthesis in Linkages for Knowledge Use." Developed for the National Institute for Education, 1984.

Hoyle, Eric. "Educational Research: Dissemination, Participation, Negotiation," in Research, Policy and Practice. *World Year Book of Education*, 1985.

Huberman, A.M. "Improving Social Practice Through the Utilization of University-Based Knowledge." *Higher Education*, vol. 12, no. 3, June 1983, pp. 257-72.

Huberman, Michael. "Steps Toward an Integrated Model of Research Utilization." *Knowledge: Creation, Diffusion, and Utilization*, vol. 8, no. 4, June 1987.

Kast, Fremont E., & Rosenzweig, James E. "The Modern View: A Systems Approach," in Blishan, John & Peters, Geoff, eds. *Systems Behavior*. London: Harper & Row, 1972, p. 19.

Kilmann, Ralph H. "Organization Design for Knowledge Utilization." *Knowledge: Creation, Diffusion, and Utilization*, vol. 3, no. 2, December 1981, pp. 211-231.

Kochen, Manfred & van Lohuizen Wal, C. W. "Managing Knowledge in Policymaking." *Knowledge: Creation, Diffusion, and Utilization*, vol. 8, no. 1, September 1986.

Larsen, J.K. "Knowledge Utilization - What Is It?" *Knowledge: Creation, Diffusion and Utilization*, vol. 1, no. 3, 1980, pp. 421-42.

Lindblom, Charles E. "Who Needs What Social Research for Policymaking." *Knowledge: Creation, Diffusion, and Utilization*, vol. 7, no. 4, June 1986.

Link, Authur S. "The American Historical Association 1884- 1984: Retrospect and Prospect." The American Historical Association, February 1985, pp. 1-17.

Lourich, Nicholas P., Jr. & Pierce, John C. "Knowledge and Politics: The Distribution and Consequences of Policy-Relevant Information Among Citizens, Activists, Legislators, and Experts." *Knowledge: Creation, Diffusion, and Utilization*, vol. 3, no. 4, June 1982.

Love, J.M. "Knowledge Transfer and Utilization in Education." *Review of Research in Education*, vol. 12, 1985, pp. 337-87.

Marvin Bernard. "What is 'Half-Knowledge' Sufficient For--And When?: The Critical Comment on Policymakers' Uses of Social Science." vol. 3, no. 1, September 1981.

Meltsner, Arnold. "Seven Deadly Sins of Policy Analysis." *Knowledge: Creation, Diffusion, and Utilization*, vol. 7, no. 4, June 1986.

Menchk, Mark David. "Knowledge and Decisions by Thomas Sowell." Book review in *Knowledge: Creation, Diffusion, and Utilization*, vol. 3, no. 2, December 1981.

Miles, Robert H. "Causal Texture of Organizational Environments." *Macro Organizational Behavior*, Glenview, IL: Scott Foresman, 1980.

Ouichi, W.G. "Markets, Bureaucracies, and Clans." *Administrative Science Quarterly*, 1980, 24, pp. 129-41.

Paisley, W.J. & Butler, M. "Knowledge Utilization Systems in Education-Dissemination, Technical Assistance, Networking Instructional Science." vol. 13, no. 1, 1984, pp. 93-94.

Paisley, W.J. and Butler, M. "Knowledge Utilization Systems in Education." *Higher Education*, vol. 13, no. 4, 1984, p. 462.

Pfeffer, J. & Moore W. L. "Power in University Budgeting: A Replication and Extension." *Administrative Science Quarterly*, 25, 1980, pp. 637-53.

Pfeffer, J., Salancik, G., & Leblebici, H. "The Effect of Uncertainty on the Use of Social Influence in Organizational Decision Making." *Administrative Science Quarterly*, 21, 1976, pp. 227-45.

Pfeffer, J. & Leong, A. "Resource Allocation in United Funds: An Examination of Power and Dependence." *Social Forces*, 55, 1977, pp. 775-790.

Rich, Robert F. "Social Science Information and Public Policy Making." *Knowledge: Creation, Diffusion, and Utilization*, vol. 4, no. 4, June 1983.

Roberts, Jane M.E. & Kenney, Jane L. "Planning: Its Evolution Through Knowledge Utilization." Paper presented at the Annual Meeting of the American Research Association, 1983.

Sabatier, Paul A. "Knowledge, Policy-Oriented Learning, and Policy Change: An Advocacy Coalition Framework." September 1986.

Salancik, G.R., & Pfeffer, J. "The Bases and Use of Power in Organizational Decision Making: The Case of a University." *Administrative Science Quarterly* 19, 1974, pp. 453-73.

Sieber, Sam D. "Trends in Diffusion Research: Knowledge Utilization." *Viewpoints*, vol. 50, no. 3, May 1974, pp. 61-81.

Tibbetts, P. & Johnson, P. "The Discourse and Praxis Models in Recent Reconstructions of Scientific Knowledge Generation." *Social Studies of Science*, vol. 15, no. 4, 1985, pp. 739-49.

Ulrich, David & Barney, Jay B. "Perspectives in Organizations: Resource Dependence, Efficiency, and Population." University of Michigan and University of California, Los Angeles.

Webber, David J. "Explaining Policymakers' Use of Policy Information: The Relative Importance of the Two Community Theory Verses Decision-Maker Orientation." *Knowledge: Creation, Diffusion, and Utilization*, vol. 7, no. 3, March 1986.

Webber, David J. "Obstacles to the Utilization of Systematic Policy Analysis: Conflicting World Views and Competing Disciplinary Matrices." *Knowledge: Creation, Diffusion, and Utilization*, vol. 4, no. 4, June 1983.

Weiss, Carol H. "Knowledge Utilization in Decision Making: Reflections on the Terms of the Discussion." *Research in Sociology of Education and Socialization*, 1982.

Whiteman, David. "Reaffirming the Importance of Strategic Use: A Two-Dimensional Perspective on Policy Analysis in Congress." *Knowledge: Creation, Diffusion, and Utilization*, vol. 6, no. 3, March 1985.

Williamson, O.E. "Transaction Cost Economics: The Governance of Contractual Relations." *Journal of Law and Economics,* 22, 1979, pp. 233-61.

Williamson, O.E. "The Economics of Organization: The Transaction Cost Approach." *American Journal of Sociology*, 87, 1981, pp. 548-77.

Witt, J.C. "Linking Research and Practice - Issues in Research Methodology and Utilization of Knowledge." *School Psychology Review*, vol. B, no. 3, 1987 pp. 274-75.

Wittsock, B. "Social Knowledge, Public Policy and Social Betterment - A Review of Current Knowledge Utilization in Policy Making." *European Journal of Political Research*, vol. 10, no. 1, 1986, pp. 83-89.

INDEX

Academic model 72
Advocacy tank
    as strategic group 74
    ideological orientation 75
Advocacy tanks 19
Aldrich, H.E. 53
American Association of Retired Persons 75
American Enterprise Institute 27, 28, 48, 72, 122
    Baroody, William, Jr. 123
    Baroody, William, Sr. 123
    Brown, Lewis 123
    case study 122
    competition with Heritage Foundation 126
    conservative voice in Washington 123
    end of liberal consensus and 42
    financial difficulties 126
    founding 41
    outputs 128
    role in policy process 41
Arthur D. Little, Inc. 28
Baer, Walter S. 15
Barnet, Richard 94, 95
Baroody, William, Jr. 123
Baroody, William, Sr. 123, 128
Boorstin, David 12
Brookings Institution 9, 16, 17, 27, 28, 133
    academic diversified group 73, 82
    analysis of strategic dimensions 84
    Brookings, Robert S. 47, 82
    case study 134
    competitors 122
    end of liberal consensus and 42
    founding 41
    funding 82
    Gordon, Kermit 135
    history 134
    institutional profile 82
    MacLaury, Bruce 48, 136
    model 48
    purposes 82
    rise of PPRI 46
    role in policy process 40
    Semerad, Roger 138
    staffing 83
Brookings Institution, 30
Brown, Lewis 123
Carnegie Endowment for International Peace 46, 49
Cato Institute 28, 75
Center for Budget Priorities
    specialization 52
Center for Educational Innovation 102
Center for International Affairs 27
Center for International Studies 29
Center for Naval Analysis 28
Center for New York Policy Studies 102
Center for Public Policy Education 138
Center for Strategic and International Studies 16
City Journal 102, 105
Commonwealth Foundation
    analysis of strategic dimensions 107
    Eberly, Don 106
    funding 106
    institutional profile 105
    outputs 106
    similarities to Heritage Foundation 77, 108
    staffing 106
    state-based model 77
Congressional Budget Office 43
Congressional Research Center 28
Congressional Research Service 43
Congressional staffs 42
Contract research 19
Contract/consulting model
    interdisciplinary research in 74

Council on Foreign Relations 16, 46, 49
Critchlow, Donald 42, 123, 136
Daft, R.L. 53, 140
Degree/non-degree granting 19
Dickson, Paul 12, 38
Dror, Yehezkel 17
Durst, Samantha 18, 30
Easterbrook, Gregg 20, 130
Eberly, Don 106
Economic Policy Institute 75
Ethics and Public Policy Center 127
Fauriol, George A. 15
   early think tanks 46
   PPRIs' role in policy process 44
Feldstein, Martin S. 87
Feulner, Edwin, Jr. 99, 129
Ford Foundation 90, 102, 140
Foreign Policy Association 16, 46
Foreign Policy Research Institute 48
Foundation for Capital Formation 27
Gellner, Winard 17
Gilder, George 102
Gilder, Richard 102
Great Society 74, 134
Hammet, William 102, 103
Heclo, Hugh 43
Heritage Foundation 20, 21, 27, 29
   analysis of strategic dimensions 99
   case study 129
   conservatism in America 53
   end of liberal consensus and 42
   Feulner, Edwin, Jr. 99, 129
   founding 41
   funding 99
   fundraising 130
   institutional profile 98
   marketing 129
   outputs 98, 131
   Pines, Burton Yale 130
   policy enterprise group 76
   politicization of PPRIs 53
   PPRI rivalry 52
   staffing 76, 98, 132
   Weyrich, Paul 129
Hoover Institution on War, Revolution and Peace 46

Huber, Peter 102
Hudson Institute 49
Independent non-profit research institutes 12
Independent public analysis organization 14
Independent research centers 16
Industry competition model 66
Institute for Government Research 82
Institute for International Economics 133
   PPRI rivalry 52
   specialization 52
Institute for Policy Studies 21
   advocacy tank 75
   analysis of strategic dimensions 95
   Barnet & Raskin 94
   end of liberal consensus and 42
   funding 94
   institutional profile 94
   outputs 95
   staffing 94
Institute for Research on Poverty 50
Judicial Studies Program 102
Kast, Fremont 62
Katherine Mabis McKenna Foundation 106
Landers, Robert K. 13, 20
   American Enterprise Institute 124
Levien, Roger 14
Linden, Patricia 20, 40, 45, 129
   politicization of PPRIs 52
Literature, review of 10
MacLaury, Bruce 83, 136
Manhattan Institute 133
   analysis of strategic dimensions 103
   Center for New York Policy Studies 102
   City Journal 102, 105
   funding 102
   Gilder, George 102
   Gilder, Richard 102
   Hammet, William 102, 103
   institutional profile 102

Hammet, William 102, 103
  institutional profile 102
  literary agent/publishing house group 76
  marketing success of 102
  staffing 102
Media 43
  influence on PPRIs 51
Murray, Charles 102
National Bureau of Economic Research 9, 27, 28, 29, 47, 86, 133
  academic specialized group 73
  analysis of strategic dimensions 88
  Feldstein, Martin S. 87
  funding 86
  institutional profile 86
  Mitchell, Wesley C. 47
  staffing 87
National Institutes for Health 28
National Science Foundation 87
New School for Social Research 95, 96
Non-profit political education groups 16
Office of Management and Budget 43
Okun, Arthur 135
Olin Foundation 126
Open systems theory 62
Orlans, Harold 11
Outputs and impacts model 17
Overseas Development Council 51
Peschek, Joseph G. 23
Pew Charitable Trusts 71, 106
Pines, Burton Yale 130
Planning Research Corporation 28
Policy research, explained 25
Policy think tanks 16
Polsby, Nelson 15, 40, 41
Porter, Michael 66
  competitive strategy 66
  industry competition factors 121
  strategic dimensions 81
  strategic group rivalry 69
  strategic groups 66
PPRI
  academic/policy maker constituency 29
  academic/policy oriented 27
  affiliated/non-affiliated 26
  characteristics 26
  competition 51, 54
  competitive trends 143
  contract/independent research 30
  customers 122
  degree granting/non-degree granting 29
  diversified/specialized 27, 32
  domestic/international 32
  environment 61, 62
  for profit/non-profit 28
  forms 26
  functions 18, 41
  funding 18
  government of experts 44
  governmental/non-governmental 28
  history 45
  industry 31
  inputs 64
  media 51
  multi-disciplinary/single disciplinary 29
  new entrants 122
  outputs 18, 26, 40, 65, 127
  partisan/non-partisan 27
  politicization 20, 27, 51, 52
  population ecology model 54
  post-war conservatism 49
  proliferation 51
  specialization 51
  staff 51
  staffing 65, 74, 76
  state-based 53
  structure 65
  tax exemption 29
  turn of century 45
  university-based 26
  working definition 31
Public Policy Institute 75
Rand 16, 17, 29, 30
  analysis of strategic dimensions 91
  case study 140

contract/consulting model 74
Domestic Research Division 90
FFRDCs 90
graduate school 91
Institute for Civil Justice 90
institutional profile 90
military industrial complex 49
R&D model 49
revenues 91
role in policy process 40
staffing 91
strategic distance 140
Thomson, James A. 91
Urban Rand 77
Raskin, Marcus 94, 95
Resources for the Future
   specialization 52
Rivlin, Alice 137
Rosenzweig, James 62
Russell Sage Foundation 9, 47
Sarah Scaife Foundation 106
Semerad, Roger 138
Smith, James A. 20, 40, 41
   American Enterprise Institute 123
   critique of role of PPRIs and elites 44
Socio-technical model 62
Stanford Research International 16
State-based model
   customers 77
   geographical focus 77
   Rand Corporation and 77
Strategic dimensions 66, 81
   interaction of 68
Strategic distance 140
Strategic groups 68
   academic diversified 72
   academic specialized 73
   advocacy tank 74
   competition 69
   contract/consulting group 74
   corporate model 75
   literary agent/publishing house group 76
   major groups 128
   market share 133
   policy enterprise 75

   representative institutions 71
   state-based 76
Thomson, James A. 91
Thurber, James 18, 30
University affiliated research centers 16
Urban Institute 49, 50
   contract/consulting model 74
   funding 51
War on Poverty 49
Weaver, R. Kent 19, 51
Weyrich, Paul 129
Wiarda, Howard J. 17, 20, 22, 139
Wilentz, Amy 28, 125
Worldwatch Institute
   specialization 52

James G. McGann, Ph.D., is President of McGann Associates of Philadelphia, a management consulting firm specializing in strategic planning and program development for think tanks, international organizations and foundations. Established in 1989, McGann Associates is pleased to count several of the leading think tanks, international organizations and foundations among its clients. Dr. McGann has written and lectured extensively on the nature and role of public policy research organizations in developed, transitional and developing countries. From 1983-1988 he directed a $10 million a year public policy grants program at the Pew Charitable which supported policy research at many of the leading think tanks in the U.S. He has served as Senior Vice President for the Executive Council on Foreign Diplomacy, a private organization that assists the U.S. Department of State by providing international affairs programs for foreign diplomats, senior government officials, and corporate executives. He also has served as the Assistant Director of the Institute of Politics, John F. Kennedy School of Government at Harvard University. He has a Ph.D. in City and Regional Planning from the University of Pennsylvania, and teaches domestic and foreign policy courses as an Adjunct Professor of Political Science at Temple University.